"PROVOCATIVE AND ILLUMINATING."
The Cleveland Plain Dealer

"While this book primarily absorbs the reader with its central narrative, it also serves a second function, providing a vivid social history of American Roman Catholic experience during the second half of this century. . . . A compelling account of Barbara Ferraro and Patricia Hussey's intellectual, spiritual and political growth, a growth made possible by the teachings, inspiration and educational facilities of the hierarchical Catholicism whose complacency they would ultimately challenge . . . A book to ponder for the implications of its core story."

The New York Times Book Review

"An inspiring account . . . NO TURNING BACK is sure to be important in America's war over abortion—and also in the quest for women's equality within Catholicism."

The Charleston Gazette

"Engrossing . . . The book will provoke the critical reader to examine a number of complex and worthwhile questions."

Newsday

"A powerful, moving and—that rare quality—even inspiring book."

San Francisco Examiner

NO TURNING BACK

*Two Nuns' Battle
with the Vatican over
Women's Right to Choose*

Barbara Ferraro
Patricia Hussey
with Jane O'Reilly

IVY BOOKS • NEW YORK

Ivy Books
Published by Ballantine Books
Copyright © 1990 by Barbara Ferraro and Patricia Hussey

Library of Congress Catalog Card Number: 90-40059

ISBN 0-8041-0871-4

This edition published by arrangement with Poseidon Press, a division of Simon & Schuster Inc.

Manufactured in the United States of America

First Ballantine Books Edition: May 1992

To our parents,
    who encouraged us through our lives to walk in integrity
    and, like the prophet Micah, always told us to "Love ten-
    derly, Act justly and Walk humbly with our God."

and

To all people of conscience,
    who have dissented quietly by their actions or publicly
    with their lives and words. When faced with adversity, be
    it in the church or society, their spirits have not been
    crushed. They have given us courage to take a day at a
    time.

Foreword

In the course of our struggle with the Vatican, many people have encouraged us to write a book. In a special way, we would like to thank Freya Manston, the agent who pursued us, and Ann Patty, the editor who believed in our story. Ann's insights led to our collaboration with Jane O'Reilly. Jane's writing has fleshed out our story. She is superb.

It has been a humbling experience. The astonishing thing about this is we are *common* women. We share many common stories and experiences with a vast majority of people. What is extraordinary is our ordinariness.

We hope that our ordinary stories and experiences will give hope and courage to all people, particularly women, who believe in a vision of justice and equality for themselves and others. The road is not easy, but if the Vatican struggle taught us anything, it taught us that it is better to walk through life with one's integrity than to lose it because the struggle becomes too difficult. We were able to remain grounded in the reality of Covenant House and allow people's lives to touch, shape, humor, and challenge our lives. We tried not to isolate ourselves from a world which often denies the human tragedies and struggles it is immersed in. We are very grateful to the people who walk through the doors of Covenant House and to our board of directors who have supported us without question and in the face of much adversity.

We lost some perceived securities which we had thought we could not live without, but we found new strengths, friendships, community, and *even* insecurities that we could live with. We became less afraid and more secure in our vision for a fair and peaceful world.

In telling our story we have changed some names and details

and places to protect the privacy of the other people involved. We have recreated specific conversations and events as accurately as we could from our own recollections, from notes we both kept at the time, and from the shared memories of other women who struggled with us. Sometimes we have had to edit and pare down the story. For example, our meeting with the Vatican lasted for three hours. Our recounting is drawn from notes and is not verbatim or complete. However, we believe it to be a fair picture of the entire meeting, as we believe our book to be a true picture of events as we experienced them.

There are many people who need to be thanked:

Our sisters and brothers, all our in-laws, nieces, and nephews who have supported us in many ways. We love them all.

Our many friends (you know who you are) who *have remained friends* with us through the good times and the hard times.

Del Spurlock and Cindy Wegman, who initially began the process of typing the manuscript, and Barbara Steinke, who so generously gave of her time and expertise as a court reporter to type and translate manuscripts!

To Beth, Betty, Diane, Sue, Nancy, Camille, Kathy, Joan, Dan, Bob, Deborah, Kristin, Sheri, Jan, Chrystal, and Sherry . . . each of you knows what you did to support us. Thanks!

Maureen Fiedler, a nun signer, who stood with us right to the end of our struggle, even when it was difficult for her.

And especially, we could never give enough thanks to Mary Hunt (Co-Director of Women's Alliance for Theology, Ethics, and Ritual) and Frances Kissling (President of Catholics for a Free Choice), who were *always* there! Their incredible insights, questions, challenges, sense of humor, and friendship were a constant source of strength for us.

Let us promise each other that for the rest of our days we will work for a world which is more justly loving.

Barbara Ferraro and Patricia Hussey   January 1990

One: The Circle

PAT

As soon as we walked into the room, we started rearranging the chairs.

A convent parlor has an iconography all its own. No matter what country it is in, no matter the age of the building which surrounds it, a convent parlor always seems to begin with polished floors and to end in the dim shadows of a lofty ceiling. The pictures on the walls have gilt frames, and they portray traditional inspirations: virgins, ascensions, and luminous bleeding hearts. The furniture, since it has usually been donated by a prosperous Catholic family that has moved on to newer styles, appears slightly orphaned, uneasy in its juxtapositions. The rugs, of a Persian sort, and the tables, of a French sort, look quite presentable but they are always slightly wrong. The tables are too high for resting a teacup, too low for holding books and papers, but perfect for nicking a visitor's kneecap or catching the edge of the carpet. The wooden chairs are either carved and vaguely apostolic or folding and sharp. The stuffed furniture is stiff and fights back. The smell of a parlor is of wax, damask, piety, and cabbage.

These spaces, these parlors, are a kind of median strip between the secret inner life of the convent and the outside world, and as such they are not planned for comfort. They are planned to terrify little girls, to impress parents, to host graduating teas, and to provide a setting for visiting cardinals. Like the front parlor of any decent nineteenth-century farmhouse, these convent rooms mostly wait, dusted and polished and empty, for events of unusual importance.

The convent parlor where Barbara Ferraro and I were moving

1

the chairs was the pride (next to the chapel, of course) of the original building of Trinity College (cornerstone laid December 1899), which itself was the pride of the school system run by the Sisters of Notre Dame de Namur. Always a girls' college, Trinity stands in the northeast corner of Washington, D.C., in the section staked out to be the intellectual heart of American Catholicism, near Catholic University and the Shrine of the Immaculate Conception. The event about to be held in the Trinity parlor that spring morning, March 22, 1986, was of such importance that a coffeepot had been brought in to provide reassurance.

It was going to be a highly unusual meeting. The hierarchy of the church speaks only in carefully calibrated declensions, from the top to the step below the top and so on downward. When it becomes necessary to address ordinary nuns such as us, the top speaks downward through the ranks until the message is given to the superiors of the religious order, who are expected to pass it—direct and unqualified and subject to immediate obedience—to the nuns in question. That day, we were the nuns in question, and a delegation from pretty near the top was coming to see why we had not obeyed earlier messages.

We were both Sisters of Notre Dame. Trinity College should have felt something like home to us. One of the people coming to see us was Sister Mary Linscott, then the highest-ranking woman in the Vatican and also a Sister of Notre Dame, a fact that was even more comforting than the coffee. But she was accompanying Archbishop Pio Laghi, the papal *pro nuncio*, or ambassador, to Washington, and, even more thunderously condescending, Archbishop Vincenzo Fagiolo from the Vatican's Congregation for Religious and Secular Institutes. The boardroom was, in a sense, coming to the assembly line. And the threat of dismissal hung in the air.

During the election campaign of 1984, we had joined a group of twenty-four nuns who signed an ad in *The New York Times* which was headlined "A Diversity of Opinions Regarding Abortion Exists Among Committed Catholics." The Vatican responded by ordering the nuns to recant or face dismissal from our religious orders. By the morning of March 22, 1986, we were the only two of the original group of nun signers whose cases had not been closed.

The Vatican wanted the matter closed. It was, it is safe to say, extremely eager to be able to present the face of unity and authority to the world.

We thought the Vatican was wrong in its teaching that abortion is always an unspeakable sin. And we had agreed to come to the meeting, to fly in from West Virginia that morning, because we wanted to explain *why* we thought the Vatican was wrong.

It is much harder to maintain hierarchy in a circle. So we moved the chairs and one unyielding couch into a ring. We would not have to sit before and beholden to the Vatican delegation. We would sit facing one another, equally.

All our lives we had formed circles, and it was as part of circles that we had found support, understanding, resolution, and transformation. When Barbara Ferraro was a little girl, she joined her parents and her ten brothers and sisters every night in the circle of the rosary. And when I was a young nun, I discovered that delinquent children could be healed and helped in the openness of a therapeutic circle. For one bright hopeful year, Barbara had worked in a parish where decisions were made in a circle of shared authority. In recent years, we had grown closer to God through the liturgies we created for the circles of our Women-Church groups. In Charleston, West Virginia, in the daytime shelter for the homeless which had been our ministry for the past nine years, the chairs were always arranged in circles.

It is much harder to ignore and dismiss and silence people who are with you in a circle. But it is not impossible.

Many women had come to the meeting with us, in spirit and memory and emotion. All the women we had met, whose stories had helped form our own life experience, who we knew were not unspeakable sinners, and who had had abortions. All the women who had stood by us, who had written to us. All the women who had never, ever had a chance to explain why, in good conscience, they too felt the Vatican was wrong.

The archbishops introduced themselves, described their mission as one of shepherds, healers, facilitators.

We introduced ourselves.

I described myself then as thirty-six years old, a Sister of Notre Dame for nineteen years, the possessor of a master of divinity degree. With curly light-brown hair and big round eyeglasses, I am often described as the shy one, a bit dreamy, cautious, and thoughtful.

Barbara Ferraro described herself then as forty-two years old, a Sister of Notre Dame for twenty-four years. She talked about earning her doctorate in ministry. She is small, intent, determined, and uncompromising. But, as usual, it was I who began the argument.

It was, said the archbishops, to be a pastoral meeting, not a juridical one, not an inquisition. It would be a dialogue. "But I must insist," said Pio Laghi, "that after our time together you must put in writing that you support and adhere to the Roman Catholic teaching on abortion."

"That does not sound like dialogue to me," I said.

For three hours, we explained our position, described our experiences, and presented our facts. We were arguing, at the deepest level, for recognition of the value and the truth of our own lives, and the lives of other women. In challenging the church's adamant opposition to abortion, we were championing women as responsible moral agents and as full participants in the life of the church.

The representatives of the church argued for obedience and the need for the *appearance* of unity.

One of the ways people can be dismissed, even in a circle, is to treat them like children. It is an old patriarchal trick. The man from the Vatican sat, and instead of listening, he stroked my arm. He got up and pinched Barbara's cheek and told her she reminded him of his grandmother. And finally, in the patient voice of an old nanny threatening to end the tantrum by sending the naughty child off to bed without dinner, he said to us in Italian, "How will your mommies and daddies feel if you are no longer religious?" We—two adult women who had given our lives to the church—were to be denied even dissent with dignity.

But women are not so easily silenced these days. This book i our own story.

Two: The Decision

BARBARA

"Why did you become a nun?" people ask me now. They try to be polite but they clearly think it was an extreme decision.

At the time I made the decision, I believed there were really only two possible choices for a young Catholic woman. I could either get married or enter a convent. Looking back, I can see myself moving toward a religious vocation as inevitably as the thirteen Ferraros would march up the center aisle of our parish church every Sunday morning.

We lived in Cambridge, Massachusetts. St. Mary's Parish Church had nothing to do with the Cambridge of the Congregationalists and William James, of Lowell and Eliot and Harvard Square. We lived in *Catholic* Cambridge. And we were *Italian* Catholics, grandchildren of immigrants from southern Italy.

Every evening at home, we would all kneel or sit in a circle around my parents and say the rosary together. If we failed to meditate properly on the Joyful Mysteries (Monday and Thursday), the Sorrowful Mysteries (Tuesday and Friday), or the Glorious Mysteries (Sunday, Wednesday, and Saturday), and began to fool around when we should have been thinking about the Annunciation or the Crowning with Thorns while we droned our Hail Marys and Our Fathers, we had to say the rosary over from the beginning.

In my family, growing up meant being able to get a job. It certainly didn't mean being able to drink, or smoke, or run around in gangs. If there were drugs in my school, I didn't know about it. If there was drinking, I didn't know it. In my senior year I heard a rumor about a girl who supposedly had gotten pregnant, but I thought that was a unique and terrible disgrace. I wasn't allowed to go out on dates until I was a senior in high school. I couldn't even go to the movies on weekends with a group of boys and girls. I went to school, I went to work, and I came home.

I was the second of eleven children. There were so many kids running in and out that the floorboards of the front porch were always scuffed down to bare wood, but it was *clean* wood. My mother ran her house according to convent standards. We each had to make our bed and dust our bedroom floor every day. We each had Friday night chores and Saturday morning chores.

My mother was very strict because she liked order, not because she wanted conformity. I can remember the nuns in school looking at me disapprovingly and saying, "Barbara Ann, you are certainly not like your quiet sister Mary." I would discover after I entered the convent that individuality always aroused disapproval. That was certainly not the way I was raised. My mother and father knew I was Barbara, not Mary; and if I was loud, they would try to channel it to some productive outlet. We had to struggle to find our own place in that line of eleven children, but our parents encouraged us to be individuals.

My dear mother. I remember her as always pregnant. She would change from summer maternity clothes to winter maternity clothes. Sometimes, when she was walking a covey of us down the street, with a baby riding in the pram and a crowd of kids tagging along on each side—and she quite visibly expecting another—the neighbors would roll their eyes and mutter, "All those children!" But to my mom, we were all *her* children, and the more the merrier. She enjoyed having a big family, and she was tremendously proud of us.

In other ways we grew up no more, and no less, innocent than the rest of middle-class America in the 1950s. Poverty was something we helped solve by donating Christmas baskets full of food to an anonymous group called "the poor." If I had heard of battered wives and abused children I would simply not have believed such things could happen. Discussions of world problems pretty much focused on beating the Russians.

A big family outing for us was a drive to the Charles River to feed peanuts to the pigeons. We chased the pigeons and my dad ate the peanuts. Or sometimes on Sunday afternoons in the summer we would visit our grandmother at the beach.

Every summer afternoon my mother would drag us all into

the living room, or out in the backyard under a tree where it was cool, and we would have what she called "the reading hour." We listened to the story of Saint Francis of Assisi and his love of the poor, or Joan of Arc and her armies. I liked the story of Saint Barbara, whose father turned her over to the Romans to be tortured and then killed her himself because she would not give up her faith. Then he was struck by lightning. But my mother tended to skip that story, and repeat the one about the Little Flower, Saint Teresa, who begged to join the Carmelite nuns at the age of nine, and died at twenty-four, sending down a shower of roses from heaven.

We believed that the Catholic church *never changed*, that the church of the Apostles and martyrs was exactly the same as the church now. And it seemed—in that historical instant when the American Catholic church reached its precarious plateau between acceptance and assimilation—to be a church triumphant. The parish church and parochial school system were intact, even complete. The seminaries and novitiates were full. John F. Kennedy, who was to us first and foremost a Catholic, was elected President of the United States.

For us, the church always and forever and everywhere was the same. We learned not history, but certainty. We knew we had The Truth. We were ignorant not only of all other religions but even of our own. The pretense was, as Garry Wills wrote in *Bare Ruined Choirs*, that the church had not a past, but only an eternal present: "It had a crystalline ahistoricity: one touch of change or time could shatter it—and did."

Ten years after I entered the convent, I took a graduate school course in family therapy, and I was asked to make a family tree and define the "system" I grew up in. I drew in all the branches and the buds and traced the quick and the dead. My father, Charles Angelo Ferraro, had his place as the third of six children of penniless immigrants who had, somehow, built an amusement park. The center of the family, as far as I was concerned, was my mother's mother, Mary Onesta DeGuglielmo. When she was only fifteen, she left her home in Italy and sailed to Boston to marry an older man from her home village. When my mother was only fourteen, her father died, and Mary Onesta, who could barely read, took over the family real estate business. There were ten children. "We never even stopped to shed a tear," my mother told me. "We couldn't. We went on. We had to survive." Not only did they survive, but all of them, including the girls, went to college.

My "system" was a portrait of the American experience, a history of perseverance and courage. But it would never have occurred to my mother to tell us the story of our family's roots during her reading hours under the tree. Saints were heroes. We were merely the Ferraros, and the strength and trust and independence I can see so clearly years later were then invisible lessons, learned minute by minute, day by day.

My whole world was that circle of Ferraros under the tree. And in that world, the most independent girls became nuns. At least, so it seemed to me. I thought of a convent as a kind of feminist commune (not that either word had ever entered my consciousness), full of strong women working in sisterhood, doing good.

When other families were going off to Cape Cod or the movies, the Ferraros were much more likely to be visiting the nuns at Emmanuel College. Emmanuel was founded in 1919 by a Sister of Notre Dame, Helen Madeline Ingraham. It was the first Roman Catholic college for women in New England. My aunts and my mother had graduated from Emmanuel, and mom loved to go back for visits. One year she won the Family Day prize for "Most Children" and our picture was in the paper—and there were only nine of us at that point!

We would get in the car and drive out on the Fenway. I was always thrilled to see the big brick central building looming over the treetops. The nuns at Emmanuel were the same kind of nuns that we had at St. Mary's—Sisters of Notre Dame de Namur— but on a Sunday afternoon, in a dim, polished parlor, they seemed more fascinating than they did in the classroom. And friendlier. Instead of banging my knuckles with a ruler they gave me homemade cookies and let me touch the long strings of rosary beads that hung from their waists.

The minute we crossed the threshold and smelled the distinctive convent odor of floor wax and cooking food, we began to whisper and tiptoe, slipping through the eerie silence of the long halls and enormous rooms. Every visit ended with a walk to the Gothic chapel that is still the centerpiece of the main Emmanuel building. As a child I knew God was living in that chapel. I felt safe there. As a freshman in college trying to decide my future, I went back again and again to the security I felt there. I would kneel in a pew and pray: Do I have a vocation? When should I decide? Will it be too hard? Would I like being a nun? Could I be happy? What does God want me to do?

Some little girls dream about having a pony or being a ballerina. I wanted to know everything about nuns. Their life was the mystery that seized my imagination, filled up my thoughts, became my secret obsession. In grade school I watched them all the time, looking for clues. What *happened* when they went behind those doors we were absolutely, positively forbidden to pass?

My older sister Mary and I went to St. Mary's Parochial School all the way from kindergarten through high school. My mother and her three sisters had all graduated from St. Mary's. It is closed now. The parish is too poor to keep it open. But then it was a big four-story building, with huge square windows, right next to St. Mary's Church. And it was run by the Sisters of Notre Dame de Namur.

I loved school. I loved my pencil boxes, new every year, and I loved the books, and the ruled paper, and I even loved homework. But the nuns were the most interesting part of all. I didn't necessarily love all of them, but I was absolutely fascinated and enthralled by them.

In high school I stayed after school a lot to work on the newspaper, and for the first time I began to get to know a nun as a friend. Sister Helen Miriam seemed to be "one of us," jovial and interested and responsive to my questions about religious life. She never laughed at me when I changed my mind about having a vocation almost every time we talked.

"Your hesitation and fear are not unlike what I felt also as a young woman," she reassured me. "You will know the answer. Just be patient with yourself."

I never could bring myself to ask her the questions I really wanted answered. She would never have allowed the conversation to become so personal. So I went on wondering: What do you do all day? Do nuns ever eat? Do nuns ever go to the bathroom? Does menstruation automatically stop when you become a nun?

It seemed to me nuns should be exempt from the everyday functions of life. After all, in my mind, they were the closest thing to God. Not the closest thing to being God, but the people in the state of spiritual grace closest to God. I began to *feel* what it would be like to be a nun, to feel peacefulness and security and holiness, from Sister Helen. Her life did not seem a contradiction. I began to trust that there were no awful things happening behind those doors.

Priests didn't interest me at all. I couldn't identify with them and I knew I couldn't become a priest. But I could be a nun, and although I certainly prayed to God the Father all the time, it was the women of the church, the nuns, who seemed to move me toward God. Maybe, looking back on it after all that has happened since, my feeling was an early understanding that God encompasses both genders.

At that time, most nuns entered the convent as soon as they graduated from high school. Still unsure about my calling, I started my freshman year at Emmanuel, traveling across the Charles River every day by MTA. I wanted to be a mathematics teacher, whether I became a nun or not. In high school I was the best in my class at math, first out of 150 kids. I really loved it. And I loved college.

The nun who made the decisive difference in my life was Sister Anne Cyril. She turned World Civilization into a pageant for her class of freshmen. I prayed to be one of the few chosen for her freshman English class, and I was. She made me ''class beetle,'' and I felt very special as I collected papers or put assignments in order for her. In the times we spent working alone together, I watched her like a hawk and not so subtly tried to find out something personal about her life. It was becoming pretty clear to me that nuns were not allowed to talk about themselves, or about their lives, although that did not strike me as a warning but as an even more enticing part of the mystery.

I had never known any career woman. The only role models I had were the nuns and the women in my family who had all gotten married and had kids. Nobody seemed to be eager to marry me. I went to proms and holiday dances with boyfriends, but no one was special. I loved children, but I had taken care of enough babies already. To me, romance was the secret of whatever went on behind those convent doors.

The fact is, I was *trained* to be a nun. Being a spinster was an unthinkable fate. It was okay to be a pious mother, but my teachers definitely gave the impression that it made more sense to sacrifice my life directly to God than it did to sacrifice it via a husband. Anyway, virginity was the highest state of life. In fourth grade I had read in my catechism book, ''It was the virginal Apostle Saint John who was loved above all others and who was privileged to rest his head on our Lord's bosom at the Last Supper. For those who follow the counsel of chastity God has ordained a special blessedness in heaven.''

I thought it would be a tremendous privilege to be accepted. It never occurred to me that nuns were like Shakers. The future of the order depended on recruitment, and one of the nuns' primary purposes was the development of "vocations."

During my visits to the chapel, I began to tell myself, Their life can't be all that bad if someone like Sister Anne seems to be so human and so happy. She was still an individual, and she seemed in touch with life as something that was good that she wanted to share with people. In her English classroom I began to believe in my own creativity. She touched within each of her students the life that was waiting to be discovered. I wanted to make a difference in people's lives, as Sister Helen and Sister Anne did.

Twenty-five years later, Sister Anne Cyril would write a scathing letter to the community about me and Pat. But she was the one who first opened up the world to me. And, as odd as it seems, becoming a nun finally seemed to me to be the best way into, not out of, the world. I expected that I would be able to live the richest, fullest, most useful life in the convent.

One day, I realized that I had made my decision.

Telling people about my decision was almost as difficult as making it. My mother, who apparently had been talking to Sister Helen about me, finally asked, "What are you planning to do next year?"

"Do?" I said. "I'm going to college, what do you mean?"

I was sitting on my bed, working on some homework. My one-year-old sister Ann was running around the room, and my mother sat down on my sister Mary's bed.

"But what are you planning?" she asked again.

"Why? What have you heard? Did anyone say something?" I said, evasively. Finally, I just blurted out, "I've been thinking about entering the convent."

Well, it turned out she had already spoken to my father about it, and they were both very pleased and proud that I had been called to a vocation. She wondered if I shouldn't finish college first, but I wanted to go ahead right away. If I entered the convent, the order would send me through school, and I could spare my parents the expense of convent clothes and my $300 dowry by paying it myself with the money I had saved up for my tuition.

The next step was to visit the provincial, the superior of the order in Massachusetts, and explain why I wanted to enter. I still remember how I felt when she appeared in the parlor. "Oh my God," I thought, "she is so big and I am so small." But she took me into another room and very kindly told me Sister

Helen had recommended I be accepted. I was tremendously relieved.

"Tell me briefly, Barbara, why do you want to enter?" she asked.

"I want to serve God and give my life to Him. I want to be able to do the many good works that I have seen the nuns in school do," I said.

It was that easy. I was set for life!

As I left that day, I stretched my neck to see down the corridors. Only a few nuns crossing the hall. I was disappointed. I would still have to wait until I entered to get behind those cloistered doors.

The last step was a surprisingly cursory physical examination. Then came an acceptance letter with a long, long list of things to buy. Towels. Facecloths. All to be marked with numbered tags. My mother and I took the list to a nun supply store in Boston called Doherty's. The most surprising thing was something called a "binder," a bra without cups that completely squashed my eighteen-year-old breasts. Some of the girls entering with me ignored that requirement and brought their own bras. But I didn't think of that. I wore what I was told to wear. I was going to do everything perfectly.

I was ready to sacrifice everything in order to follow God's call to be a nun. My faith told me I would be able to do anything and give up everything.

What did I know? I was only eighteen years old. I had no idea what I was getting into.

I entered the Sisters of Notre Dame on Wednesday, August 1, 1962. Entrance day. It lives in my memory as if it were only yesterday. Entrance day! In big bright shining letters. The summer morning seemed to drag on endlessly. My trunk had been packed for days. My small suitcase could be closed as soon as I put my toothbrush into it. Everything was ready to go. Especially me. I was eager to begin. If I kept moving, the bright promise of the adventure ahead of me overshadowed any fears or sense of loss I felt that day. Anticipation dulled even the strange eerie realization that I would never set foot in my home again, that I was leaving my family forever.

"Forever" is not a concept that means much to an eighteen-year-old. As far as I was concerned that morning, "forever" felt like the time I had to wait before we could set out on the hour's drive north to the novitiate in Ipswich. From Cambridge to Ipswich, with a stop to say good-bye to my grandmother and a detour to say good-bye to the Atlantic Ocean—make that two hours.

But there were still another two hours to wait. I sat down on my bed and looked around the room I had shared all through high school with my older sister, Mary. We were the big girls, the two oldest. Our desks and bookcases stood between the large front windows of the bedroom. On top of a bureau between the beds were my teenage treasures: my jewelry box, my lipsticks, a big bottle of Jean Naté after-bath lotion.

Good-bye, I thought, I won't be needing any of that any longer.

Very formally, I had asked my sister Mary to choose something she would like from my jewelry box. She picked out some bracelets and a gold chain with a cross. My few other bequests were completed when I gave my high school ring and my charm bracelet to my parents to keep for my little sisters.

Good-bye, I thought, as I pulled up my bedspread and patted it smooth. I emptied the wastebasket and straightened my books on the shelf. It would never do for a Ferraro to leave behind a messy room, even if she were leaving it forever.

Finally, it was time to get dressed. I took off my familiar pink cotton bathrobe and put on the clothes that would mark me for the next six months as a postulant. Neighbors and relatives had been dropping in for days before this, saying good-bye, wishing me well. "Show us what you are going to look like as a nun, Barbara," they would urge. And I would dress up in my new outfit, turning slowly in the middle of the living room, trying not to enjoy the interest and attention.

But on entrance day, it was no longer make-believe. I looked at myself for the last time in the full-length mirror. There would be scarcely any mirrors in the convent, certainly none in our rooms. Good-bye, mirror, I thought. And good-bye, Barbara. Even without my new habit there wasn't much of me to reflect. I was only five feet tall (I still am!). I saw a tiny figure weighted to the ground by black, clumpy nun shoes. My body had disappeared inside a heavy black cotton and Dacron skirt that showed six inches of black cotton stockings beneath the hem. On top, over my bound bosom, a matching black blouse buttoned up the front. A white plastic collar circled my neck. I swung the postulant's cape over my shoulders and stared at the only part of myself that was recognizable—my face. I saw my thick wavy brown hair, the familiar determined set to the corners of my mouth, my brown eyes staring earnestly back at me.

"I know I am going to be a good nun," I whispered. "God will be with me."

When I turned away from the mirror, I left behind, along with the bottle of Jean Naté and the copy of *Black Beauty*, any lingering sense of myself as a young college woman on a road that might lead to marriage and family.

Good-bye, good-bye, good-bye. All my brothers and sisters were waving and shouting. My trunk and my suitcase were in the back of the station wagon, the beach wagon, as we call it in Massachusetts. My parents were in the front seat. The rules were that each postulant could be accompanied by only three adults, and we would pick up my Aunt Joan at my grandmother's house. Aunt Joan had been in the convent and left.

Mary held up my baby sister Ann and waved her tiny fat fist: "Say 'bye-bye' to Barbara." Jody, Janet, and Joan walked around the car waving and giggling. "Good-bye, good-bye." Somebody must have been holding on to Arthur, who was only four years old. Maybe it was Jimmy (only eleven months younger than I am) who had just decided not to become a priest. The little kids, Clare, Charlie, and Johnny, were jumping off the porch steps and running up and down the sidewalk. I was inside the car, folded into my seat in my stiff new clothes, feeling a little self-important, a little scared, a little solemn. They didn't seem to realize I was leaving *forever*, that my going was not just a chance to divide up my clothes and belongings. After all, the extra space in the bedroom would be there because I was *gone*. I remember a long, long minute, as though I were dissolving in slow motion into black and white as my family exploded like a loving fireworks display all around me.

And then we were driving away. As I turned around and waved I knew I would always remember the sight of all those Ferraros jumping up and down on the front lawn before the big old wooden house under the maple trees. At least I was right about one thing. I do still remember the scene.

I turned out to be wrong about a lot of other things. For example, according to the rules of the time, I expected that I would never be allowed to come home again. I would never again see my entire family together because we were allowed only four adult visitors (which they counted as anyone over twelve) at a time, and only once a month. My sisters and brothers would get married without me; their children would be baptized without me. I accepted all that, and I was willing to make the sacrifice. But one of the things I didn't know on entrance day was that once I became a nun I would be allowed to attend only one of my parents' funerals. I would have to choose. Luckily, both my parents survived until the rules changed. The rules are still changing, and my parents, thank God, are still surviving, steadfast and supportive through it all.

We didn't talk very much on the ride to Ipswich. I was so starry-eyed, so idealistic about what life in a convent would be, that once my parents were certain that I was sure of my decision they probably wanted to support me in my choice. We didn't spend a lot of time talking about what I would be giving up. I used to think that they had been very wise not to harp on the sacrifices I would be making. Now I think that they didn't know, any more than I did, what I would discover behind the closed door of the cloister.

The entire month before I left had been a combination wake and celebration, and we had carefully done all the sentimental "last" things. My father made his special fruit cup for the family's Sunday breakfast. Both Mom and Dad took me to a last lobster dinner at Jimmy's by the Sea. Today would be my last visit to my maternal grandmother's house. Mary Onesta was a great heroine in my life. What an amazing woman she was, and what a legacy of strength and independence she passed on to the women in my family.

Whenever we went to her house when we were little, she gave us some of her famous Italian anise cookies. I don't remember if she did on that last visit, but I do remember it wasn't an especially dramatic parting. "Well, Barbara, let me look at you," she said. And she twirled me around, looked me over, hugged me, and at the end she just said, "Good-bye, dear, I hope you'll be fine."

And then it was good-bye to the ocean. We walked down to the beach at the end of my grandmother's street to sniff the salt air and listen to the waves. It was August, and the beach was crowded with families. Mothers struggled to set up playpens for their babies, teenagers shrieked at the edge of the water. When I got back in the car I noticed sand under my feet. It was old sand, left from all the earlier picnics my family had taken. We could never get it all out of the car. By that time, I was beginning to get very, very quiet.

* * *

In 1962 there were about 2,500 Sisters of Notre Dame in the
United States, and 5,000 internationally. There were 1,000 of
us in Massachusetts. Along with the Sisters of Saint Joseph, we
were still the mainstay of the parochial school system in the
state. The convent in Ipswich was the provincial house. At that
time we were one province of Massachusetts. The nun at the
top of the state pyramid was called the provincial, and she lived
at Ipswich with her governing council. All the records for the
state were kept there. And it was there that new sisters came to
stay as postulants and remained as novices in the next stage of
their progression toward their first vows as professed Sisters of
Notre Dame.

My entrance day was the first that had ever been celebrated
at Ipswich. We were new, and so was the convent—brand,
spanking, sparkling new. It had been built on the fields surrounding the mansion of an old North Shore estate which had
been left to the Boston diocese. The estimable Richard Cardinal
Cushing had seen to it that the Sisters of Notre Dame had
been able to construct everything they might need for the en-
largement and perfection of the order for a very long way into
the foreseeable future.

As my family drove up the long, long driveway to the entrance, none of us could ever have guessed how short the foreseeable future would turn out to be. In 1973, the Massachusetts
province split into the progressive Boston province and the conservative Ipswich province. The place built to enfold young
women into an ever-growing order now houses elderly nuns and
offices.

The building was huge. Three wings stretched out from the
central section, which contained the main entrance, the chapel,
and the visiting parlor. One wing was for the professed sisters,
one for the postulants, and one for the novices. The original
mansion stood up on the hill, a kind of rest and recreation center
used for retreats and conferences. The grounds seemed endless,
green and rolling under the August sun.

A large group of people was gathered on the circular driveway
in front of the main entrance. Cups of punch and plates of cookies were set out on tables on the lawn. It was easy to pick out
the other postulants. We were all dressed alike, and each of us
was surrounded by a little group of people who were getting
ready for a last good-bye. Still, there was more laughter than
tears. Nuns from all around Boston had come for the event, and
they were greeting relatives and old friends.

"Well, well, you have brought us Barbara," said Sister Virginia Saint John, a nun I had visited many times with my mother. When I was a little girl, she had been my baby-sitter. My father said to her, "We will miss Barbara. I know we have other children at home, but we will miss her. Can you promise me you will take good care of her?"

Sister Virginia went with us when my turn came to be presented by my parents to the provincial, who was at that time Sister Eleanor Joseph. "Welcome, Barbara Ann," she said. "I know you will be very happy here." I knelt before her. On a table next to her there were little piles of folded veils, the short black mesh veils of postulancy. Another nun handed one of the veils (Mine! I thought) to the provincial, and she opened it up. A breeze caught it briefly, a little puff that seemed to lift it magically over my head, and then she fitted its headband over my hair.

I knew I was there to stay!

The postulants were gathered together for a group photograph before the enormous glass entrance doors. Cameras snapped. I knew my father was out there with the movie camera that had recorded every important family event since I was a little girl. For a moment, I couldn't see him. Then I saw Mom, all dressed up in summer silk, and Dad with his camera in one hand and his other arm around my mother's shoulders. His tie was crooked from all the farewell hugs. I am sure there were tears, but they were proud and happy tears.

And then it was time to go. The mistress of postulants rang a brass handbell for silence.

"Postulants! Postulants! Quiet, please. Girls! Quiet, please," she said, in the decorous shout of a well-trained nun. "Please take your suitcases and line up to go inside. No one else is allowed to come in. Say good-bye now."

The last, very last good-byes were said. Mom said good-bye, and I said, "I'll see you in a month, on visiting day." And then I said, "Good-bye, Dad." Finally, I picked up my suitcase and joined the line of young women I thought would become my new family.

That entrance day was a long time ago, more than twenty-seven years. I often think now, as I was never allowed to think at the time, of what a glorious group of women we were. A long shining line of vigorous, dedicated, enthusiastic young Catholic women, ready to give God all we had.

Little did we know what waited for us on the other side of the door. Sixty-two hopeful postulants entered with me that day. Only half were still there two and a half years later when the time came to take our first vows.

Three: Behind the Doors

BARBARA

We lined up, one behind the other, each girl carrying a suitcase, and marched through the front door of the novitiate.

"Don't look back," warned a nun posted along the side of the corridor. As we shuffled into the enormous visitors' parlor, nervous chatter bounced off the rows of green and orange plastic chairs and sofas.

Suddenly, as though we were all attached to the same switch, the chattering stopped. Sister Mary Kevin had stepped to the front of the room and silenced us with a look.

Sister Mary Kevin, mistress of postulants who later became our mistress of novices, was in charge of directing the rigorous process known as "sister formation." The first stage, at the time I entered the Sisters of Notre Dame, was a six-month period spent as a postulant (a petitioner or candidate).

Postulancy was like boot camp. I had no idea, as I sat there on a green plastic chair that summer afternoon, that I was about to begin a program designed to break my will, destroy my sense of self, and cut off all my loyalties to anyone or anything in the outside world. At the end I would be, in theory, a blank slate, ready to learn to live only for God. Or else (and I was painfully aware of this possibility in my future), I would be a failure, a disgrace to my family, a girl who somehow didn't have the guts to answer God's call. The fault, I knew from my own family, lay always with the person who left, not ever with the church.

If I made it through the first six months, I would receive a new name, a nun's habit, and the white veil of the novice which I would wear for two years. During the first year as a novice, the "canonical year," I would study only theology from other

Sisters of Notre Dame in classrooms inside the novitiate. The second year I would take secular subjects from teachers who came to us at the convent. The last sixty days of that year would be concentrated on studying the history and rules of the community. At last I would go before the provincial and ask to be professed. After making and signing a will turning everything over to Notre Dame I would make my first temporary vows. Five years later I could take final vows.

Through every stage of the process I would be pruned, corrected, mortified, and punished. At the end, the line of young women who had just walked through the front door of the novitiate would be brainwashed, indoctrinated, "formed" into good little Sisters of Notre Dame.

Sister Mary Kevin must have been fairly young, still in her thirties. She went straight to work, using a tone of voice that could have been heard across a parade ground.

"You will go to your cells to unpack your suitcases and as quickly as possible return to the study hall. IN SILENCE," she announced.

"Cell," I whispered to myself as I scurried down newly waxed halls. It turned out to be one of four cubicles in a room divided up into curtained alcoves. Each cubicle had a bed, a straight wooden chair, a small sink, and a closet.

For the first time in my life, I had my own space. As I put away my new white cotton nightgown and black bathrobe, my underclothes and slippers, I felt as though I had truly grown up and left home. At last, I had my own things, and no sisters and brothers were going to interfere with them. I put my piano music, the only sentimental thing I had brought from home, in my trunk, and then I started looking for the study hall.

The stairs were full of black-clothed figures, grinning and gesturing and pointing out the way to each other in silence. Eventually we found the study hall and sat down at our desks. Sister Mary Kevin came in and, in a voice like a thunderclap, let us know that we had already, before even the first hour had passed, failed to meet her standards.

At top volume, Sister Mary Kevin roared, "Postulants, the front door swings both ways! As easy as you came in, you can go out."

My stomach began to feel nervous.

"Some of you," Sister went on, ominously, "went upstairs and started to have a good time."

It seemed that some of the girls actually had introduced themselves to each other, passed around boxes of candy, started making friends. I hadn't even imagined that I could do those things.

That evening I learned the first and most important lesson of convent life. If I was going to make it I needed to be obedient to every rule and regulation. I needed to keep the letter of the law under all circumstances.

And I did!

I would like to forget those first days and years. Sometimes they seem like a bad dream. "Did that really happen?" I ask myself even now. For a long time I couldn't talk to anyone, not my family or my friends, about those early days. The rule of secrecy sat on my tongue.

Sister Mary Kevin had an advantage the Marines would have envied. She spoke for God. God was speaking to me through her as my superior. When she taught me the Rule she was teaching God's will for me.

Every day we got up at 5:30 A.M. and went to bed at 9:00 P.M. Every hour of the day was scheduled, even the one hour of recreation when we could walk and talk (but only in groups of three). The convent bell—an electric buzz instead of a peaceful clang—ruled my time. Mass, benediction, the rosary, and sixty minutes of meditating on scriptural passages took me into the chapel three times a day. Plus lauds, vespers, and compline.

I was supposed to feel close to God and I did. After all, I spent hours every day praying and thinking about God's will becoming manifest in my life. The idea was to empty my mind of everything but the thought of God. Sometimes the effect was simply an empty mind, which was a confusing contradiction to the fact that the hours I enjoyed most were spent in the classroom. I still loved school.

God's will for me involved a lot of housecleaning. I had chores after every meal. Morning, noon, and night I dragged around enormous buckets, huge mops, giant cans of wax, bundles of dust rags. One of the Ways of Notre Dame was to clean for the sake of cleaning. Every day we swept the back stairs. Every day we cleaned all the toilets. Immaculate was only a starting point. Everyone, including the professed sisters, cleaned.

Some jobs were nicer than others. Working in the professed sisters' quarters or in the visitors' parlors was pleasant. The most prestigious assignment was cleaning the chapel and the sanctuary, polishing the silver candlesticks and dusting the stations of the cross. I never quite figured out why I never got those jobs, why I was always crawling around mopping the bathrooms or the back stairs. There seemed to be an unspoken image of how a "perfect" nun should look and act, and I wasn't it. Years later, when I could talk about that period with my friends, we discovered that the ideal usually matched whatever the mistress of novices at the time was like. The favorites when I was a novice were tall and stately. They looked pretty and could glide along as though they had ball bearings instead of feet.

One day I came charging down the stairs in my usual way, and I heard Sister Mary Kevin's voice, cracking out across the hall like a whip.

"Barbara, dear, come with me."

When a nun says "dear"—watch out.

She called me into her office and began making fun of me. "You walk like a little Italian kid running across the street. That is not the way a nun walks. A nun walks *modestly*. You swing your arms, like this" (she mocked a windmill). "A nun clasps her hands, bends her head, and casts her eyes downward. You sound like Sister Jeremiah, who weighs three hundred pounds."

I weighed 110 pounds.

The scorn and sarcasm and the saccharine smugness of the "for your own good" corrections were hard to take, but not as hard as the fact that I very rarely knew what I was being corrected for.

"Barbara, dear, we don't do that here."

I would look around nervously. Were my legs crossed? Were my elbows on the table?

"Look at your posture, dear."

I looked. Both feet were on the floor. I wasn't slumping.

"Your *back*, dear. Sit upright. Your back must not touch the chair."

Who would ever have thought of that? I couldn't have been forewarned by the other postulants because we were rarely allowed to speak to one another, and when we were it was against the Rule to talk about ourselves.

I was definitely not a favorite. Disapproval haunted me. For example, I loved to play show tunes on the piano. Five or six of us who had studied music were told to prepare a favorite piece for the music teacher. We could take turns practicing in the auditorium at certain scheduled hours. It was just wonderful. I was really rolling again with my old favorites from *The Sound of Music* and *West Side Story*. Finally, the day came to play for the teacher. We went in, one at a time, and there sat Sister Claire

Marguerite, about five feet tall and as mean as she could be. I put my favorite piece of music on the rack, sat down on the bench, drew a deep breath, and started in, *con brio*. I was pedaling away with my foot, pounding away at the keyboard.

"Oh, the HILLS are ALIVE WITH . . ."

"STOP!"

Mid-chord, I stopped.

"Thank you. Put your music away, Dear."

And that was it for *The Sound of Music*.

I couldn't have asked why she stopped me, or whether I could go on practicing, because questions were not allowed and explanations were rarely offered. No wonder then that years later the idea of dialogue as a way to discern God's will and to find solutions to conflicting views became overwhelmingly important to me.

I was being made to detach myself from everything in the outside world that meant anything to me.

Our families were not to be talked about.

We would relinquish even our memories of the past.

A box of candy passed around the dinner table was an opportunity for renunciation. Visitors were always leaving enormous boxes of chocolates "for the good nuns." It was nice to be sitting at the head of the table when one was brought out to share for a special occasion. Then I could get first pick. But even as my hand went toward the vanilla cream, a new voice in my head said, "No. Deny yourself. For Christ." It wasn't enough to deny myself the one I liked. I had to take the one I hated—chocolate-covered raisins. "Offer it up," whispered the voice, "for the sins of the world."

Twice a week we had nightly instructions on the Ways of Notre Dame. "Guide your eyes. Do not look at people. Keep yourself focused, in silence, on God and what you are meant to be doing."

We were each assigned one evening a week to ask for penance. My name would be posted on the bulletin board with my Wednesday-night penance group. At dinner we would line up next to a long table with the mistress of novices sitting at the head. Everyone else at the table could hear what was going on. When my turn came I would kneel beside her and say, "Sister Mary Kevin, please may I ask forgiveness for . . . looking in the mirror . . . speaking on the stairs." Or whatever. And she would tell me to say the Stations or three Hail Marys or something, as penance. And then I would kiss the floor.

If something extraordinarily bad happened I would have to tell her as soon as I saw her. I remember one day I knelt down in the corridor and said, "Sister, please may I ask forgiveness, I was outside and I ripped my habit."

"Kiss the floor, Sister," she said. I can still see the disgusted, prim expression on her face. "Maybe you are not ready to have a Sunday habit if you can't take better care of it than this." I knew better than to argue. Arguing was a sign of willfulness and required curative humiliations.

The most innocent things became sources of baffled shame. All our letters were censored. One time I wrote to one of my brothers, and I said I hoped he would have a good time on his honeymoon. The letter came back with directions to change the sentence. I had to scrape off the ink and write in something else, and I couldn't imagine why. Finally, I realized the nuns thought I was making a sexual joke about honeymoons. I was mortified.

Mortification was the point. The admission of sinfulness was the beginning of the road to a higher spirituality.

One day after I had become a novice the mistress took me into her office for a little personal instruction. After she had asked the usual perfunctory questions—"Are you keeping the silence? How are you doing?"—she introduced me to something new.

"I think it is time for you to be shown the disciplines," she said, and she pulled out a whip. It was made of a short cluster of rope with knots. I was told to take it to my room and once a week to whip myself on my naked hips in the spirit of the suffering of Jesus. We were never to speak to anyone about the practice, which is why it was years before I discovered that some of the girls who were novices with me simply went to their rooms and whipped their pillows.

But I, with my passion to become a good nun, was so successful with my whip that I received permission to use, in addition, a celice—a chain with sharp pointed links which I wore on regularly scheduled days around my upper arm. It hurt a lot, but not as much as the crown of thorns had hurt Jesus.

My self-esteem was being knocked out of me. I had come into the convent as Barbara Ferraro, an intelligent human being. My parents had raised me to ask questions, and the enforced silence in the convent was running against my very nature. I had won awards in high school and had my picture in the paper. I had been working since I was a freshman and I knew I could have had a good career. And here I was kissing the floor.

And yet, I was happy. It is hard to explain how I could have been happy. My new sense of closeness to God kept me oblivious to what was really happening to me. Each new step in my formation was exciting. In my enthusiasm and eagerness to begin what I thought was a wonderful vocation, I went along with what I was told to do. I conformed.

My clearest emotion was the fear that I would be sent home. Looking back, I think it would have been a blessing if I had been, but I didn't want to be a disgrace to my family. My brother Jimmy had left the seminary just before I entered the convent. He was only eleven months younger than I, and he had been a regular villain in grade school. In the eighth grade he changed schools and met a nun he liked, and she decided he should start becoming a priest right away. So he went to the Franciscan Seminary in Andover, Massachusetts, as a freshman in high school. Of course he was much too young for such a decision (now he is a probation officer in Boston who has won acclaim for standing up to an allegedly corrupt judge). He came back home in his senior year, and I sensed that my parents were really disappointed. I certainly wasn't going to disappoint them again.

Over and over I heard phrases such as "You must forget all and put all your trust in God" or "The only feelings you must have are spiritual feelings for God," and I actually began to lose my feelings, both emotional and physical.

Even friendship was forbidden, which now seems an odd way to create a spirit of community. I didn't know why we had to walk and talk in threes. When I tried to spend more time with Claudia, I was scolded and told to consider my lack of charity in excluding others. When we were told never to enter the cell of another nun without permission, I was totally baffled. In my family we shared everything. Years later, when we could talk freely with other nuns, someone finally explained to me that the great fear was that Something Would Happen if particular friendships developed. Even then it hadn't occurred to me that the something was sexual. And indeed, the fear was of something deeper and more important than physical intimacy— sinful though that would be. Particular friendships could become dangerous and intemperate indulgences of feeling. Chastity required a close guard on *all* the senses. Gradually I was taught to restrain all the behavior that had been so natural for me as a loving sister, an exuberant friend, and a happy daughter. My womanhood was being taken away. On the very first visiting day with my parents after I had entered, I was ordered, "When you go to the parlor, postulants, do not push a baby carriage or pick up young children."

"Why not?" I wanted to ask. But I had already learned that questions were not part of the regimen. Can you imagine how foolish I felt when my baby sister, Ann, came running up to hug me, and I couldn't pick her up? The worst of it was I couldn't explain to my parents why I wasn't hugging Ann. I wasn't even allowed to tell them what I ate for breakfast in the convent. Personal things were not to be talked about. The fact that things were not to be talked about was also not to be talked about. So at best I was evasive, and at worst I had to lie to my parents. Even today I am not sure they know why the communication we had so treasured began to break down.

Another thing that was not to be talked about was the fact of an empty place in chapel, or an empty bedroom cubicle. Silence was the only farewell to those who went home.

My body rebelled. In the first weeks of my postulancy, hideous boils broke out everywhere except on my face, my hands, and my neck. The rest of me was covered up by the black material, to which I may have been allergic. More likely the boils were the result of repressed anxiety, doubt, and the stifled suspicion that my life was more horrid than consecrated. But instead of asking to see a doctor, I was grateful that none of the oozing sores were visible. I was terrified that if they found out I was sick they would send me home.

I stopped menstruating for several months. Some of the novices who later became my friends told me they had stopped having their periods for over a year. After the boils went away I began having nauseating stomach cramps which eventually turned into the beginning of ulcers. If I had told the mistress of novices about my pain, she might have called a doctor, or she might have told me it was all in my head and I should offer it up for suffering sinners. As it was, I offered it up and kept quiet.

After six months I lost my name. We could each submit three choices for our permanent religious names, and my first choice was Barbara Ann. I was told someone else already had my name. Only when we knelt in front of the provincial and our mistress of postulants on name day did we find out, in effect, who we would be.

"Barbara Ann Ferraro, from this day forward you will be called Sister Charles Marie."

It was my third choice. But at least I had gotten my father's name. I hoped he would be proud. (It is interesting how many of us chose male names.)

Shortly after my name changed, I received the habit. I was very excited. Now I would look like a sister, except for the white veil signifying I was still only a novice.

Fifty of the original group of sixty-two postulants remained to move on to the next stage of formation. It was time for me to lose my hair.

In silence we lined up outside the bathroom doors. One by one we went inside where three professed sisters standing behind three chairs waited for us. No one spoke, which was not unusual. Although the postulants, novices, and professed sisters all lived under one roof, we had separate quarters and separate dining rooms. I had a friend, Janice, who had entered six months ahead of me, and I could never speak to her. If we passed in the corridors, the senior nun could say "Praise be Jesus Christ" and the other could respond "Praise forever. Amen." I suppose sometime in the past, centuries ago, the source of that bizarre absence of communication was the idea of cleansing a novice's consciousness of everything but a connection with God (and of safeguarding the older sisters' recollection). But it was lonely, and somehow spectral, like meeting ghosts in the corridors. It also cut us off from any ability to compare role models. Sister Mary Kevin's version of a nun was the only one offered me.

The great symbol of entering the sisterhood was the shaving of the novice's head. Yet when my turn came the scene was eerie, almost unsisterly. In silence I took my place. In silence one of the sisters clipped off my hair. Then she shaved my head. It wasn't especially traumatic for me. My hair had always been short, and at that point I couldn't wait to wear the headpiece of the habit. Anyway, there wasn't a mirror so I couldn't see how I looked.

We rushed back to our cells, trying not to scratch our itchy heads. I laced up my stiff new corset and tunneled into my new habit. It was made of fourteen yards of heavy black synthetic material and I looked, and felt, as though I were dressed in a Barnum and Bailey tent.

One older novice slipped into my cell and in silence helped

me put on the headpiece. There were no buttons and no zippers—I was held together by fourteen pins. My dress was fastened with three pins down the front. Then she pinned a square piece of material over the dress and closed it with four pins. A white plastic bib tied in the back and was held down with a pin through a loop. The underbonnet of the headpiece was pulled together with a string and a white pin at the back of my head. Over that she put the stiff black bonnet. It stuck out in front of our faces like an old-fashioned sunbonnet and cut off all peripheral vision. We called it the "blinders." Finally, the veil was attached to it with three pins. Then, with extreme delicacy, she reached under the black bonnet and attached it to the white one with two more pins. Usually those were the pins that did some damage to my head.

Over the years, as we followed the directives of Vatican II and began to change, that voluminous habit was cut up into all kinds of pieces. The massive skirt became a couple of ankle-length skirts and a blouse, and then a shorter skirt and a kind of jacket.

As we moved down the aisle of the chapel that afternoon, all the novices and professed sisters sang "Come Holy Spirit" ("*Veni Creator Spiritus*"). We were stumbling and tripping in our new skirts, our new three-foot-long rosary beads clattering from our waists. Our headpieces hung perilously to left or right. And we thought we looked absolutely beautiful! Only as I cut my archaic habit into something suitable for the twentieth century did I realize how truly bound and blinded I had been inside it. I could barely move, and psychologically the effect was to dim my ability to respond to people, to understand their lives.

As I crossed the yard to the novitiate where I would live for the next two years, my individuality as Barbara was fading away. My name was changed—I was number 878—and I was one of one hundred novices who all looked alike. I remember I felt so proud, so eager to be holy Sister Charles Marie. Unfortunately, I was a nineteen-year-old anachronism, about as practical in the world of 1963 as a dinosaur.

For the two and a half years of my formation, I was cut off from all contact with my own time. There were no newspapers, no radios, no television. Even as we were told to kiss the floor, we were assured that we had chosen the most glorious life, a "higher life" of virginity. Inevitably the message came across that a life that included men and children was not so glorious. We were suspicious of the "outside," even afraid of it. But too often we were cranky and childish and dependent inside our convent walls. Only rarely could the world not be avoided, and then the encounter was sometimes funny and sometimes tragic.

I will never forget my first birthday as a novice. My parents wanted to make the day special for me, but they had no idea if birthdays were celebrated in the convent. And, of course, I couldn't tell them. The rules were never revealed to outsiders. That evening Sister Mary Kevin, who strictly followed the rule of never showing any feelings, actually laughed when she told me that one of my aunts had arranged for a singing birthday telegram. Of course, I never heard the telegram (I never even saw a phone until years later). Sister Mary Kevin received it.

Then she told me, with a grim little smile, that my family had delivered enough lasagna and Italian rum cake for all the hundred novices. As I walked into the refectory that evening, I went as usual to my assigned seat and waited for everyone to arrive. I hoped we would be surprised with a ring of the bell and the mistress's "Praise be Jesus Christ." That would mean we could gleefully respond "Praise forever. Amen" and proceed to have recreation—to talk—at table during dinner.

It didn't happen. After all, it was Advent and our penance that evening was the usual silence while we ate and listened to someone read an inspiring passage from the lives of the saints. It also happened to be one of the two nights a week during Advent that we knelt for meals. We said grace, put our chairs under the table, and knelt. I was so short that my chin barely reached the edge of the table. So there I was, in that ludicrous position, trying to eat my birthday lasagna and munch on a slice of rum cake. In silence.

That month, when I wrote the one letter I was allowed to my family, I thanked them for the birthday treats. Of course I didn't give them the details. If I had, the letter would have come straight back to me from Sister Mary Kevin to be "corrected."

Thanks to my parents' insistence, I had gotten a driver's license the summer I graduated from high school. Because of that, I could occasionally pin back my "blinders" and drive another novice to the doctor or dentist. Even though we had to keep silence during the ride, it still seemed like a delightful outing.

I was sitting in the waiting room of a dentist's office the afternoon of November 22, 1963. Suddenly the news of the shooting of President John F. Kennedy came over the radio. I was too shocked even to pray. All I could think about was that I had actually *seen* him. My senior year in high school I had joined the political process in a big way, pasting posters and banners all over the school and the neighborhood. With my sister Mary I had pushed through the crowds and waited, and waited, and waited in the Boston Garden just to catch a glimpse of him. He was a hero, a *Catholic* hero.

Incredibly, we drove back to the convent, bound by silence, without speaking. I went to the mistress and told her what I had heard.

"You are to tell no one," she said. "The other novices will be told during chapel time tonight, and we will pray for the President and his family."

The day of the President's funeral, we were brought into the auditorium and for the first and last time we were allowed to watch television. I felt very sad but I didn't cry. We weren't supposed to cry. I was already losing touch with my emotions and it would be a long, long time before I would feel them again.

By January of 1965 there were only thirty-two novices left in my group. But I had survived! I would be among those receiving the black veils of professed sisters at a special Mass. Our parents would be invited, and our pictures would be taken to present to them. As a special celebratory dispensation we would be allowed to sit down to a banquet with our parents. We would be eating with "outsiders"!

Why did I stay? It wasn't only because I am a very stubborn person. It wasn't just because I didn't want to disappoint my family, or because being a nun was one way to be special. Certainly, I did not fully understand the vows. I didn't know what it meant to promise to be chaste for the rest of my life. I'd never been in love, never been deeply moved by a man.

I stayed because I believed this was my calling.

And so, on January 27, I stood at the altar in the chapel at Ipswich and said:

Almighty and eternal God, Adorable Trinity, I, Sister Charles Marie, humbly prostrate before you and in the presence of the most Blessed Virgin Mary, vow and promise to your Majesty through the hands of Sister Provincial,
Poverty, Chastity, and Obedience,
according to the constitutions for *one year* and according to

obedience a particular care of the Christian and Apostolic Education of youth in the congregation of the Sisters of Notre Dame.

And I hope through the merits of Jesus Christ who inspires me to make these vows for the grace
                         to accomplish them. Amen.

I believed then, as I still do today, that my vows were spoken to God and not to the institutional church. I did not make them to the pope. I was speaking to God and to the people I would work with, and live with, and teach.

Luckily (or perhaps through divine providence), at that very moment Vatican II had begun to change the church. For almost the next two decades I would have the profound satisfaction of being free to search for a way to live my vows as I myself understood them.

Four: Harvest of Daughters

BARBARA

When I had firmly decided to become a nun, my Uncle Arthur, a Franciscan priest, suggested I join the Carmelites. He knew them, but he didn't seem to know me. The Carmelites spend their days praying, they never talk, and they are completely cloistered. "No, no," I said. "I could never spend my entire day in silence. Besides, I know the Sisters of Notre Dame. They are like family to me." I never bothered to find out about other religious communities. The Maryknolls, the Mercies, the Saint Joes, the Charities were not the nuns I knew.

What I "knew" was what I had learned in school. The order of the Sisters of Notre Dame de Namur was founded in 1804 by a French peasant woman, Marie Rose Julie Billiart, who later became Saint Julie. The sisters had become, by 1962, an international group of about 5,000 who lived and worked all over the world. Most of them taught, and a few of them were convent cooks and seamstresses.

Saint Julie was an extraordinary woman—independent, determined, a brilliant administrator and negotiator. Raised in the turmoil of the French Revolution, she began her order at almost the very moment that Napoleon crowned himself Emperor of France. A colleague of Saint Julie's remembered: "The principal end in view was the training of teachers who would go, never less than two, wherever they would be asked for, in order to instruct poor children free of charge."

The great question, then as now, was who would control the order. Napoleon wanted all nuns under the jurisdiction of his mother, Letizia. In each French diocese, the local bishop wanted to decide the convent rules, control its resources, and compel obedience to himself. When the bishop of Amiens grew particularly insistent and it became clear there would be no dialogue (how strange it is that some things never change!), Saint Julie established her motherhouse in Belgium, in Namur, where the bishop was sympathetic to her goals. She was determined that the order must have a central government headed by a nun who would be superior general, pooled community resources, and great autonomy so that they might expand wherever they were needed.

Eventually, in 1844, twenty-eight years after Saint Julie's death, her goals were codified into the first *Régles et Constitutions des Soeurs de Notre Dame*, approved by Pope Gregory XVI. Over the years, the constitution was revised, each time with a laborious struggle to reconcile modern necessity and experience with Saint Julie's vision. The most recent revision was undertaken in accordance with directives following the Second Vatican Council, which freed religious orders for self-examination and experimentation "in the light of the gospel, the spirit of the founder, the needs of the members, and the signs of the times."

The Sisters of Notre Dame were established, thanks to Saint Julie's ingenuity, as a papal, religious institute. Many congregations have a similar direct connection to the Vatican. Many others are instead tied to a diocese. The Sisters of Saint Joseph, for example, who taught Pat in high school, are answerable to their local bishop, archbishop, or cardinal, and generally do not move outside of their diocese.

Our order of itinerant teachers is, in effect, given permission to exist by the pope. The Congregation on Secular and Religious Institutes (CRIS)* in Rome must approve its constitution. Ultimately, the order is accountable to the Vatican. These organizational points may seem arcane, but they are exactly the details which determined where we would work, with whom we would live, and from whom we would receive our orders.

Every religious community takes its own unique constitution extremely seriously. It is the Rule, the inspiration, and the definition of the congregation's mission. Every word is considered and can be brought up as defense in the double acrostics of Vatican debate.

*CRIS, as we called the office when it governed our lives, has since changed its name to Congregation for Institutes of Consecrated Life and Societies of Apostolic Life (CICLSAL).

"In the spirit of Saint Julie Billiart and the tradition of the Congregation we, the Sisters of Notre Dame, see ourselves situated within God's continuing action in history," announces the draft constitution of 1984. For those not fluent in nunspeak, this sort of pronouncement may seem high-flown and obscure. But for us, it was a call to justice through action, an interpretation received in Rome about as joyfully as Luther's ninety-five theses.

"We commit ourselves to live the Gospel in community." Of course. But . . . what is "community," and what does it mean "to live the Gospel"? Discovering the answers to such questions has been the great effort of my life and of Pat's. Trying to practice our answers has been the joy, the satisfaction, and the meaning of our lives.

When I entered, I did not know there were any questions. I didn't even know there was such a thing as a constitution. Outsiders were never permitted to see a copy. Instead of debate, there were rules. Instead of history, there were "the Ways of Notre Dame," which stressed such points of appearance as the proper way to fold our hands into our sleeves when walking down a corridor.

No wonder in 1962 the good Pope John XXIII thought it was time to let a little fresh air into the cloister!

I joined an old and honorable profession, one that had, over nearly two millennium, been a refuge and an opportunity for women. In the earliest Christian times, both men *and* women preached the gospel. When in 312 A.D. the Emperor Constantine was converted, patriarchy reasserted itself as the "natural order," and the organization of the Christian Church became the same as the hierarchical, male organization of the Roman Empire.

For the next nine hundred or so years, the only chance any Christian—man or woman—had to lead a scholar's life was inside a cloister. But men, having decided that only they could be priests, considered themselves also entitled to dictate how women religious should live. The women constantly resisted outside direction, with varying degrees of success, and continue to resist to this day.

Sometime between 343 and 420 A.D., Saint Jerome kindly allowed the daughter of a friend, one Laerta, to study. She won the privilege by pledging herself to virginity. The first known convent was founded in 512 by Archbishop Caesarius of Arles, who placed his sister Caesaria in charge. The bishop also composed a "Rule for Nuns and Monks" which briefly preceded the Rule of Saint Benedict of Nursia, Abbot of Monte Cassino. The Benedictine Rule eventually governed life in virtually all monasteries and convents.

Vows of poverty, chastity, and obedience were required for membership in a religious order. Because the world was full of evil and temptation, and women were frail (being not only easy to tempt, but a temptation in themselves), claustration was decreed. Women were to be enclosed within the convent as much as possible, and the world was to be kept strictly out of the community's "cloister." All activities—prayer, work, sleeping, eating—were to be done together, and, except for the daily business and disciplinary meeting in the chapter house, in the greatest possible silence. Over the centuries, these rules were subject to cycles of lapse and reform. What remained constant was the horarium or holy office which was the prayers said together in the chapel every three hours, day and night, from matins at midnight to compline at the end of the day's work. These prayers were the heart of the structure, the very reason for the convent's existence.

Most medieval nuns were upper class. Poor women who felt a need to withdraw from the world, but could not read, were allowed in to perform the necessary manual labor—an arrangement which continued almost to the present day. There were gardens and books in the convents, and, in the best years, in the tenth and eleventh centuries, there were power and influence.

There were far, far more monks than nuns in the Middle Ages, and the monks were much richer. The women always struggled, both economically and for recognition of their right to exist. Not only were they "mere" women, but they were largely restricted to living in their convents, and to prayer as their occupations. Most nuns did not teach, or nurse, or take on the administration of charities until the early eighteenth century.

"Get thee to a nunnery" was not for everyone the bleak banishment Ophelia felt it to be. Many women *wanted* to be nuns. The hope of seeking spiritual perfection and union with God was real to them, as was the hope of easing not only their own salvation, but that of others through prayer. The church fathers were relatively tolerant as long as nuns appeared to live according to the medieval ideal they were meant to exemplify: silent, secluded, and subordinate. But many women entered a convent because their intelligence and energy could find no safe

expression in the outside world. (Look what happened to Joan
of Arc!) Those women were, by their nature, nonconformists
and troublemakers. The correspondence of the mother superiors
through the centuries is a long record of beseeching, imploring,
and explaining letters to bishops, cardinals, and the Vatican.
The nuns agitated always to be included as adults in the life of
the church.

During the great monastic reforms of the thirteenth century,
the men began studying at universities, and the nuns were left
angrily behind. Even the reformers, the new mendicant orders
of Dominicans and Franciscans, wanted no connection with
women. Saint Francis objected (futilely) to the pope's insistence
that the Poor Clares be included as "sisters" of the Franciscans.
"God has taken away our wives, and now the devil gives us
sisters," he grumbled. They offered the usual excuse for cutting
women out of the action—an excuse cited in all cultures: nuns
are women, and women are a temptation against chastity, so it
is women who should be enclosed and excluded.

Celibacy, in theory the heroic vow, an act of consecration and
denial so supreme as to cast a kind of spell of protection around
its professor, was not an invention of the church. The Vestal
Virgins of ancient Rome were buried alive if they broke their
vow, but after thirty years of service they were free to marry.
Unchaste nuns were not killed (although they were threatened
with eternal hellfire), but neither were they ever free of their
vow.

In fact, celibacy is not necessarily the extraordinary sacrifice
it seems to most people of the twentieth century. A nun's sanc-
tioned virginity (as opposed to a spinster's unconsecrated re-
dundancy) could be an escape from subordination to a husband,
from early death in childbirth, from distraction.

As the centuries rolled on, each age would leave its mark, a
moment of history embedded, as in amber, in immutable custom. In the fifteenth century, the forehead was considered a
feature of great beauty. Modesty required that it be covered.
And so it remained covered, *in the same fifteenth-century style*,
until nuns began to abandon their habits after the Second Vatican
Council in 1962. Not until 1950 was the complete subjection of
the day and night to the schedule of the horarium revised to
allow some flexibility for work. The Sisters of Notre Dame wore,
for one hundred and sixty years, an approximation of the garb
worn by the peasants of eighteenth-century France, the dress of
their founder, Saint Julie.

From time to time, a man would urge that women should be educated. Erasmus, at the beginning of the sixteenth century, did, and he struck a chord in France. The Ursulines were founded in 1534 to prepare women to be educated mothers, but the women who wanted to be educated tended not to want to be mothers, and the Ursulines ended up producing nuns. At the same time a woman in England named Mary Ward began offering a Jesuit education to girls, but her effort was quickly suppressed by Rome as unsuitable for women.

The French Revolution, and the subsequent repression of religious orders, had the contrary effect of prompting women to found orders specifically for the purpose of educating girls.

The founders always planned to include poor girls, but economic necessity usually resulted in upper-class, or, in time, middle-class students. Religion and the ladylike skills of value to a gentlewoman were, almost inevitably, far more important in the curriculum than academic subjects.

Many nuns found a fresh outlet for their adventurous spirits in the missionary opportunities beckoning from the New World. They set off, often with rather vague plans of converting the Native Americans. Between 1790 and 1920, 38 new orders were founded in the United States, and 118 European orders arrived to set up convents. There were 200 nuns in the United States in 1822; in 1850 there were 344 nuns and 1,109 priests. By 1920 there were 88,773 nuns—almost four times more than there were priests. In 1988 there were 106,912 nuns and only 53,522 priests.

Instead of preaching to the besieged Native Americans, the nuns—often on the orders of a bishop—began founding hundreds of female academies. Their schools offered virtually the only secondary education available to women—either Catholic or Protestant—in the nineteenth century. As the population grew in the new cities along the rivers of the Middle West, so grew the academies, bringing a genteel culture to the frontier. Those academies left the sweeter memories of "going to the nuns": the embroidery lessons, the snatches of Latin and passages of French, the classes in catechism muddled up with instructions in deportment.

Back in the East, a movement was growing to educate women as adequately as men, or well enough to allow self-sufficiency, at least, and at best a reformed world. Unfortunately, the convent schools stopped short of that degree of revolution. They aimed for salvation in the next world, and they concentrated on teaching convent virtues to achieve it: self-sacrifice, humility, submission. The sentimental, highly feminine, rather smug, and often childish piety they valued was not specifically Catholic. After the Industrial Revolution, as Ann Douglas brilliantly described in *The Feminization of American Culture*, men took over the hard, masculine, commercial and industrial sphere. Women, in alliance with a declining clergy, were relegated to being cultural custodians, the "beautiful influence." A middle-class Victorian frailty became the feminine ideal, in most glaring contrast to the way most American women actually lived. But who better to reinforce the ideal than nuns, who were themselves the ultimate custodians of virtue? For centuries nuns had taken upon themselves the task of wiping away the sins of the world through prayer. They had become static forms, totems of clarity who absolved the rest of the world from confronting its own paradoxes. They had become—and not only to Catholics—an *idée fixe*, women whose job was taking care of virtue—like the Vestal Virgins. Not until the Second Vatican Council did real women begin to step out from behind that immutable image, and when they did, the world reacted with the same shocked confusion it might have shown if the plaster statue of the Blessed Virgin Mary had stepped down from its pedestal and begun to dance.

In the middle of the nineteenth century came the great flood of European immigrants—poor, despised, and Catholic—to a nation that was all but officially Protestant, whose historical memory was anti-Papist. They came—indeed, they built—the cities of the northeast and the Great Lakes. Catholicism was the only thing they had in common, and the church rose to the challenge. Rarely before or since have priests been so priestly. They organized, ministered, led, succored, civilized. And built churches.

In 1884, at the Third Plenary Council of Baltimore, the United States bishops voted to require a Catholic education for every Catholic child. In some parishes, priests withheld the sacraments from parents who sent their children to public school. The parochial school system unified urban Catholics, sustaining and increasing the faithful. But convent life changed drastically. Nuns, unpaid—the serfs of the Catholic church—were needed to teach in those expensive new schools and parishes. A great harvest of daughters began.

Nuns were no longer teaching only the daughters of the middle class. Suddenly they were transferring a Catholic heritage to both boys and girls, and many of those the urchins of the lower class. Many of the new nuns had once been urchins themselves. It is those nuns, and the atmosphere of those schools, which haunt several generations of Catholics still alive today. The romanticized, loving resignation of the nun played by Ingrid Bergman in the movie *The Bells of St. Mary's* was the ideal, so important to the sentiments of Catholics that Bergman was driven out of the country when she was revealed, after all, as an adulterous movie star. In hindsight, a truer image of those parochial school wardens is probably the ferociously cruel, ravingly abusive nun in the play *Sister Mary Ignatius Explains It All for You*.

Nuns, in general, are not particularly well liked in the United States. And yet, even people with the most terrifying classroom memories hold on to the ideal. They insist that nuns (alone among all God's people) should, having chosen to be nuns, remain static—as icon, symbol, artifact. But the nuns themselves managed to sustain the power that came from being different only by the most rigid refusal to reveal their true condition to the outside world.

The nuns in those parochial schools were Catholics of their time, suffering from a ghetto fear and a terror of contamination by the Protestant elite. In too many parishes the dominant emotions were the confusion and cruelty and contradictions of Irish Catholic alcoholism. Piety and conformity were more important than academic excellence. Worst of all, the nuns were not educated themselves. The priests boasted of the school buildings but quite deliberately discouraged the nuns' efforts to improve the teaching inside them. In the classroom the nuns were unprepared, afraid, and overwhelmed. Not until well into the twentieth century did standards of teaching in parochial schools begin to meet public school requirements, as the nuns, forbidden entrance to male Catholic colleges—forbidden even to study theology until halfway through this century—began founding their own colleges.

There were so many more nuns than priests that by default the nuns became in charge of teaching religion. The priests were preoccupied with fundraising. Had the different orders of nuns ever gotten together to pool their talent and resources, or even to discuss their problems, the entire history of the twentieth-century American Catholic church might be different. But they didn't. Instead, they competed for recruits and students. The academies merrily expanded into colleges, despite the nuns' lack of higher degrees. By 1962, of 276 women's colleges in the United States, 155 were Catholic (and offering higher degrees).

For nearly two thousand years, nuns had maintained the extreme delicacy of their position: not priests and yet not lay people; not dependent women and yet not independent. What sustained them was the great bond of community. Unhappily, in time custom calcified the rituals of community into a shell that suffocated individuality. By the 1950s not only the convents but the entire Catholic church in the United States had grown stagnant. And it was rapidly growing irrelevant. The faithful would not have recognized themselves as moribund, but Pope John XXIII did.

Five: Burning the Whips and Chains

PAT

I entered the Sisters of Notre Dame on September 8, 1967—our Lady's birthday—five years after Barbara Ferraro. The trunk I brought along to the Connecticut novitiate in Fairfield was full of regular clothes—skirts and blouses and jackets, in dull tones and baggy shapes. I was glad to know that the rules were changing and I would never have to wear the traditional habit. It looked hot.

In high school I had been taught by the Sisters of St. Joseph. A nun we called the Little General had once spent an entire study period explaining the iconography of her habit. The fifteen pleats on the front of the long dress represented the different mysteries of Jesus' life, birth, and resurrection. The white triangle on the forehead framed by black veiling stood for the Trinity. I certainly didn't choose to enter the Sisters of Notre Dame because their habit was less symbol-laden, but it helped.

The real reason I chose the Sisters of Notre Dame was because I had had them as teachers from the fifth to the eighth grade at Holy Cross School in Springfield, Massachusetts, and I liked them. They seemed down-to-earth, and they enjoyed the lay teachers and got along with each other. They even played basketball in the gym. When the windows of the gym were partially blocked with brown paper, we'd peep through them and spy on our teachers doing what we thought was prohibited. And my God, how they laughed! They didn't have that glazed-eyed look of women communicating with a distant deity. They were grounded on earth, and I knew that was good. When I was in grade school I began to think I might be like them someday, but I never spoke it out loud. I was afraid people would think I was weird.

41

Also, the Sisters of Notre Dame were an international order, and I wanted to be a missionary. I dreamed of spreading the good news of Jesus Christ in the poorest parts of the world. If I should become a martyr, thrown to the crocodiles, so be it.

I arrived at the novitiate with name tags sewn on everything. By this time, nuns no longer gave up their own names. I would always be Patricia Ann Hussey. There were three Patricias in my group of nine postulants. Plain Patricia, Patricia Eileen, and me, Patricia Ann. Only two of us were still around to take our first vows in 1970. I was the last to leave the order, but I held out until 1988, and when I left it was for the same reasons that I had become a nun. I wanted to make the world a better place, to commit my life to God and the people of the earth. I wanted to be part of a larger agenda.

I was seventeen years old and my grasp of the particular aspects of the world that might need improvement was pathetically limited. If someone had asked me what, exactly, I saw myself doing in the future, I probably would have talked about going to Africa, where I had read about missionaries being killed by the guerrillas. The people there seemed a likely object of good works. Clothe the naked, feed the hungry, and suffer joyfully for the Lord. No one had told me about the snakes and bugs.

Nor had anyone told me about colonialism and structural poverty. Or about wars of liberation.

It was 1967. My entire generation was on the march. In the spring of that year, ten thousand hippies painted themselves in Day-Glo colors and held a "be-in" in New York City's Central Park. It was a preposterous and wonderful collective celebration of peace and love. In March, Martin Luther King, Jr., spoke out against the Vietnam War, saying it was wrong in itself, and its cost was destroying the hopes of the civil rights movement and of the poor.

On April 25, the governor of Colorado, John A. Love, signed the nation's first law legalizing abortion.

The Six-Day War between Israel and Egypt and other Arab states happened in June. There were riots in Buffalo and Detroit. In July, General Westmoreland asked Secretary of Defense NcNamara for more troops to be sent to Vietnam. In August, Stokely Carmichael called for a black revolution in America, and American planes bombed the suburbs of Hanoi.

In October, the first black justice, Thurgood Marshall, was sworn in at the Supreme Court. And seven white men were convicted of conspiracy in the brutal murder of three civil rights workers, Andrew Goodman, Michael Schwerner, and James Chaney. In Washington, D.C., clouds of tear gas rolled over thousands of people marching on the Pentagon to protest the war.

On October 27, a priest, Father Philip Berrigan, was arrested in Baltimore for pouring duck blood on files in a local draft office.

And in September of that year, I, Patricia Ann Hussey, went one evening into the chapel of the novitiate to say compline. It was nine o'clock at night, and I was feeling very, very holy. There I was, very self-conscious, completing the schedule of a nun's day, on my knees in an enormous dim chapel. Very piously, I made the sign of the cross, genuflected as I stepped out of the pew, and started to walk veery slooowly down the side aisle. Suddenly I saw a dark figure fall to the floor. Now, I had already learned that we were never to speak to an older nun unless she spoke to us first, and even then we were restricted to replying "Praise forever. Amen." But that lesson went entirely out of my mind.

"Are you all right?" I whispered, leaning over the recumbent form that turned out to be a novice named Barbara. Was it a fit? Had she fainted? Maybe she was dead!

She turned her head to the side, her arms stretched out flat, her cheek against the marble floor, and looked at me through her one visible eye as though I had just reversed the earth in its spin. Slowly she gathered herself up and stood facing me. She was astonished. I was astonished. We stared at each other.

"Of course I'm all right," she said, finally. "I'm just kissing the floor."

Kissing the floor? I had already spent the afternoon wondering what on earth an admonition to "practice modesty of the eyes" could mean. And now kissing the floor seemed to be a routine activity. I wondered what would come next.

The days passed in a pleasant enough cycle of chores, prayers, and lessons; lessons, prayers, and chores. I was learning a part, the role of a nun, but it didn't seem quite real. I was waiting for it to connect to my vision of myself, all in white, bringing grace to the lands of the equator, a kind of Lady Bountiful of the Beatitudes. What was odd—although I couldn't have identified it at the time—was that everyone seemed to be waiting for something. It was like the moment before the weather breaks, or the tide turns.

What we were waiting for was direction. The Second Vatican Council, which began in 1962 and closed in 1965, had called for *aggiornamento*, renewal. Most astonishing, it had called on nuns to discover our own renewal, in effect to reinvent ourselves according to our own deliberations. By the time I entered the order, the idea of self-determination had just begun to sink in, and we were standing, nervous and excited, on the edge of change.

One afternoon during the winter of my first year as a postulant, I happened, quite by accident, to be present for one of those seemingly unremarkable moments that prove in retrospect to be turning points. I had gathered up the trash on the third floor of the postulate and taken the elevator down to the incinerator room in the basement. It was cold outside, and the furnace was going full blast. I walked in with my bag of trash, and there, before the roaring, crackling flames, stood the mistress of novices, Sister Patricia Agnes. In full habit, her black skirts whirling in the heat, she was dropping into the incinerator, one by one, an armload of what were quite obviously whips. We stood there, me burning the trash, Sister Patricia Agnes burning whips.

By the time I entered the convent, postulants were allowed to ask questions. Since I clearly had questions about the whips, we had quite an interesting discussion about the spirituality of women and the traditions of self-denial and identification with the scourged and suffering Jesus that had been passed on from the early Middle Ages. Until, apparently, that very moment.

Kissing the floor, according to Sister Mary Josepha, was a way of showing reverence for the earth. That explanation was radically different from the one Barbara was taught, that kissing the ground was an act of great humility because the sinful earth (and all its works) existed only to be overcome in the great task of perfecting a spiritual life. That version would have made no sense at all to me. I *liked* the earth. I thought it was one of God's best ideas. Too bad human beings had so far proved to be such poor custodians. I more or less imagined my spiritual path as trying to be a better custodian.

From the start I was a "new" nun. In 1967, Barbara Ferraro, whom I would not meet for another eleven years, had begun testing her fledgling Vatican II wings in Salem, New Hampshire, where she was teaching fifth grade. Thanks to Pope John XXIII, my wings, unlike Barbara's, were never clipped. Plucked a little perhaps, with a loss of some of the downy underlayer, but the primaries remained intact.

Sometimes I wonder what path I would have chosen if I had been at the "be-in" in Central Park, or marched on Washington to protest the Vietnam War. But there was never any chance of that. Becoming a nun was, oddly enough, the only way I knew of to become a radical—even in 1967.

My mother always liked to say that she grew up in an ecumenical household. Her father was Lutheran and her mother was Irish Catholic. In the Springfield, Massachusetts, of the early 1900s that was cross-cultural clash. My mother, whose name is June, was the fifth of six children. A few years before her father died he finally made the rest of the family happy and was baptized a Catholic. I'm sure it made my father's family even happier because the Husseys were the kind of strict Catholics who believed non-Catholics would have a lot of trouble getting into heaven.

I was born first, on November 7, 1949. Two years later my brother Walter came along, and in 1955 my sister June was born. My hometown of Milford was a small place on the shore then, not yet swallowed up by its neighbors in New Haven and Bridgeport. In the 1950s all families were supposed to look alike, and, while few of them were the happy little group that was beginning to appear on television as the "norm," my family actually matched the ideal. We were middle class, white, with three children, a mother at home, and a father who left for work every morning and came home almost every night for supper. My parents were deeply committed to their religion and to trying to live in a Christian way. They were very loving, very affirming, and nothing was more important to them than spending time with us children.

The most vivid picture I have of my early life in Milford is of us kids setting out for our daily walk with our mother. In the winter she would put the youngest into the stroller with blankets and extra mittens, and then she would tuck us all into our snowsuits, patting and hugging us. She still does that whenever she is with us, strokes and pats and gives little loving tugs to our hair or our fingers or whatever she can get her hands on. In the summer she would load pails and shovels and little water wings on top of whoever was in the stroller. Then we would head off down the hill. My mother was a firm believer in exercise. "Got to get the kids out!" she would say. And we would walk, a little convoy of Husseys, almost two miles a day.

We had two favorite stops, Bayview Beach and the local bookstore. Eventually I think we bought and devoured every children's book ever published. My favorite book was called *The Poky Little Puppy*, about a puppy who was always lagging behind his siblings and getting home late, but in time to eat all the dessert they had been sent off to bed without. My mother began to call me her Poky Puppy. She says I was a very slow and deliberate child. I even threw baseballs very thoughtfully. I dawdled along beside the stroller, and sometimes she would ask me what on earth I was thinking about. Then she would say, "Oh well, Tricia honey, you go right on thinking. I know when you have it figured out we will all hear about it."

Bayview Beach was on Long Island Sound, not on the Atlantic Ocean. The Connecticut shoreline is one of the most beautiful in the world, full of coves and tidal marshes and sandy strips, and I loved it. Even today I need to feel salt spray on my face and breathe the sharp sea air to be truly at peace with myself. Whenever I have been very troubled I have always tried to reach the ocean. Its overwhelming greatness heals and calms me.

I think I first felt what I would later describe as a spiritual experience by the sea. It struck me the way contemplating the stars on a clear summer night has struck other people I know, or the way some of the astronauts talked about how they felt when they gazed down upon the earth as it hung revealed in the universe. It is a feeling not so much of closeness to God, as a kind of astonished yet restful willingness to believe God exists.

Just before my tenth birthday my father got a promotion and we moved to Springfield, Massachusetts, back near our family. My Hussey grandparents began to visit, as regularly and "normally" as a kind of Catholic Norman Rockwell illustration. They would go to confession on Saturday afternoon and drop by for Saturday night supper, and then come back after Sunday mass for breakfast and a big Sunday noon dinner.

My youngest brother, Michael, was born that year. I didn't know until very recently that my mother nearly died when he was born. At one point during her labor the doctor told my father that he would have to choose between the baby and my mother. Catholic doctors were not supposed to present such a choice in 1959. They were supposed to save the baby, and rejoice that God had taken the mother to heaven. But my father, murmuring something about needing my mother to help raise the children (he didn't want to sound selfish and admit that *he* needed her), told the doctor to save my mother. As it turned out, they both lived, but my brother would never quite catch up. He is today a happy, cheerful, willing young man, but he has had great difficulty learning to read. He is also, truly, the most dearly beloved member of our family. It would take me many years to realize that not all of the accidents which so often accompany birth turn out so happily.

When I was in high school I was a volunteer at a place called Brightside, which was a home for abused and abandoned children run by the Sisters of Providence in Holyoke, Massachusetts. The idea of volunteering came through a program run by my high school, and I drove up once in a while to take the kids swimming or out to the movies. I remember how astonished I was to discover that not all families were like mine. I had been thinking about poor little orphaned children before I started, and instead I met kids like the five Harrison children. They were very young, from eight down to three, and they had blue eyes, blond hair, and freckled faces. The nuns told me the Harrison parents were both alcoholics and could not take care of their children. I just couldn't understand how such a thing could happen, how the children would ever deal with their loss or how the parents could leave them.

I was sheltered and protected in my youth, but in a way that resulted in security, and it is for that that I am most grateful to my parents. It was not the kind of security that would have made me fearful of the world, but the kind that allowed me to go out into it. I was a quiet young girl, but I had a challenging and rebellious spirit, and my parents always helped me to channel it toward discovery rather than trying to nip me into conformity.

For example, I learned in my very earliest catechism classes that Catholics who did not attend Sunday mass were doomed to eternal damnation in hell unless they repented of their mortal sin. The idea seemed okay to me until I began to notice that Mr. Moran, my best friend's father, never went to mass.

As far as I could see, Mr. Moran loved his wife and his daughter Mary Ann. He was always cheerful when the neighborhood gang tore up his grass and filled his before-dinner hour with shrieking as we played Capture the Flag in his yard. All year he coached the girls' sports teams and drove us to games. He was a wonderful man, a good and generous and loving man, and I decided he was certainly not going to be condemned to the eternal fires because he missed mass sometimes.

That was the first time I found myself in direct conflict with the official teachings of the church. The problem was, the teaching conflicted drastically with the lived reality of a real and good human being. I knew Mr. Moran, and, even more important, I knew that the God my parents had taught me about was a good God, compassionate and sensible. I decided the rule, not God, was absurd.

Every school day from 1963 through 1967 I walked to Cathedral High School. I wore the girls' uniform: a green pleated skirt, a white blouse, and a green jacket with green patches on the sleeves. The boys wore gray slacks and blue blazers with white shirts and blue ties. There were 2,800 students at Cathedral High School, and we all looked exactly alike except for one boy. He was black. Only one black in a city with a growing black Catholic population, in a school that cost each student only twenty dollars a year for books and uniforms!

I was somewhat lost in my class of 692 people. I had never traveled beyond New England, and even though half the class was male, I didn't go out on dates very much. My folks were pretty strict, and in junior high school when a lot of my friends went off to take cha-cha lessons, my parents couldn't afford to send me. I did manage to go to the senior prom with someone I was fixed up with at the last moment. My social life sounds pretty pitiful, but I didn't feel like a nerd. In fact, I wasn't a nerd. It was just that other things were more important to me.

I graduated sixty-seventh out of those 692, and I was a member of the National Honor Society. Girls didn't have organized sports teams then, but I played on the intramural teams, and I even joined the math club—I can't imagine why; I hated math. All my friends were going to college, and whenever any of them asked me what I was going to do after graduation I would say, "Go to college, what else?" How could I explain I was going into a convent? The prospect left me speechless myself. And I suspected that some of my friends wouldn't be surprised. I didn't want to give them the satisfaction of being right.

I was not always at dawn mass, or constantly dropping into the chapel for a word or two with God. In fact I wasn't any more pious than they were. But I wasn't very interested in marriage and I was pretty idealistic—and with those attitudes, what else could a good Catholic girl do?

I wasn't at all interested in money or things that money could buy, such as cars, houses, boats. I knew some girls in my class who were living for the day they would get married. They walked up and down the corridors carrying copies of *Modern Bride*, and they talked about china patterns. I thought they were taking on a huge responsibility, but I also had a vision of their future that I couldn't get out of my head—I saw them marching up to the altar in a cloud of white tulle, and then walking out of the church and disappearing for the rest of their lives. I didn't want to disappear. I wanted to make the world a better place.

What was important to me was to try to make a difference with my life within the world, within the church, and to my God. And the Sisters of Notre Dame seemed to be the best avenue through which I could channel my life, time, and energy. In grammar school I had been impressed by the way the sisters reached out to the marginal kids. The idea of working together with a warm community of women, as I imagined a convent to be, was very appealing. Some of my aunts and uncles talked about nuns as though they were a special, sacred group, but I thought of nuns as regular women who had chosen a different life-style. Who wanted to be put on a pedestal? Pedestals are as confining and limiting as any other small space.

I wish I could say that an angel sat on my shoulder and whispered, "Patricia Ann Hussey, you are hereby called to consecrate your life to God." If there was an angel, the part was played by Julie Andrews. As Maria Von Trapp in *The Sound of Music* she listened so intently as her mother superior sang "Climb Ev'ry Mountain." Since I was thinking about becoming a nun the song was a great inspiration to me. (I scarcely noticed that after Maria heard it, she left the convent, married the baron, and lived happily ever after.)

I was ready to conquer the world with my enthusiasm. If I had been born two hundred years ago, and born a boy, I would have run away to sea. But given who I was in 1967, the most challenging and adventurous life I could think of was to enter a convent. Becoming a nun was my romantic way of living.

I remember I once saw on television some nuns in full habit taking part in a civil rights march, and I thought they were slick. They were the part of the church that was alive for me, that had something to say about what was right and just, and what was wrong and evil. Even though the real world was just shadows to me, I was absolutely clear that I did not intend, by entering a convent, to escape the world. I certainly wouldn't be able to feed the hungry by sticking labels on jelly jars in a Trappist monastery.

If I had been in public school, if I had never known any nuns, if I had not been taught that my only options were marriage or the convent—I might have been attracted to the Peace Corps. But of course, at seventeen, I had no skills to offer. And the Peace Corps wouldn't have been permanent enough for me. I was looking for a long-term commitment. And I figured the only way to do things was to go flat out, all the way at once, forever. My parents wondered if I wanted to finish college first. "I know what I want, so why wait?" I said.

The first challenge was to be admitted to the Sisters of Notre Dame. Things had changed since Barbara slipped in with just a quick physical and a statement of purpose. I had to go through months of psychological tests. Rorschach blots and Minnesota Multiphasic Personality Inventory. Draw the person and connect the dots. The tests seemed endless and nerve-wracking. I began to wonder if I was, in fact, normal.

The purpose of all that probing was to find out if I was psychologically balanced and fit to live up to the demands of nundom. Sometimes, when I think about the women who left nundom over the succeeding years, and when I think about the strange ones who stayed, I wonder what kind of personality traits they were looking for. Whatever those were, I passed.

My family drove me to the Fairfield novitiate. The nuns were suspiciously welcoming. "Hi! Mr. Hussey, Mrs. Hussey. How are you? Would you like a tour? These are the gardens. This is where your daughter will be sleeping and here is where she will be eating." I had been taught by enough nuns to make me wonder when the cozy tea party atmosphere would stop.

I had never been away from my family before. I don't even remember ever having been left with a baby-sitter. As we toured my new home, my mother was crying and patting my head and my shoulder. Finally, it was time for them to leave. I had been planning to be a big brave person and not shed a tear, but as they drove down the driveway, Michael leaned out of the car window and howled, "P-A-A-A-A-T. . . ." My eyes filled up with tears.

From then on I would see them only once a month, for exactly two hours on a Sunday afternoon. But that first day, I stood there, swallowing my tears, holding the dime my mother had just given me.

"If you ever need me, Tricia, or need to talk to us, this is just to make sure. Get to a pay phone if anything happens," she said. I still have that dime.

The tea party stopped by dinnertime. September 8 was the Feast of Our Lady, and as a celebration all the nuns had steak to eat. The new postulants had little frozen pot pies. The difference must have seemed a bit extreme even to the nuns because someone explained that our stomachs wouldn't be able to digest steak after such an exciting day. The reality had begun. I was now actually with the people who were going to change the world with me.

When I entered the convent it was not as archaic a decision as it might now seem. Convents all over the country were expanding. The tide would very soon begin to run the other way, but in 1966 there were 181,421 nuns in the United States, the most there would ever be. Change was in the air—positive change— and the Catholic church was part of it.

There was a brief moment, and for me I will date it 1967, when it seemed as though we would at last become an inclusive society.

The civil rights movement was about inclusion.

The poverty programs, with their idea of maximum feasible participation of the people, were about inclusion.

The protests against the Vietnam War were about the people demanding to be included—and heard—in the formation of policies that were deciding matters of life and death for our youth and the population of an entire country.

The ideas of Pope John XXIII, in his encyclicals and in his guidance of the Second Vatican Council, were about inclusion of the faithful. The Catholic church was becoming open. The Mass was to be in a language people could understand. The priest had turned around to face the people, and to face the world. "You are us, and we are you," the church seemed to be saying.

You are us, and we are you. It is the most important principle, the Golden Rule, Christ's message. If we understand that, no one can be excluded, starved, murdered, scorned. If we understand that, the world can really be changed.

I understood the idea, and although I was completely ignorant of the incredible difficulty of applying it, I became a nun to try.

I was a young girl in 1967, sheltered and naive. Mississippi and Da Nang were very remote to me. But change for the better was in the air I breathed, and my church was part of that change. For a very long time it seemed that the church and I were changing together, and in the same positive direction.

Six: *Aggiornamento*

PAT

Most of the turmoil of the sixties in the United States took place in the streets. But for American Catholics, the most revolutionary change of all began under Bernini's gilded bronze *baldacchino* in St. Peter's Cathedral in Rome.

There, on October 11, 1962, Pope John XXIII convened the Second Vatican Council. In 1869, the First Vatican Council had been called to reassert the church's authority against "the heresies of modernity." This time, the cardinals and bishops and the great Vatican bureaucracy known as the Curia had been called together to bring Catholicism into the modern world.

"We are going to shake off the dust that has collected on the throne of Saint Peter since the time of Constantine and let in some fresh air," announced Pope John. It was to be an *aggiornamento*, a bringing up to date. A renewal.

When Angelo Giuseppe Roncalli was elected Pope John XXIII in 1958, the Curia expected him to be a genial interim figure, an appealing personality after the long and highly rigid reign of Pope Pius XII, but not quite a full-scale pope-like leader. His encyclicals, *Mater et Magistra* and *Pacem in Terris*, however, gave fair warning that he was impatient with the state of the church and eager to use his new authority. The Curia, surprised, found itself preparing to argue for the preservation of the status quo.

And so the men gathered in Rome, row after row of them down each side of the nave, all in white satin robes, each with a white satin pointed bishop's mitre. They arrived as representatives of a church that stood for uniformity, certainty, and an absolute central authority. But many of them were all too aware that the rigidity of that structure was about to collapse under the pressure of reality.

The Catholic church of the 1960s had become the world's largest religion. But it was no longer a European religion. It had become a world church, and above all a Third World church.

There were, by the way, fifteen women auditors at the Second Vatican Council. They appeared on November 2, 1963, presumably as part of the confrontation with reality. Only one of them was an American, Mary Luke Tobin, a Sister of Loretto from Kentucky, who was head of the Conference of Major Superiors of Women Religious in the United States.

In June 1963, Pope John XXIII died, and Giovanni Battista Montini was elected to succeed him as Paul VI. He pushed the work of the Council forward.

Decisions and documents and pronouncements began to reach the faithful. In 1964, Latin was abolished as the official language of the liturgy. Mass would now be said in English, or Swahili or Chinese, whatever the language of the people. The change forced a rude awakening. Instead of seeming sacred and mysterious, the Mass seemed arcane and hollow.

Nuns repeating their holy office found themselves gravely declaring in unison, "My enemies will be ground into powder under my feet. Glory to God, the Son, and the Holy Ghost." They could scarcely avoid wondering about the point of such prayers.

Wondering was the point of Vatican II. "Why are we doing this?" was the great question. "Is it because it has always been done, or because it illuminates our faith today?"

Priests and participants were forced to begin thinking about creating a liturgy that would be meaningful for our times. But the first step, the most important step in the transformation of the church, had already been taken. Vatican II told the priests to turn around and face the people during the Mass. They, and the church, turned toward the people and toward the world, forming a circle of the People of God. The monolithic, authoritarian Roman church was signaling that it wished to be one *with* the people, to be a community of equals, a servant of the poor. A declaration on the freedom of individual conscience signaled that the church was even willing to trust the people.

The church was admitting that it could, and must, change— and reminding the people that they were also responsible for defining the change.

On October 28, 1965, the Council declared that the Jews

should not be held accountable for killing Jesus, an extremely belated official dismantling of the justification for anti-Semitism.

After the Council closed, in December 1965, the declarations continued to pour out. The Index of publications Catholics were forbidden to read was abolished in 1966. A Catholic could now be married to a non-Catholic without fear of excommunication.

Pope John XXIII had called for honest dialogue among Catholics, and between Catholics and the other religions of the world. Experimentation was an essential part of that dialogue. Nuns and priests were specifically directed to try out new ways of ordering their lives, and to contribute to the reform of canon law according to the results. That process turned out to take almost twenty years.

"Charity, justice, and community" were the watchwords of Vatican II. Interpretation, dialogue, and experimentation carried us forward—and apart. Within the Roman church, Pope John XXIII's "renewal" has now become Pope John Paul II's "restoration." Today, the church is divided between the People of God and the men of Vatican City.

Meat on Fridays, mass on Saturday night, nuns in short skirts! It was all very startling. So startling, in fact, that many nuns allowed themselves to get bogged down in arguments about details; what to wear and when to eat, instead of how to define a mission.

The recommendations of Vatican II to nuns were a kind of carte blanche for self-discovery. We were told to rethink our role in the church, to redefine ourselves as "witnesses to the Resurrection and to the life of the Lord Jesus as a sign that God Lives" (and first we would have to define that bit of church talk). All of a sudden we could meet people, instead of rejecting them as worldly and dangerous. We could speak, telephone, watch television, eat in restaurants. We could go home to visit our families. We could be *with the people*.

We were encouraged to rethink our vows. We were suddenly entitled to ask WHY? as though we were grown-ups, instead of practicing "cadaver obedience." We could even decide for ourselves when to turn off the lights at bedtime.

Pope Paul VI urged us to be "overtly loving," but what did that mean in terms of chastity? We could admit that we were sexual beings, and that we had emotions . . . but then what?

He said we were to be with the church of the poor. What did poverty mean in that context? Was it morally right for nuns to live as a cheap labor pool teaching middle- and upper-class Catholic students?

Nuns were told to get into the world, educate ourselves, give up our medieval robes if that would make our mission easier, and take more responsibility for ourselves both collectively and individually.

Nuns, as we surely have demonstrated by now, were trained to obey. And so, when we were told to educate ourselves, we did it. There were already more of us than there were priests, and we rapidly outperformed them in higher education. Today, 65 percent of American nuns have master's degrees and 25 percent have doctoral degrees. Only 24 percent of American *bishops* have masters' degrees, and only 10 percent have doctorates.

Pope John was the only pope in history to encourage women to be all we could be. Alas that his reign was so short. It took us quite a while to realize that the rest of the hierarchy had no real understanding of the implications of what we were being encouraged to do. Probably they thought we would pray a little and decide that the old ways were the best ways. We were the daughters of the church and they were the fathers, and we were expected to be dutiful, as always. Their surprise, and discomfort, and eventually their fury as we developed different ideas was as ferocious as any husband's was in the 1970s when he discovered that his wife was no longer interested in folding his socks.

By 1984 we would immediately understand why the American bishops so bitterly attacked Geraldine Ferraro when she was running for vice president. But in 1965 we nuns were only beginning to learn to think of ourselves as individuals. We still thought the problems that seemed to exist because we were women could be fixed by a simple explanation of the necessary changes. In 1965 the Leadership Conference of Women Superiors petitioned Rome, asking for representation on Vatican commissions dealing with the lives of religious women. Instead, the superiors were allowed to be "a downward channel of communication." The Vatican would be willing to dictate directly to the superior, instead of to the local bishop or priests, and she would then dictate to the affected nun.

Even now there is still no structure through which an individual nun can deal in an adult way with a bishop, the bishop's conference, or the Curia. When, in 1984, we called for a dialogue on abortion within the church, we forgot that the lines had not yet been opened for women's voices to be heard.

* * *

Barbara would never have lasted as a Sister of Notre Dame if the balm of Vatican II had not come along to heal her ulcers and restore her enthusiasm. But for me, the turmoil seemed quite natural and exciting. It was what I expected. In fact, I was rather impatient that things didn't move faster. I have a picture of myself taken when I had just entered the novitiate. I am wearing a transitional habit all of black with a little round white collar at the neck, and a veil with my bangs slicked across my forehead. Perched on my nose is a pair of definitely post-conciliar glasses with tortoiseshell harlequin frames.

The sad part was that for many nuns, the turmoil was more than they could bear. The older ones liked being able to visit their families and some of them were even happy to give up their cumbersome habits. But the structure they had lived by for so many years was dissolving. Their profession had been to be a nun, and their most important work was offering prayers around the clock; ants whose compulsive duty was to transfer the earth to heaven bit by bit. Without the horarium, what was their identity? Even some of the younger nuns had trouble with parents who seemed to want their daughters to be living scapulars, identified by the old habit and reliably praying the family into heaven—the ultimate gift to God.

Understandably, many of the older nuns resented the sudden switch. One year all Catholics agreed that nuns' lives were meaningful and holy, and the next year the pope was saying they should renew themselves and be different. They were losing their sense of identity. Later, in the seventies, when I discovered that nuns did not invent the women's movement all on our own, I thought that the changes of Vatican II must have threatened the older nuns just the way feminism threatened women whose security was in being a housewife.

It also turned out to be much harder to keep a convent running smoothly without the old rigid rules. I remember one morning soon after I had first entered the convent, when I passed the laundry room at about six-thirty in the morning on my way to chapel and I thought I would be helpful. The laundry was the assigned charge of plain Patricia, but I thought I would just give it a start.

Unfortunately, I did something wrong and the machine started to eat the clothes and then with a horrible grinding it stopped. I had to go to lauds and then I had to sit through breakfast in silence. Finally, I could go up to the mistress of postulants and say, "Sister Mary Josepha, I broke the washing machine."

"What do you mean, *you* broke the washing machine?" she demanded, really puzzled.

"I tried to start it," I said.

"But the washing machine is not your chore," she said, and then she immediately began to scold plain Patricia.

My reflexive independence had thrown a cog in the well-oiled machinery of rules and obedience. Everything external was simpler and more orderly in the old ways, but everything internal was stifled. After Vatican II we had to talk, and respond, and cooperate. It was exhausting. Consider the effort of mind and spirit it took even to imagine, still less to implement, the idea that it might be equally desirable for each nun to have time to nurture her own private prayer life instead of being bound to static prayers with the entire community.

And it was so slow! It could take months for us to decide to extend our bedtime twenty minutes—and it took many more months for us to realize that a universal bedtime was ridiculous.

Vatican II had called on all religious orders to hold a General Chapter Meeting within three years of the close of the council to consider renewal. The great hope, as expressed, was that the orders would rediscover their roots in order to discover the principles that would govern their future.

For the Sisters of Notre Dame (SNDs) the first of a series of General Chapter Meetings took place in Rome at the end of 1967 and the beginning of 1968. There were about sixty delegates, representing what were then about five thousand SNDs worldwide. It was tremendously exciting for me as a new postulant. Every morning we would gather at nine o'clock for instruction, and we would read and discuss whatever section of the new rules—the Chapter Acts—had arrived. We even discussed the revisions. Instead of being presented with an edict, we spent every morning sharing our doubts and hopes and frustrations. We were truly scrutinizing the core of our existence as a religious order, and in the process we were redefining who we were and what we wanted to commit our lives to. We were becoming responsible, as adult women, for the life of the Sisters of Notre Dame.

As we talked, we changed our language. We began to talk about our self-government in terms of "collegiality" instead of a chain of command beginning with "superiors." We began to see our vows as freeing us for service in the world instead of locking us into an archaic life behind convent walls. The concepts of poverty, chastity, and obedience were beginning to evolve into those of responsible stewardship, responsible intimacy, and responsible sharing of authority.

Long before I had to take any action, the words we used challenged me. Words can be smoke and feathers, or they can be the means of claiming and defining our own lives. As nuns we spent an enormous amount of time choosing words, because we expected to say what we meant and live what we said.

The most important words I ever read as a nun, because they seemed to define my own desires, were written as part of "The Acts of the Special General Chapter of the Sisters of Notre Dame," a document that was published in 1969 to serve as the direction we had all been waiting for. They read:

> We must be prepared to be the unwelcome disturbers of the false peace and complacency, our own as well as others, that conceal the often inarticulate misery of two-thirds of our brothers and sisters.
>
> . . . Therefore, as a congregation . . . our preference is to serve the poor in the most neglected places.
>
> Sisters of Notre Dame share in the prophetic mission of the Church. We are called to become engaged with the elements of conflict in society; to reflect alone and with others upon the conflict . . . In the face of this, neutral living is counter witness to the gospel.

Those words demanded a radical commitment from me and I knew I wanted my life to measure up to those demands. I was generally determined to make my prophetic mission the task of afflicting the comfortable and comforting the afflicted. But I hadn't even finished college yet. How would I find "the most neglected places"? Often, I prayed I would be open to all the experiences that life and its people had to offer and that I would not be afraid of them.

Seven: My World Had Been So Small

PAT

My first year was spent as a postulant, cocooned in the Fairfield, Connecticut novitiate. Compared to Barbara's experience, my formation period was a trip to the beach. But those first sequestered months were a weird contrast to what was going on in the outside world. At least I, unlike Barbara, could read newspapers and watch some television so that when I ventured forth in the fall of 1968, dressed in a short black dress and a veil, to begin as a sophomore at Sacred Heart University in Bridgeport, Connecticut, I wasn't completely overwhelmed by the Age of Aquarius.

Martin Luther King, Jr., and Robert Kennedy were dead, martyrs to the cause of social justice. On television the image of a defeated Lyndon Johnson gave way to that of Chicago's Mayor Richard Daley, with his apoplectic, swollen face, and then to Richard Nixon in triumph. I met a veteran at school who talked about having made a lei of ears he had cut off the Vietnamese, stringing the ears on a piece of cord and wearing it around his neck. Blood and smoke and fear and rage swirled around the globe, from Washington, D.C., to Saigon to Paris. And overhead, on Christmas, three men circled the moon.

I was bewildered, and afraid, and hopeful all at once, yearning to seize hold of it all, to find my part. The most memorable event of that epic year for me was the day I finally plunged in to join a crowd from campus protesting the war in Vietnam. By that time protests were practically weekly events, even in Connecticut, and I had been longing to join in, but I hadn't told the director of novices what I was going to do.

What if I get arrested? I remember thinking. How in God's

name am I going to explain this one? Up to then, my only infractions had been unladylike things such as taking the stairs two at a time.

Then I realized I was actually *afraid*. It wasn't the thought of my novice director that had been keeping me on the edges, it was my own fear of what might happen.

"Be a good United States citizen, Pat," I scolded myself, "and practice your right to dissent."

Many protest marches have followed, but that was my first, and my first as a nun. It would never be as hard again. I was beginning to learn that the only way past fear is through it.

Two years later, on August 27, 1970, I made my first vows, or promises as they were called by that time. Only Margaret Kilmartin and I were left of our original group of nine. The cut-and-dried formula vow that Barbara had recited five years earlier had been changed. I wrote my own vows, trying to express exactly how I wanted to live my life.

Every word was chosen deliberately, chosen instead of another. I particularly wanted to update the words "poverty, chastity, and obedience." There had been hours of discussion in the convent about what it meant to choose to live in poverty. Poor people would not choose to be poor. Nuns had the luxury of being able to choose simplicity, but we would never be in real need.

The idea of obedience was fairly simple to resolve (or so it seemed at the time!) but I balked at putting the word "celibate" into the vow of formulation. The word "chastity" seemed a more positive statement.

Finally, the whole promise was looked over by a canon lawyer, and the great day came when I stood in the great Fairfield chapel and said:

Lord, strengthened by your love, I, Sister Patricia Hussey, come before you today. In the simple spirit that was Julie's [our foundress], I pray for the courage to give you my life— free and fearless in service of your poor. Filled with hope, I give you my life—chaste in love and for love; poor in fact and available to your people; obedient to the Spirit who directs me toward justice as the Acts of the Sisters of Notre Dame express. And, in trust, supported by a God-touched and frail community, I say "yes" to you today and tomorrow, and I ask for your help that I may remain faithful to you. Amen.

"Free and fearless." How those words have come up in my prayers over the last twenty years. I experience fear as paralysis, and my personal litany has often been:

Let me not be paralyzed.
Be not afraid, for I am with you.
Let me act despite my fear.
Let me know what I am afraid of.

One answer to those prayers was the realization that denying fear is part of being paralyzed. If I acknowledge my fears, face them, almost as if I am saying "How do you do?" and then hold them up for inspection, I can overcome my paralysis and move ahead. The important thing is to know, as clearly as I can, what I fear. Once I can name it, I can deal with it.

After making my first vows I was truly a "new" nun. I felt fairly bursting with openness and eagerness to embrace the world. And then I got a terrible shock. The world, in the person of my oldest friend, saw me differently.

Millie and I had known each other so long we could remember fighting over a yellow sponge duck at the beach on Long Island. We had shared everything all our lives until I entered the convent. I hadn't seen her for four years, and I was thrilled when she asked me to meet her for dinner at a little Italian restaurant just outside of Hamden.

We both pulled into the parking lot at the same time, jumped out of our cars, and hugged. Inside, everything was perfect. Linen tablecloths and napkins, a candle reflecting in our glasses of wine, wonderful smells of garlic and tomato sauce in the air. Millie toasted me, saying, "Here's to you, Pat, the first nun I've ever shared a bottle of wine with." I laughed and felt smug about how modern we new nuns had become.

We sipped wine and twirled spaghetti and slipped more and more into our old companionship. Pretty soon we were ranting and raving about Richard Nixon and Vietnam, the death penalty and the prison system. Having dealt with the problems of the world, we moved on to topics closer to home. We talked about schools and careers, my relationship with my new community and hers with her husband. The topics of abortion and birth control came up, as remote theoretical issues. Millie said she considered herself "anti-abortion," and she had problems with women who thought abortions were okay.

I think I must have said something like, "I can't imagine ever choosing to have an abortion, but it's a serious problem and I guess people deal with it in serious ways." The fact is, I don't think I had ever really given any thought to what it would be like to actually be in that situation.

I was so happy that Millie had invited me to dinner. Things now seemed to be the way they always had been with us. Ever since I had gone into the convent, I had felt a distance between us. Sometimes she wouldn't meet my eyes. I had worried, and yet I hadn't known exactly how to ask what was wrong. Was it because I was now a nun?

No, that can't be it, I would shrug. I decided that whatever was wrong, she would fill me in when the time came. And the time had finally come that night at dinner.

"Pat, I have something I want to tell you," Millie said, solemnly putting down her glass.

Uh-oh, I thought. She's going to tell me she's getting a divorce. I began adjusting my "openness" systems to hear about a divorce. I was ready to cope.

It was not a divorce. It was an abortion, I was to learn. Our earlier vague chat about abortion and birth control had been Millie's test to see if I could be trusted to respond sympathetically.

"We want so much to have children," she started, "but there is a genetically transmitted deformity in my family, and we wanted to be as sure as we could be that it wouldn't be passed on to our kids. I went to a hospital in New Haven for genetic counseling."

I nodded encouragingly.

"Before the results of the tests came back I thought I was pregnant." She looked at me warily. I nodded again.

"When I went to another doctor for a pregnancy test, I explained my situation to him. He told me I wasn't pregnant, and he gave me something to drink. Of course I never questioned him about what it was.

"A month later my regular doctor told me I was in fact pregnant. God, I was so scared. The first doctor wouldn't even tell me what I had taken. We had to call a lawyer to find out. Then we learned it was something that was supposed to abort the fetus. My own doctor told me it could have caused severe fetal damage. I was panic-stricken. I talked to the doctor, Paul talked to him, we all talked together. Finally, together, we decided that the only thing to do was to have an abortion."

I was stunned. I felt suspended in space indefinitely until I thought of something to say. And what a dumb thing it was!

"And did you?" I asked.

She nodded, looking at me anxiously.

I took her hand, and said, "Oh, I'm so glad you told me."

Two great emotional currents were rushing through me at once. One was: how could it have been wrong for Millie to make that choice? And the other was: why hadn't she been able to talk to me about it before? In the half-minute before I took her hand, a lifetime of reconsideration was whirling around in my head. I knew Millie as well as I knew anyone, and without any doubt she was a good and tender-hearted woman.

"Oh, Pat," she said, holding my hand and wiping her eyes at the same time, "I've felt so guilty. I've been so afraid you wouldn't understand, that no one would understand. Everyone will think I am a bad person. I hope when I die God will forgive me."

"Good grief, Millie, you aren't even a Catholic!" I burst out. "Where did you learn such guilt? God could never be as hard on you as you are on yourself. Certainly God has forgiven you. It's time you had some peace."

She laughed a little bit and sniffled.

The Catholic church's teaching on abortion began to fall apart in front of my eyes, just the way the teaching on Sunday mass had fallen apart when I was confronted with the real-life case of my neighbor Mr. Moran. Here was Millie, my friend, flesh and blood, and therefore, abortion could not be simply a case of right or wrong, or absolute distinction between morality and immorality. People's lives were involved here, and their lives didn't fit into the neat rules of the church's pronouncements.

I had never felt so helpless. I couldn't fix her anguish. I had no solutions, and I was too young to know that by asking me to dinner Millie had decided to move toward resolution for herself. By just sitting there and listening as she poured out her story, I was helping. With all my grandiose schemes of setting the world to rights I had certainly never recognized the comfort just listening can give.

Millie described the waiting room in the hospital before she had the abortion.

"Every one of us knew why the other women were there. You know, Pat, none of us could meet each other's eyes to offer even silent support. There were no words of comfort or encouragement spoken. Why? Why didn't we speak? God knows I could have used some kind words then, even from a stranger. Maybe we were all too scared, or too scared of what the other women thought.''

This was in 1969, before abortion was legal. Every woman there had had to go through a long and humiliating process to persuade the doctors—male—that she desperately needed an abortion. The picture of the waiting room flashed through my mind, and somehow it didn't fit the church's caricature of evil women who had abortions. Millie was still a good person. In fact, she seemed to have become more compassionate because of her own experience. She certainly didn't lose her heart and soul when she had an abortion.

We talked and talked, and finally we ended up laughing about the fact that in high school we had never been offered any sex education at all. There was one very odd experience in our sophomore year when a priest asked each girl in his religion class how long our menstrual periods were. But other than that the presumption was that the subject of responsible sex was covered by the word ''abstinence.'' The only time I remember having a discussion about abortion was when we read some soppy piece from the *Reader's Digest* by someone who was counting the birthdays of ''the child that might have been.'' The tendency of Catholic teachers at the time was to dilute ethical discussion with sentimental homily.

''I'm so glad you told me,'' I repeated. ''I was afraid something was lost between us.'' I paused, and I looked at Millie, her tears still glimmering in the candlelight. ''Something was wrong, wasn't it?''

She nodded.

''Oh, Pat,'' she said, ''you're a *nun* now. I thought you would just give me the party line. I didn't know if you could forgive me.''

''I was much more upset about the wall that had gone up between us than I could ever be about your deciding you needed to have an abortion,'' I said.

And I realized that I meant it from the bottom of my heart. But I was beginning to wonder how I would respond to someone who was not my best friend.

Eight: Learning

PAT

By 1970 the Vatican Council had begun to open up our lives beyond the prescribed limits. Work in all kinds of areas seemed possible: medicine, social work, music and art therapy, the law. The bright and emancipating idea dawned that a woman who felt happy and fulfilled in her work could only enhance the effort to build a world where all people would have dignity and justice.

The change was revolutionary. For hundreds and hundreds of years nuns had subjected themselves to a kind of automatic living, moving in lockstep to the Rule, and offering up to heaven such parts of their spirits as were amputated in the process. Now we began to try to live as though each woman's talent and inclination was part of God's plan for her life, and as such should be followed.

This wonderful, exuberant, Christian, humane notion came at an especially lucky time for me. I liked being a nun, but I had discovered that I did not like school. And I *hated* teaching. Nursing was completely out of the question.

So far, I had made one small turn toward my own path. I had decided to get a degree in special education, to learn how to help the emotionally disturbed, the mentally retarded, and those with learning disabilities. My order was very supportive, and sent me to Southern Connecticut State College. I had my doubts about the usefulness of college, but found that the classes in my own field would take me directly to the kind of people who needed me most.

One day my little group of student visitors from the special education department was given a tour of Southbury Training School, one of the state institutions for people with developmental disabilities. The social worker who was guiding us talked about the routine followed in the ward: when to change diapers, when to force-feed, how to move people to prevent bed sores.

"It will be instructive for you to understand the permanence of these problems if you read the charts attached to the cribs. Each person's birth date is noted," she said.

Rows of cribs were lined up under the windows running along the two side walls of the ward. The cribs were ordinary baby beds, the kind that have high barred sides that slide up and down, and are fairly big—big enough to hold a small child and a large collection of stuffed animals. There were few toys. I walked along a row.

It was 1972, a few years after the great famine in Biafra. These patients looked like the news photographs of starving Biafran children. They had the same frail, shrunken arms and legs, the same swollen bellies, the same vacant look in the eyes. Most were tiny, the size of a year-old child. I remember standing over one strangely twisted little figure, and looking at the chart on the crib. He had been born in 1950. He was twenty-two years old!

For several days after that visit I was so physically upset I couldn't eat. The classroom capers of my irritating professors made me madder than ever. I wanted to shout "WE can think! We have minds! Don't waste our time. Don't waste us!"

I kept wondering, Why are those people in those cribs alive? *Are* they alive, or is theirs some kind of living death?

I didn't know. I still don't know. The image of those lost children kept coming back to me years later when I was trying to figure out an answer to the question of abortion. But the memory didn't help make it any clearer, one way or the other. By the time I started actually working in an institution, medicine and educational methods had improved to the point that some children who would have spent their lives in an institutional limbo were able to go to classes and develop some self-reliance. But not all of them, and for those who fell so tragically and hopelessly short of adequate, the questions remained.

While I was going to school I lived in my first real community of professed Sisters of Notre Dame, at the Convent of St. Rita in Hamden, Connecticut. I was lucky to be with such a warm, supportive group of women.

At college, the courses in my field of study were excellent. But the rest of my teachers made me restless, disenchanted, sometimes angry. I couldn't believe the kind of silliness we were expected to sit through. I was sure I could be learning more on my own. As a matter of fact, the more time I spent out in the world the more I was learning, and I felt that school was a time-wasting series of empty lectures and stupid rules. I certainly sound like I was a college student of the sixties, don't I? Well, I was.

After three years, I graduated in 1972 with a bachelor of science degree in special education. My order then assigned me to a job as a regular school sister, to see how I would do. The provincial thought I needed some structure. I taught the fourth, fifth, and sixth grades at St. Teresa's in Providence, Rhode Island. I greatly admire good teachers, but I was distressed to discover that I was not going to be one of them. Working one-on-one with a student was grand. But when I faced an entire classroom of expectant little faces, I mostly felt inadequate.

I loved Fridays and detested Sunday evenings. At the end of the weekend I would begin sinking into a depression. I checked hopefully for fevers, cramps, spots, nausea. One night I found myself praying for a serious but not life-threatening illness. Alas, I seemed to have the constitution of an ox. Even though I lived in a brick convent that was a hundred years old, where the wind whistled through my corner bedroom windows on the third floor and I huddled on the bed inside a sleeping bag all winter, I was never sick. And, because I lived in the convent with the school principal and the rest of the faculty, I could never call in sick, or declare a free day for the recovery of my mental health. I don't even remember a single day when the boiler broke, or a blizzard shut the school, even though I remember plenty of snow.

Demoralization began to set in. I felt inept and exhausted and to make matters worse I had a shattering confrontation with the nun who was the school principal. She had also held on to the role of mother superior in our convent residence, although we were trying to experiment with a new form of collective government.

It started with what I thought was a routine request for the use of the convent car.

"I want to take John Christmas shopping," I said, conversationally.

"No, you may not have permission to use the car," snapped the principal.

Until that moment I had not thought I was asking for permission. Rather, I had been informing the group, in case anyone else wanted to come along, or needed some errands run. John was a boy in the sixth grade. Some of my students were abused and neglected, but John had a really tough homelife. His father was a mean drinker and John got the worst of it. He was the family scapegoat, and he brought all his anger and frustration to school. He fought everyone but me. For some reason he and I were friends. A couple of days before, he had asked me if I could help him find some Christmas presents for his brothers and sisters.

"Well, if Saturday isn't okay, how about Sunday, after mass?" I asked the principal.

"We do not have a car so that young sisters can relieve their sexual frustrations by taking young men shopping," announced the principal, her chin shaking with disapproval. To hide her quiver she picked up her water glass from the dinner table and took a prim little sip. Her lips were so tightly pressed together she could scarcely open them enough to let the water slide through. I noticed all those details, because I had turned to stone on the spot. I had never heard anything so unfair, and humiliating, and cruel in my life.

What is going on here? I remember thinking. And I finally unfroze enough to turn on my heel and run out of the room. I galloped up the stairs, two at a time, and found my allies, Sister Roberta, who had taught my sister June in the fourth grade, and Sister Catherine, who had been my seventh-grade teacher back at Holy Cross.

"What in the world is going on here?" I shouted. "I don't get it. How could she say such a thing?"

I solved the problem by going home and borrowing my parents' car to take John shopping. I suppose I had learned a lesson about not being afraid to go against authority when authority doesn't make any sense.

Even more important was the lesson I learned that to hate someone is to let them control me. For two or three days I fully, flat out hated the principal. I had never felt anything like it before, a black seethe chewing away inside of me, eating me up.

At last I let a little grace come into my mind, and I realized the principal's problem was not my problem, and it certainly wasn't worth losing all my energy and concentration. I prayed to be willing to give the hate up, and it dissolved.

A good thing it did, too, because a few years later I would find myself living in the same community with the principal again, where I discovered that both our attitudes had much improved.

Thanks to the steady friendship and wise guidance of Roberta and Catherine, I got through my year as a parochial school teacher. But I was sure I would not make it through another.

Thanks to Vatican II, I did not have to spend the rest of my life doing something I hated. The concept of holy self-sacrifice no longer required that a nun live in abject misery. I was determined I would never be unhappy at work again. I knew it would never be physically or mentally healthy for me or others if I was not content. But what was I going to do?

Sometime in my first few years in the convent I had given up my determination to become a missionary sister. Whenever a Sister of Notre Dame came to the Connecticut province from one of the order's missions I tried to meet her and find out if the reality matched my girlhood fantasies. Almost always she would tell me that while the work could be very interesting and certainly very romantic in South America, what was really needed was to change things in the United States. Those missionary sisters brought to me the same realization that the returning Peace Corps volunteers carried home in the sixties: the foreign and economic policies of the United States were (and still are) suffocating the hopes of the Third World.

And then one day I realized that the same patterns of oppression and exclusion existed at home. Even in Connecticut. My mission was to the Third World in the United States.

Very slowly, my political consciousness was being developed. As I studied the Vatican Council's call for human dignity and justice, I started to figure out that I would have to begin to respond by going out and looking for the people who needed dignity and justice most. Then, through the grace of God, I discovered that I was already moving toward an answer. There was a way to do what I liked, to do what I had already been trained to do, and to serve the poor in the most neglected places.

I wrote to the Long Lane School, a state institution in Connecticut, and asked for a job.

Nine: Long Lane

PAT

Long Lane School was a Connecticut state institution for that
category of misfits known as "juvenile delinquents." Built in
the late 1860s as a home for wayward girls, it had once been
known as Long Lane Farm, and some of the knives and forks
still had LLF engraved on the handles. By summer of 1973,
when I arrived, there were only a few acres of meadows left and
the town of Middletown was beginning to crowd Long Lane at
the edges.

There were no fences or bars around the two-story brick
"cottages" that were scattered over the grounds in a way that
looked as though the original architect had been trying to achieve
the effect of a quiet country rest home. Many of the youngsters
at Long Lane—now including boys as well as girls by the time
I arrived—had never lived in any place so nice. They were not
kids from upper middle-class or wealthy homes, who, when they
got into trouble, were sent to private therapists or private schools
in the Berkshire Mountains.

These kids, my kids, arrived at Long Lane by court order.
They ranged in age from eleven to eighteen, and they came,
almost all of them, from poor homes or no homes at all. Some
were runaways. Some were truants. And some had been involved in serious crimes such as murder, assault, automobile
theft, prostitution, or robbery.

Many, many of them were throwaway children. No one cared
about them, or ever had cared about them. They had no choice
but to live on the streets or be committed to a place like Long
Lane, to be a ward of the state until they reached the age of
eighteen.

The juvenile justice system made no distinctions. The most disturbed and violent children were mixed together with those who were merely lost. The ones who had committed crimes were there because they were too young to be sent to jail. The truants, who were usually also runaways, were there because the law said anyone under sixteen had to go to school. The throwaways were there because there was nowhere else for them to go. And the runaways? I couldn't figure out why they should be committed, under the law, to what was in theory a reformatory. But of course at that time, only sixteen years ago, almost no one in the courts bothered to ask *why* the child was running away before convicting him or her of being "incorrigible" or "unmanageable." I discovered to my horror that it was the parents of many of those children who should have been locked up.

My first day at Long Lane was July 7, 1973. I was not quite twenty-four years old, and I had been hired to be the cottage parent in Smith Cottage. I had arranged to live in Hartford at St. Justin's Convent, and to use the community's car to commute the twenty miles. I worked one of three shifts, from 7:00 A.M. to 3:30 P.M., or 4:00 P.M. to 11:00 P.M., or 11:00 P.M. to 7:00 A.M., and that half hour each way in the car quickly became a lifesaving quiet time when I could clear my head. For three years and one summer I traveled to work at Long Lane, and I loved almost every minute of it.

The first morning I went to the administration building and the superintendent introduced me to the woman who would be my immediate supervisor. Her name was Ida Billingslea. I have only two or three real heroines, people whose life I admire, and who gave me a vision of what I could do with my own life. Ida was one of those women. She was in her early fifties, tall, and black.

Later, as I got to know her, she would reveal parts of her life. She had been born very poor in South Carolina, but by the time I met her she was definitely middle class: married, a Protestant, with two children—a son and a daughter.

Much later, after we had become friends, she told me that her work had grown out of a promise she had made to God when she was in her early twenties. She and her husband, John, had just had their first child, John, Jr., and she was very seriously ill. When she woke up from a major operation she thought she had been dreaming, but years later she realized she had had an out-of-body experience. As she remembered it, she was dying and she went up to a door. She looked across the threshold but did not cross it; through it she saw all the dead members of her family sitting in a circle with one empty chair. Her mother came to the door and said, "Ida, we've been waiting for you," and she pointed to the empty chair.

"Mom, I can't come right now, I've got John and John, Jr., to take care of," Ida said. And her mother said, "All right."

And then Ida said, "I promise you, Mom, that if I go back I will give my life to humanity."

And she fulfilled that promise.

The morning I met Ida she was interested only in observing what I might reveal about myself as she took me on a tour of Long Lane. We walked through the cafeteria, then we looked in the door of the chapel. She pointed out some of the different cottages, and I began to be impatient to see this Smith Cottage which would be my responsibility. But first Ida took me into a cottage named Kimball. There were only about ten youngsters living there, each locked alone in a room, which to me looked like a cell, a tiny space ten by fifteen feet.

Kimball was the most jail-like of all the cottages, and Ida wanted to see how I would react to the toughest kids and the worst conditions. I was shocked to see teenage girls locked up, and I suppose it showed, but I managed to ask quite calmly, "Why are they here?"

Ida unlocked one of the doors, and introduced me to a tall girl with several Band-Aids stuck to her face.

"Daphene, this is Pat. Would you tell her what happened?"

"Bitch had my shades," growled Daphene.

Later, Ida gave me a fuller explanation. Daphene had been in a violent fight over a pair of sunglasses with someone in her regular cottage. The other girl had lost a chunk of her hair and had to have stitches taken in her arm where Daphene had bitten her.

When we opened the next door, a sweet-looking girl in a pink sweater was sitting on the bed. She greeted Ida with a hug.

"So you've come back to us, Gayle?" Ida said. Gayle grinned and said, "I'm not going to any home."

Gayle had run away. The punishment for running away—whether the kids were caught by the police and brought back or came back by themselves—was to be locked up for some length of time. Gayle's only stable "home" was Long Lane. She had been placed in foster home after foster home and had always managed to be sent back. Now she was old enough to be trained to live in a group home (a kind of halfway house) but she didn't want to go. So every time she knew the people at Long Lane were getting ready to send her into the outside world she ran away. Then she would come back and have to start her cycle all over again, beginning with the lockup period. She was plainly delighted to be back in her cell, safe and cared for.

I couldn't begin to comprehend the reasons for the children's behavior, but I managed to remember to avoid judging and keep an open mind. What really impressed me that day was the way Ida spoke to and about the girls. She treated them as human beings, and she never for a moment behaved as though they were unhearing, unfeeling "cases." She had taught me the first of many important lessons: every person deserves to be taken seriously.

The miracle of Long Lane, to me, was that it could have been a snake pit—or a battleground between the keepers and the kept—but instead, Ida made her cottage work as I had always imagined a community should work. The staff did not think of themselves as custodians. They really liked the kids, and they tried their best to teach them how to live.

In the years since then I have been frustrated, infuriated, and humiliated by all kinds of institutions: ecclesiastic, academic, and helping. And I know *it doesn't have to be that way.* At Long Lane's Smith Cottage the rules were merely a guide, not a barricade erected to shut out all acknowledgment of a petitioner's humanity. It was not easy remembering that each of the youngsters I worked with had a name and a history and a soul—but it wasn't nearly as hard as it would have been to forget, because forgetting would have undone all my efforts and eventually would have blighted my own soul.

My world had been so small! The staff at Smith Cottage was like an ecumenical council for me. They were old and young; single and married; black, Puerto Rican, and white; Jewish, Protestant, Catholic, and atheist; born of both the poor and the middle classes. They knew I was a nun, but I dressed in regular clothes, and I did not wear my Notre Dame cross to work. I'm sure everyone else would have thought it was just a pretty, modern cross, but for me the decision not to wear it signified something very important, something I myself didn't fully understand at the time. The cross was part of our habit, and eventually it became the only remnant of the habit, the prime symbol of our vocation.

It was bronze, with *Ah qu'il est bon le bon Dieu* engraved on it, and was worn around the neck. My conscious reason for not wearing it was that I was working for a secular institution, and I did not feel I was working "as a nun." But unconsciously I think it was because I wanted to be myself, Patricia Hussey, not someone special and separate. I didn't want to be put in a category. And I was so happy when I felt included.

I was working with atheists! And foul-mouthed atheists at that. From Laurie the social worker I first heard the "F" word. When I was growing up I never even heard the word "hell" at home. Now, every morning I was greeted in the most loving tone of voice with "Hey, motherfucker, how ya' doin' today?" The first time, I thought my ears would catch on fire, but since most of my kids seemed to have one-word vocabularies—their conversations sounded like a barnyard: "Uck, uck, uck, uck, uckooo"—after about two years I stopped noticing. And of course the terrible day came when I forgot myself and said something in the Long Lane vernacular when I was visiting my parents. The only way I could calm down my father was to tell him some of the stories I had heard.

On the average there were twenty girls in residence at Smith Cottage. About half of them were white, and the rest were black and Puerto Rican. Each had her own bedroom and was responsible for keeping it clean. They each had a daily community chore to perform for which they were awarded points. (It was kind of like the convent, except that we never got any points.) Twenty points for cleaning their rooms, twenty points for doing the morning chores. Points added up to the right to visit home or go to dances.

The point system was part of a program of behavioral modification, a way to make the children experience limits and discipline. For emergencies, we had a system of "time-outs." "Time-out!" we yelled if someone was about to smash someone else with a broom. Then the enraged person would have to go sit down in a chair in the corner of the room until she could cool down and get in some fragile touch with her more adult self. Behavioral modification worked pretty well, but I think its success depended on the reinforcement we gave through personal contact with the kids. Actually, each depended on the other.

Ida deeply believed in group therapy. Every day after school, the staff and the residents of Smith Cottage would gather in the living room on straight-back chairs arranged in a circle so that we would feel the energy and power of the group. We all talked about what made us feel good or bad, or about whatever had happened in our lives that the staff and the girls wanted to share. Ida usually was the leader, and she worked from whatever was happening that day. If the mood was angry, we talked about anger. The more trust grew, the more the youngsters felt they were in a warm and caring atmosphere, the more they shared their life histories.

I think in the beginning I must have imagined those children as coming from a place looking like my own mother's kitchen. I suppose my sympathy was organized around the assumption that something had gone tragically wrong *within* the children. Imagine how naive and confused and frightened I felt when I heard their stories.

"Well, like, you know, I'd been in ten or fifteen different foster homes by the time I was twelve. When the last old man started climbing into my bed, I split."

"My guy took real good care of me. He made real sure my tricks were okay, not weird or anything." This from a fourteen-year-old who had been so starved for anything that looked like love that she could be exploited beyond endurance by a pimp who "cared" for her.

At first I couldn't believe their stories; I couldn't quite process what they were saying. Then I could not believe the world still turned when such things happened. And finally, most horribly, I could not believe that the stories were *routine*, that I was hearing them again and again from different children.

Children spoke of abuse, both physical and sexual. They spoke of becoming pregnant by their fathers, pimps, or their mother's boyfriends. They whispered or cried about being tied up or tied down. They wept about their hands being held to flames or hot stoves so they would "learn their lessons." Over and over I heard children tell of trying to escape their parents' murderous rages. "He held my head under water until I couldn't breathe anymore."

One day Ida asked me to think about taking in a girl named Ruby. She was from the Hartford inner city. Her mother was an alcoholic who had once tried to hang all three of her children from the shower curtain rod. She got them all up in the air, but luckily she wasn't very good with knots and they just hung there until the rod broke and they escaped. When Ruby was thirteen she had a child, which meant she had gotten pregnant at twelve. When she came to Long Lane she was fourteen, and she had killed her boyfriend with a knife. It was especially horrible to think of that knife, of the physical directness of stabbing someone. She killed him because he had begun to strangle her by the gold chain around her neck. He was dragging her through the kitchen by the chain, and he shouted, "You better grab that knife because it's either going to be you or me." She did grab the knife and plunged it into his heart and he died. She was devastated to lose him. I remember the day she arrived. I expected someone about 250 pounds, maybe six feet tall. And she was just a girl, just a gawky adolescent girl.

Sitting in that circle, we tried to let the girl-children sweep away enough of their past so that they could touch the good part of themselves and try to nourish it. But sometimes I could not imagine how any hope had survived. I will never as long as I live forget the afternoon that a girl named Elizabeth finally spoke in the circle. From a small town in Connecticut, she was sixteen years old, tall, with long, dark hair. She had already been with us for a couple of months. Other kids gravitated toward her; she was a kind of leader, direct and articulate. But she had never spoken about herself.

I could not imagine what she held within her. She always spoke in a soft voice, but with an edge to it, as though her rage might come boiling out at any moment. With India Ink and a pin she had tattooed herself across her thighs: "EAT ME."

Ida must have sensed that Elizabeth was reaching a breaking point that day because she leaned forward in her chair and said, "You can only begin to be free if you possess your own reality, Elizabeth. Say it, and let it go."

"My father has dogs," she began, holding her head down. "He taught me to 'do it' with animals. He showed me by doing it himself with one of the dogs and then I had to do it."

There was not one snicker, no nervous laughter, only quiet.

"He made me do it a lot . . . and then one day he did it to me too. Over and over again, he did it. When I got old enough to take care of myself, I ran away."

Old enough? She had been committed to Long Lane by the state of Connecticut's juvenile judge for being a runaway at the age of fifteen. Her father had reported her as a runaway, and her school reported her as a truant. No one, as far as I ever knew, had asked her why she had run away.

As Elizabeth spoke, I felt sick to my stomach. I hoped my face didn't reveal my disgust. I was surprised by the way she told her story, in a kind of detached, flat narrative, as though she were watching a play unfold. At the time, I didn't know that detachment was protection, but I would learn it during my last four years as a nun.

My mind kept rushing to thoughts of my own father, the man who came home to dinner every night when his children were young, who turned down promotions because they would require too much travel. The man we Hussey kids called "Sergeant" because he handed out lists of Saturday morning chores. The man who had always been ready to listen to me, and who would support me through all of my battles. Now it seemed so unfair and so confusing for me to have been so lucky. No wonder people look for the easiest explanation and blame the child.

There was more to Elizabeth's story.

"My boyfriend was a biker," she said. "You know, motorcycles. To get to be someone's old lady you have to make it with all the guys in the gang. All at once. I mean, one after another, in front of everybody. It's kind of like rape." She looked up at that point, and then she ducked her head again.

"I'm pregnant," she said. And she lifted her head. "I'm going to have an abortion."

It's all right, I kept thinking. It's all right.

In time, I would learn, as Barbara also did, that people don't ask permission when they are going to have an abortion. They may share the information with someone they trust in the hope of being supported in their decision, but the decision itself is so uniquely and primarily personal that notions of "consultation" and "approval" ultimately have no bearing.

For several months, I acted as the Long Lane social worker, and I remember Ida making it very clear that I could not let the fact that I was a Catholic affect my response to the girls who asked to get an abortion. On January 22, 1973, the Supreme Court had declared, in the case of *Roe* v. *Wade,* that an American woman had a legal, constitutional right to choose an abortion. It was not my job to stand in the way of the law. I didn't have a problem with that, nor did I say "That is an area that someone else will have to deal with.'' It was my job to support the girls as much as possible, whatever their decision.

I saw children happily bearing children, hoping that they could provide their babies with all the good life and family they themselves had never known. I saw children bearing children in homes for unwed mothers, taking on one more stigma in a society that jumps at any chance to label and then reject people. I saw children bearing children and, knowing they could never care for the babies, giving them up for adoption.

And I saw children deciding not to bear children because they could not deal with the harsh reality I called ''life'' and they called ''survival.'' They had abortions. And I could no longer judge them or be so certain of God's will. It wasn't so easy anymore to declare a woman right or wrong, moral or immoral.

I probably should have left the Sisters of Notre Dame in 1976. It would have saved them, and me, a lot of trouble if I had. I had discovered the obvious but painful truth that it was not necessary to be a nun to be committed to humanity. The women I worked with at Long Lane were motivated out of all their different religious traditions, or no religious tradition at all. They treated the children with respect and reverence, and they challenged and sustained me. I had a whole new idea of community, and a vastly enlarged view of the world.

Very often, as I think back on those years, I wish that more nuns had allowed their parochial world to be expanded. There was nothing to be afraid of. My experience enriched my life, and I believe it made me a better nun—at least according to my own understanding of what made a nun.

At home, at St. Justin's Convent, the question of what made a nun was destroying my primary community.

St. Justin's was once the pride of the Irish community in Hartford. But by 1973 it had become a poor black parish in a declining neighborhood. The school was financially poor, but the eight nuns I lived with who taught there were excellent, committed teachers.

We tried to develop a meaningful program for nuns too. Almost every morning we attended mass in the convent chapel. We experimented with our morning and evening prayers, creating mixtures of readings drawn from secular work and biblical passages. I was very conscious of being on a spiritual quest.

"I don't like the term 'God the Father,' " I grumbled to my spiritual director one afternoon. She was astonished.

"But why? Your father is a good father," she said.

"I know, but the idea of God as Father seems exclusive somehow. Exclusive of me, I guess."

Pretty soon I would start reading books about God as Mother—and that was the most inclusive idea I had ever come across.

I began to discuss the matter with the spiritual director. A spiritual director was a kind of post-Vatican II version of a novice director. We would meet once a month and she would ask some questions: "How do you see God moving in your life? In what direction do you see yourself moving? What are the different challenges in your life as far as work and community goes?"

The last was the most pressing question. We were a community of young women, and I deeply valued their support when I came home with the confusion and despair I sometimes felt after a day at Long Lane. But only two of us had already taken our final vows. The rest had to face an annual period of evaluation we all went through before renewing our vows.

Our weekly community business meetings became more and more strained. Sometimes I wished I could bring in Ida with her therapeutic skills, and sometimes I wished I could work the evening shift at Long Lane permanently so I would never have to attend another community supper at St. Justin's. Without the old narrow rules we developed friendships, and connections beyond the convent, and opinions, and we didn't seem to be able to solve the resulting problems in our own circle.

The real problem was that my sisters had also realized they could live committed lives without being nuns. Some were disillusioned with community living, and some wanted to get married and have children. Toward the end the only topic at our meetings was whether to leave or to stay. Donna and Peggy left, and then Mary Anne, Laura, and Julie. I began to have conversations with myself as I drove to Long Lane.

"Do you want to stay?"

"Are you sure you want to be a nun?"

"What about these vows you are supposed to be taking soon?"

"Who's going to be left?"

Why did I stay? My best friends had left, taking some part of me with them. But their arguments were not my answers. And I could not, for myself, assemble enough reasons to leave. I was still committed to my own spiritual path.

If I was not going to leave, I would have to go forward. And, of all things, I would have to go forward by going back to school. I had tangled with reality, and I needed to make sense of it theologically.

I applied to the Jesuit School of Theology in Chicago for a three-year course that would make me a Master of Divinity.

Ten: Teaching

BARBARA

No sooner was I "formed" in the old ways of Notre Dame—or at least half-set as Barbara turned Sister Charles Marie—than the directives from Vatican II began to loosen me up again. Apparently the old ways had not been an immutable demonstration of the will of God after all. The whole life of the church was being turned upside down. The first things to be affected were the length of my skirts and the extent of my education. But in time, I was forced to examine my understanding of God, church, and my vocation. Vatican II enabled me to define the kind of religious life and commitment to God I had deeply sought when I was eighteen, but was then still too young and inexperienced to name.

In 1966, the year I graduated from Emmanuel College, it was not possible to choose for myself what my work would be. The educated Sisters of Notre Dame were teachers, the uneducated were cooks and seamstresses. That was that. But the teachers' own level of education was extremely spotty.

For decades nuns had been assigned to teaching jobs as soon as they took their first vows, and had been left to complete their degrees as best they could in the summer, one term or even one course at a time, whenever it was convenient for the schedule of the entire order. Some had managed to finish doctorates, but I knew others who had been teaching for twenty years and still had not gotten a B.A. The first step toward reform was to make sure we all had degrees before we began teaching.

I graduated with a major in Spanish, not with the degree in mathematics that I had planned. I was really disappointed, but we nuns were on a kind of predetermined assembly line and had to take whatever we could in order to graduate on time. There was no going back to pick up courses or to fill in gaps. Math got lost in the shuffle. I tried to make myself feel better by taking one course in Portuguese, thinking I would go to the Brazilian missions one day.

Instead, I went to Salem, New Hampshire.

In those days, the late summer was a period of extreme anxiety in every convent. Hidden behind closed doors, the superiors and school supervisors were engaged in the wearying task of "filling slots": deciding who would go where, live with whom, teach what subjects in what school. And the rest of us, unable even to express a preference, much less make a request, grew more edgy and nervous every day as we waited for the moment when everyone at once would receive their "mission assignment."

I was longing to teach the first grade. Who knows why? Maybe I was still homesick for the din of my family's house in Cambridge. Maybe I knew from experience that I could take care of little kids, and I wasn't at all sure of what would happen in a classroom without tiny chairs, and big alphabet letters on the walls. But I had already scuttled my chance for first grade by refusing to major in education. Even with a half-baked Spanish major, I had been put on the high school teacher track. The first stop would be the fifth-grade classroom at St. Joseph's School in Salem, New Hampshire.

It was a modern school in a yellow brick building about five years old, with the convent built on the top floor. Eight other nuns lived there, eight really wonderful women who were also excellent teachers. The first day of school we all trooped across the street to early morning mass at St. Joseph's, and then we came back to open the doors. For days before, I had been arranging my classroom, sharpening the pencils, unpacking the chalk, and putting up pictures of autumn foliage in the White Mountains. It had been scary enough just sitting at my desk staring at the rows of empty desks. What was I going to do when those chairs were full?

Every desk had a little name tag I had taped on top in strict alphabetical order. At least that way I would have some chance of remembering their last names for the first few weeks. By the second week I would already be rearranging. There would be at least one incident a day of: "Jimmy! Move your desk away from Angela Marie right now! Come right up here to the front row where I can keep an eye on you."

On that first day I had stood by the classroom door, still in full habit, looking welcoming. Then I stood in front of the room, led the class in a pledge of allegiance and an "Our Father," and successfully made the students go around the room introducing themselves. There were forty-five kids—looking at me, waiting for something, and all I could think of was the horrible fact that they were all bigger than I was. Never in my life had I been so glad to hear the recess bell.

That afternoon I trudged back upstairs to the convent and threw myself down on a chair in a little den where I met with the fourth- and sixth-grade teachers. "What am I supposed to do with these kids?" I groaned. After a couple of hours of encouragement and suggestions from the nuns teaching in the classrooms on each side of mine, I felt better. That night, as I was going to sleep, just after I had prayed feverently for inspiration, I thought, It would be fun to teach them math. Eventually, most of the day, every day, was fun. I put down my ruler and concentrated on learning how to evoke those wonderful, infinitely rewarding moments when a student would suddenly "get it." Sometimes I felt as though I could really see a light bulb click on above their heads, and it clicked in my heart as well.

In the fall of 1969 I was, for some reason known only to the provincial, assigned to my first choice: teaching the first grade at St. Lawrence's in Lawrence, Massachusetts. I loved those children, and I would teach in that school for five years. In Lawrence, my world, already expanding, enlarged in astonishing ways.

The fact is, I was at last beginning to grow up. Vatican II allowed us to change from childlike, protected creatures of a separate world into responsible, vital women. And I would soon want a mission that would further challenge an adult.

Eleven: Experimenting

BARBARA

Lawrence, Massachusetts, in 1969 was a declining town: blue-collar, depressed, and tough. Many of the old red brick textile mills appeared to be in the last stages of decay, their roofs falling in, windows shattered, weeds springing from the gutters. Mile after mile of them stretched, strangely elegant and poignant, along the murky, choking flood of the Merrimack River.

Straight north of Boston, almost at the New Hampshire border, the old mill towns follow the river: Lowell, Lawrence, Haverhill. Generations of immigrants had been drawn to those clattering halls: Yankee farm girls from northern New England; the Irish, Italians, Poles, Syrians, Armenians, French-Canadians. In the late twenties the companies had begun moving to North Carolina and Georgia, where labor was cheap and unions non-existent, but still people came, hoping to find work where once work had been. In my classroom I learned the meaning of "multi-cultural." I had first-generation Italians; immigrants from Mexico, Puerto Rico, and Cuba.

St. Lawrence's, my new school and parish church, had been built in the early 1900s. Both buildings were of soot-streaked brick. I remember high ceilings and dim rooms. It was not, in fact, so very different from St. Mary's, my childhood parish in Cambridge. It would be a *challenge* to work there, and a challenge was what I most wanted. The convent, where I would live, turned out to be a big old frame family house. To me it felt—for the first time in so long—like home. I knew I never wanted to go back to the old institutionalized ways again.

There were only six Sisters of Notre Dame in my Lawrence community. The other nuns were mostly young, although at twenty-six I was the youngest. By a wonderful coincidence, one of them was a woman who had been to college with my sister and who had grown up with her six sisters right around the corner from me in Cambridge. Several years later she would fall in love and leave the convent to get married. But we would have many stages of adjustment to face before that happened.

We had all already moved through the first phases of changing nundom. We were wearing skirts and blouses and colors, and our hair showed beneath our smaller veils. The first time I had ventured out into a schoolyard in my new habit I felt naked. Actually, what was really being exposed was Barbara, the person. I was reclaiming the self I had left at the door of the Ipswich novitiate.

After I entered, my connections with my family had withered down to exchanges of news and pleasantries. My younger sisters and brothers didn't know who I was, except that I was "the nun." My little sister Clare had been in the third grade when I left home. It seemed a miracle when Clare decided to attend Merrimack College in Lawrence—and to live with us two days a week. As I got to know her I began to feel like an older sister again, sharing questions and problems. Watching her grow, I felt I had been given back a precious gift. Through her I became involved again with all my siblings. I helped prepare their wedding ceremonies, and I even played the music, because I had taught myself to play a guitar and become a singing nun. If only Sister Clare Marguerite could have seen me strumming away during folk masses.

In the summer of 1970 the Sisters of Notre Dame of the Massachusetts Province tried an experiment. They decided that the twenty-five of us who were about to take our final vows would gather in Rome at the motherhouse. We hoped to "catch the Notre Dame spirit" at the source.

As a novice I had been taught that my "self" was sinful and deficient. Everyone's was. Mortification and repression of what was natural were the only possible approaches to God. That old system was totalitarian and abusive. Even though I had only had a few years of it, my sense of possibility and hope had been badly damaged. Thanks once again to Vatican II, I was learning to value myself and others as human beings, God-touched and miraculous in our creation. To nurture the best part of myself, to be all that I could be, I would have to know myself. And so going to Rome was a gift that came at exactly the right moment, a journey to my roots.

The plane landed in Rome and I presented my brand-new passport. We took a bus to Namur, Belgium, to our foundress's first home, and then to her birthplace in Cuvilly, France. At both places I looked at the relics, so carefully preserved and displayed: books, reading glasses, embroidered altar clothes, and page after page of letters. She seemed to have been a bit like me—small, bustling, and determined.

We spent six weeks in Rome. Back in the United States we were all wearing secular clothes, but in Rome we were advised to look like nuns—wear black and bring a veil. There were twenty of us and I was the only one to wear a dark green dress. I certainly was not going to be obliterated in a group again. Anyway, it was the only dark dress I had.

Oh, what a grand time it was! We went to Assisi and I bought all the slides in the souvenir stores so I could give talks when I got back home. We went to the catacombs, and I would often remember those dank chambers when I began to study the early Christians—so democratic, non-hierarchical, inclusive. Truly Christian, in fact.

One day a man proposed to me in the middle of the street. I couldn't understand much Italian, despite my parents' conversations at home, but I could understand his message. He was actually proposing marriage—I suppose it was such a respectable offer because I was wearing my veil.

On September 13, 1970, I was back in Cambridge, making my final vows at St. Francis of Assisi, a church founded by my DeGuglielmo grandparents when they came to the United States. My sisters sang and after mass my family celebrated in my parents' backyard. Many more women were leaving religious orders than entering in 1970, but as far as I was concerned, never in the history of the church had it been a better time to be a nun.

We could read newspapers! And magazines! There were radios and a television set in the house, and I could turn them on whenever I wanted to! I remember the night of July 20, 1969, when Neil Armstrong and Buzz Aldrin landed on the moon. We had just driven back from Boston where we had *eaten in a restaurant* and we rushed into the house to watch. We got so excited that I put a record on the phonograph and taught everyone how to do the cha-cha. I felt *Italian* again.

We even had an automobile! I could drive home to visit my family once a month. Another huge new "privilege" was a personal monthly allowance of twenty-five dollars. Out of that we bought our clothes and our personal supplies such as toothpaste and shampoo. Obviously we didn't buy very many clothes, but each of those little changes made an enormous difference in my mental attitude toward my work and my life as a nun, the difference between growth and stagnation.

The evenings were for discussing ideas. We sat around the dining room table and examined everything. No one frowned and put a stop to the conversation as we ventured closer and closer to our deepest thoughts and feelings. Most of our sentences began "Why?" or "How?" or "What if?"

"Why do we need a superior in our house?" "Why don't we experiment with sharing responsibility as a collegial group?" At the annual meeting of our province there had been talk of such an arrangement, and we wanted to try it. It was silly to have a superior in a house with only six people.

Rules and regulations were no longer the controlling factors of our daily life. We became bonded by our evolving vision of community and commitment. Community was beginning to mean not only the people we shared our lives with as Sisters of Notre Dame, but also the people we rubbed shoulders with in school, in the parish, in the town of Lawrence, Massachusetts.

We realized that the world was our community. Our commitment to each other and to the structure of our religious order was only the beginning, the foundation of our broader commitment to make a difference in the world.

First, we became something we had never been allowed to be. We became *friends*. An essential step toward world peace, one would think.

If we had become Bolsheviks we couldn't have upset some of the other Sisters of Notre Dame more. Before Vatican II, nuns had been leaving the order because it was too conservative. After Vatican II many left because it had become too radical. Those that stayed fought to establish the middle ground.

One night we were upstairs in the den watching television. The doorbell rang and when we looked out the window we saw an SND named Mary standing under the front porch light with a suitcase in her hands. When we got her settled into a comfortable chair with a cup of hot tea, we waited for her to tell her story. She was clearly very upset, almost in tears.

"Would it be possible for me to come and live with you?" she asked.

"Why not?" and "Why?" we all said at once.

"I can't bear to stay in my community one minute longer," she said. "They watch television *all* the time and they never talk. I think they want to go back to the days of the Grand Silence. When I try to talk about defining a mission they just look at me and say, 'You are a nun, dear, that is mission enough.' "

In our house we talked about defining mission from dawn to midnight, so of course we took in Mary, a runaway nun. The strange thing about it was that she had run away from two blocks up the street, from the school and convent in the next parish. By now the entire Massachusetts province was splitting into factions. People in the parishes identified the various groups as the "no-no's," the "so-so's," and the "go-go's" depending on how eagerly each was welcoming the changes of Vatican II.

In the early seventies, there were still about 900 SNDs in the Massachusetts province. We began to meet in different groups. For the no-no's and the so-so's, the meetings were a little like caucus gatherings, but for us, the go-go's, they were like the feminist consciousness-raising sessions that were beginning in the secular world. We shared our experiences and found that strength and courage came from the discovery that our stories were so similar.

By 1973 the no-no's and the go-go's were finding it impossible to live together. We petitioned the leadership of the order of the Sisters of Notre Dame in Rome for the establishment of a new province. Mary Linscott, who would be present at our encounter with the Vatican years later, was the superior general then, and I believe she gave us permission to break apart because she knew that without the freedom to discover our own ways of living, a flood of sisters would leave the order.

Our Massachusetts province split in two. Three hundred experimentalists formed a new Boston province. The old Massachusetts province, with the traditionalists, was renamed the Ipswich province.

The Boston group wanted to try new ways of governing, new ministries beyond being teachers, new ways of using our resources. We would be *making our own choices*. But we were still bound together with all the other SNDs by our common constitution, our common motherhouse in Rome, and our loyalty to our founder's spirit. We were all living by the same principles, the determination to "stand by the poor in the most neglected places," as expressed in the Chapter Acts of 1968 which had so excited Pat. Our differences lay in the ways we began to put those principles into practice. My little community in Lawrence was growing impatient. We had reflected on renewal, we had begun to accumulate lived experience. It was time to act.

We spent hours and hours talking about the key words of Vatican II: peace and justice. We taught Christian doctrine to our school classes, and we were expected to spend our after-school hours and evenings teaching catechism to the Catholic children in our parish who did not attend St. Lawrence's. Yet, for years after I entered the convent, I had not seen television or read the papers. If that had not changed I would have been teaching ethics as just a remote hypothesis. (Even the women who taught current events classes could not read the papers— talk about irrelevant!) Imagine how astonished I was when I was finally allowed to turn on the television and see great moral leaders engaged in making a difference. Martin Luther King, Jr., was a prophet—relevant, righteous, and real. And he lived and died before my very eyes.

It was a wildly exciting time to be a Catholic nun. Every weekend that we possibly could, some of us from St. Lawrence's piled into our little car and drove all over New England to one of a never-ending series of conferences on religion and theology. I heard men and women from all over the nation talking about doing the same work I was trying to do, about getting out from behind our closed doors and finding out about the lives of the people. I was not alone in believing that our actions must begin to match our words. This is my experience too! I thought. God is among the people and they have something to teach us.

God began to come alive in my own life. During my formation period I had dutifully spent an hour a day with a book in front of my face, sitting in the chapel and "meditating." I would read a passage from scripture and then try to think about it—which was what I understood meditation to be. Pretty soon I would be sneaking glances at the other novices and wondering what they found to think about for all that time. Later, as I moved out into the world, I began to find God—not "out there" but much closer, in other people.

Talking to people, getting to know what their lives were really about, trying to understand their hurts and joys, was the way I began to touch moments of sacredness. I saw the spirit of God working through people, alive in our moments of goodness, uniting us all by our struggles to live day by day. God was not something outside, but something living and breathing and operating through all of us. The very aims of Vatican II—peace and justice—depended on appreciating the God-life within one another.

We tried to translate our new understanding of God into our prayer life. Once again we sat around the dining room table, trying to find words to explain ourselves to each other, choosing readings for new celebrations and liturgies.

"What if next Sunday the eighth-grade confirmation class reads the offertory petitions?"

"Let's sing 'Amazing Grace,' and Mary Margaret can read the letter to the Ephesians."

"What if Mary Margaret offers the thanksgiving on her birthday? Or maybe we should offer the thanksgiving in honor of Mary Margaret."

There were parishioners who hated our experiments. The last thing they wanted was to be involved in creating the expression of their own spirituality. They wanted Latin and Gregorian chant and they wanted it on Sunday morning, not Saturday night. I remember one time the parish priests, my group of nuns, and the seventh and eighth grades spent months creating a folk mass. Probably we should have called it a "people's mass," which is what it was, but we were still not comfortable with radical language. I thought it was a joyous celebration, but afterward one elderly lady, her rosary and missal held out in front of her, stepped up and told me, "Sister, every time you pick up your guitar I want to scream."

I wonder what she would have thought if she had been with us on our retreats?

A retreat is a period of time, a few days or a few weeks, spent away from the world in prayer and meditation. It is an excellent way to clear psychic space for thinking things through, or for sitting quietly and waiting for inspiration. In the old days, we would have spent the time in silence punctuated by a priest who would "direct" us with endless homilies—some of them extremely shopworn. Now, we began to structure our own retreats. The priest was welcome to say Mass but the rest of the time we set our own agenda, with time for meditation and for walking, and plenty of time for gathering in a circle and sharing our visions of what we had begun to call "the journey."

In those circles, and in the circles around our tables at home, we discussed the new feminist theologians, particularly Mary

Daly's essay, ''After the Death of God the Father: Women's Liberation and the Transformation of Christian Consciousness.'' A new and astounding idea began to transform our vision of God and our vision of our own place in God's plan.

What if God was not male?

In 1971 I was a twenty-eight-year-old Sister of Notre Dame, and I was being asked a lot of questions.

''Why are you still a nun? You are young, energetic, you enjoy life. Why don't you leave?''

''What does it mean to be a Catholic these days?''

''Why are we having Saturday night masses? What does Vatican II mean?''

''Why are you asking parents to help teach our children religious education? You nuns are supposed to be the experts.''

''How can you keep your vow of celibacy and go to conferences with men? Where is your obedience? Where is your poverty if you are riding around in cars? If you are going on vacations?''

Good questions, as Pat would say. Some of the answers began to evolve in all those hardworking circles of talk. I wanted to remain a Sister of Notre Dame. I believed I knew what my mission was supposed to be. I would have to *do* what I had been praying about. My job was to bring about justice by helping people to work together to cross racial lines, class lines, economic lines. I was going to try to live out the gospel, rather than reflecting on it in nice secluded meditation. To *do*, I would have to get involved in people's lives. And the people who were before me, waiting, were the people in the parish of St. Lawrence's.

Something was wrong in that parish, and in many of the older urban parishes in the United States. The consolation and support and unity the church had provided for my grandparents' and even for my parents' generation was missing. ''Inner-city parishes'' was the phrase used to describe churches abandoned by the prosperous and left as an expensive burden to newcomers who would find prosperity more difficult to achieve.

The Catholic church does not spread its money around so that all share equally according to need. St. Lawrence's was poor and getting poorer. People sent their children to our school if they could, because they hoped it offered a better education. But the parish was losing its feeling of community. There were only two priests and six nuns. It seemed obvious that we, who at least knew the children, should try to bring people together. Vatican II seemed to have shown the way by encouraging parents to join in teaching their children to prepare to receive the sacraments. We began leading adult education classes, teaching people who were not nuns or priests to become involved in the life of the church. I particularly liked the new way we celebrated First Communion, with parents coming to the altar and receiving Communion with their child.

One day one of the mothers, a woman named Anna, stopped me after class. She was obviously very upset. It took a few minutes before she could start speaking. Finally, she blurted out, "Sister, I had an abortion five years ago."

Everything I feel shows immediately on my face. On that day I am sure my eyes became wide-opened and surprised, although I tried hard not to show any reaction. Abortions were not yet legal—certainly not in the state of Massachusetts. I had never before met anyone who had had an abortion. I had never before even had a conversation with someone about having an abortion. My parents had welcomed every baby with love and laughter.

"Tell me about it," I managed to say. Those magic words! I had said the right thing!

We stood together in the schoolyard and we talked. She told me she had several older children who were teenagers. Her marriage had begun to fall apart, and when she found she was pregnant again she felt too frightened and exhausted to have another child.

"I know I made the best decision for me. Do you think, Sister, that God understood?" she said.

How did I know?

"I don't think God would judge you as harshly as you are judging yourself," I said. Then I asked her, "Why are you worrying about it so much at this moment?"

It seemed that she had gone to confession, in another parish, at the time, and the priest asked her if she was sorry for her sin. And she stubbornly said she didn't feel sorry because she had done the only thing she could do. Since she had refused to murmur a few words of contrition, the priest had told her she could not receive Communion.

"What am I going to do?" she said. "I've been so happy to be part of my son's First Communion classes, but how can I explain I cannot go to the altar with him?"

I knew Anna was a good woman—and a wonderful mother.

Somehow her marriage had survived. How could I judge her? I remember thinking "There is no easy answer to this," and being surprised. The priests had always sounded so *certain*. They sounded certain when they thundered from the pulpit against birth control too. They never hesitated to repeat: "Wives, be submissive to your husbands."

Some voice in my head was saying WHY NOT? Why couldn't a woman choose to practice birth control, or choose an abortion? Why was the Catholic church so rigid on these matters?

"Nobody in this parish knows about the decision you made," I said. "Keep coming to the classes, and receive Communion with your son." As the words were coming out of my mouth, I was hoping they were more convincing to her than they were to me. Yet, I could not believe that the God I was coming to know would say anything different to Anna.

As I walked across the street to the convent I kept going over the conversation in my mind, hoping I had said the right thing, worrying that I had gone too far. As I opened the front door, I said out loud, "My God, Barbara, you have so much to learn. If you are going to get involved in peoples' lives, you'd better learn and understand all sides of the dilemmas people find themselves in."

That night, as I said my prayers—including a plea for Anna's peace of mind—a tremendous wave of joy swept through me. An adult woman had believed *me* to be an adult woman. She had turned to me for spiritual counseling. I was no longer separated from people by the forbidding veneer of the habit. Anna had seen me as someone who could understand and respond. And I had not walked away!

Once I had seen a woman approach a priest, and I heard him say "I don't want to discuss it" before he bolted for the sanctuary. No wonder he was so frightened. Before Vatican II, a priest's introduction to counseling included such advice as "Never let a crying woman in the same room with you. You will feel sorry for her, and she may seduce you."

Even the nuns, in my early years in the order, had too often said to me when I needed comfort, "It's not appropriate for me to talk about that, dear."

But *I* hadn't walked away. I knew I didn't have the answers, but I knew that Anna trusted me and was hurting and that I needed to listen. I had found my mission, but I didn't yet know what to call it.

I wanted to do parish work. I wanted to work equally, as part of a team, with the priests.

Did I want to be a priest?

Well. Yes. That did seem to be the job I was imagining.

At that point in my conversation with myself, my thoughts would always conclude: It's bound to happen soon. After all, there are more nuns than there are priests. We are better educated. We are closer to the people—the priests have been managing parish real estate instead of tending parishioners for too many years. It is a crazy, bizarre waste of talent and energy not to ordain nuns. How could we have let ourselves be shut out?

And then I would mentally hug myself and think, I am so lucky to be a nun at this moment in history.

As it turned out, the church had no use for my commitment.

One day one of the teachers, Martha, brought a Protestant minister named Alice to the convent. She had been unhappy living at her parsonage and without a second thought we offered her a haven. Not until some of the parents spoke to us about the amount of time Alice and Martha spent together did we begin to question their relationship. We had noticed that Martha and Alice seemed emotionally involved: they had long, low conversations together, and sometimes snapped irritably at each other in the way only people who are very close do. But we simply had never allowed ourselves to think they might be sexually involved.

We talked, earnestly and awkwardly, about the necessity to be open to "new situations." The trouble was, we were not able to talk to Martha or Alice. The one person who had been Martha's closest friend tried to reach her and was pushed away. It ended one dreadful night as we sat eating dinner. We watched Martha carry her boxes one by one down the stairs and out the front door. She wouldn't say anything, and we still didn't know what to say. In June, after the school year ended, she left the order.

We felt as though we had failed. There we were, trying to get involved in people's lives, in new experiences, and we couldn't even handle one when it touched our own family. My world had been so small!

I realized that merely listening was not enough. What I wanted to do required professional skills, and I would have to learn them. I began to look for a program that would admit women who wanted to learn practical pastoral work.

Loyola University in Chicago offered a master's degree in pastoral studies. The course descriptions in the catalogue were exactly what I was looking for: new ways of teaching theology, pastoral counseling, organizing at the parish level, feminist spirituality. And liturgy! How to celebrate the rituals of the sacraments in the new forms. It would indeed be a new form if I, a female, were celebrating. The degree could be earned by attending school in the summer (it would take me five summers).

I applied. I was accepted. The Sisters of Notre Dame denied my request to study. No explanation. This was before the province split, and consensus-style decision-making was still a thing to come. I am almost sure, looking back, that the reason I could not go was because the order could not afford to send me at that particular time—but it would have made so much more sense to tell me that.

"Apply next year," they said. I did. I had a partial scholarship, and a partial grant from the Sisters of Notre Dame. Permission granted.

And so in the summer of 1972, when I was twenty-eight, I left for Chicago. Brave new world, here I come!

Twelve: Twenty-Eight Going on Eighteen

BARBARA

Three of us from the convent in Lawrence were going to spend the summer of 1973 at Loyola University in Chicago. Ellen, Rosemary, and I would share many adventures in the years to come. We had discovered, through the nuns' network of thrifty tips, an organization called Drive-away which would let us drive someone else's car for free if we delivered it on a certain date. If we left on Friday, we were sure we would have plenty of time to register at school, settle in, and deliver the car by Monday.

What could be better for an anxious owner than to turn his car over to three nuns who never drove above fifty miles an hour? We were sure the Drive-away people would take advantage of the opportunity and give us something special. They did. They gave us a car that couldn't possibly have gotten up the speed to go more than fifty miles an hour.

I was so excited I didn't even mind that the backseat smelled ominously of cat. I had never taken a long automobile trip before. I had never been further than New Jersey, and the land of the Great Lakes was terra incognita.

We arrived, exhausted, on Saturday night. The light was fading as we first caught sight of Chicago—glowing, enormous, and intimidating against the twilight sky. Somehow, I had not expected the city to be *so* much bigger than Boston. The skyline got closer and closer and suddenly we were lost inside the city. It grew pitch dark, and we were in the car huddled over a map by the flickering light of the overhead bulb, trying to figure out where we were going.

I like to foresee all events, to know exactly what I am going to be doing on the afternoon of this day a year from now. "Plan ahead'' is my motto. Pat has been known to use the words ''painfully well-organized'' about me. I have tried to loosen up, but planning makes me feel safe. And that night, the plan for my summer in Chicago was already beginning to fall apart.

''But I wrote to the school and told them we would be there on Saturday evening. We are going to be late,'' I said, in my Sister Charles Marie–tone.

''Barbara, we will be lucky if we get there at all,'' said Ellen.

Finally, we spotted a small sign: Loyola University. *Deo gratias!* We drove under arches of trees, through some gates, and into a dark and apparently deserted campus.

''What are we going to do?'' I wailed. We were in a strange city. We didn't know anyone. None of us had ever stayed in a hotel in our lives, and in 1973 we certainly had no charge cards or extra money.

Finally we found a guard who checked with a security office and allowed us in. We spent a miserable night in a cold dormitory with no sheets or blankets. If anyone had heard our grumbling they would have thought we were spoiled brats instead of nuns who had once dreamed of the glories of enduring the hardships of missionary lands.

In an odd way we actually were spoiled as nuns. Or at least I was. I had never had to take care of myself. I turned the little money I earned as a teacher over to the Sisters of Notre Dame, and in exchange, my rent, my grocery bill, my health insurance, and my electric bill were paid for me. I had learned to think of everyone who was not a Sister of Notre Dame as ''the outside world,'' and I had no accurate idea of how ''they'' lived. My suspicion that I was ignorant of both the practicalities and the subtleties of real life had brought me to Loyola, but I soon realized I had even more to learn than I had thought. It would take me eight more years of hard struggle before I paid my own light bill for the first time.

Can you imagine how dramatic that first summer in Chicago was for me? It was the first time that I was not entirely surrounded by Sisters of Notre Dame. My classmates were nuns, priests, and lay people from all over the United States. (It would be quite a few years before I realized that life in the real world necessarily involved rubbing shoulders with non-Catholics.) And my colleagues were asking the same questions I was! In class I could explore the experiences I had had in St. Lawrence's Parish, and no one shut off the discussion with an abrupt "right or wrong" answer.

"A woman in our parish was left alone with two young children," I began one day. "Her husband just up and left her. He disappeared. She had really been struggling to survive until she fell in love with a Catholic man and they were married. He was a wonderful guy, and he was great with her kids."

It was a hot Chicago day and the leaves on the trees outside the windows hung motionless and dusty. Somewhere out on the lake a thunderstorm rumbled. I discovered I was standing up, turning as I spoke as though I wanted an answer from everyone in the room. I continued.

"The pastor refused to let her become a member of the women's society of the parish because she couldn't go to Communion. Now this woman's faith was very important to her. Her kids went to our school. We had even wanted her to run for the parish council. But the pastor said she wasn't a legal member of the church. She had been *divorced*. He told her—he actually told her—that she was living in sin."

The class nodded. It was an old story to most of them.

"Well, I have a lot of questions about that," I said. And then I surprised myself by shouting, "Where was the Catholic church for this woman? Why were they blaming her for her ex-husband's behavior?"

A couple of people in the class laughed. I scowled, furious. I can remember standing there, one fist clenched at my side and my other hand raised with the index finger out and ready for a deadly Sister Charles Marie–style point, when some more people laughed—and I realized they were *with me*!

"I know, Barbara," a laywoman from St. Louis who was sitting in the chair next to mine said. "It happened to me. That's why I'm here."

At that exact moment, a thunderstorm broke directly over the campus. I felt as though a lightning bolt had run right into the top of my head. Kaboom! I was shouting out loud all the questions that my little circles of Sisters of Notre Dame had been discussing for years.

"Why isn't the church getting in touch with *women's* experiences?" (crash!)

"What kind of twisted theology excludes the experiences of half the people in the world?" (crack!)

"WHY can't women practice birth control?" (rumble!)

"Why can't women be *ordained*?"

People were laughing as I shouted one final question: "WHAT IF GOD IS A WOMAN?"

The women in the room applauded.

I was swept out of the building and carried off through the summer downpour to a coffee shop with my new friends.

My questions turned out to be everyone's questions. Well-known church scholars such as Rosemary Radford Ruether, Elisabeth Schüssler Fiorenza, Daniel Maguire, and Charles Curran had begun to develop a whole new understanding of God and of life in the church. Almost every time I went to a class I found myself writing in the margins of my notebooks: "Wow! There is a place for my thinking and believing." I was discovering a new and much larger community of people whose lives were committed to realizing justice and love.

I had missed so many of the experiences of growing up that I felt as though I was twenty-eight going on eighteen. And, like an eighteen-year-old, I spent a lot of time that summer laughing and crying. A *lot* of time—after all, I had been repressing my feelings for ten years.

Four summers later, in 1977, I would receive a master's degree in pastoral studies from Loyola. But that first summer of 1973 the most important course of study turned out to be something that could have been catalogued as

Socializing 101: a make-up requirement for those who missed out on group interaction in high school and college. Course will include field trips to restaurants and bars, college dances, late-night bull sessions on the meaning of life, heterosexual encounters. For students willing to move ahead rapidly, course offers the possibility of experiencing a broken heart for extra credit.

I wasn't the only person at Loyola that summer who had missed out on ten years of normal development. The classes were full of priests and nuns who had all lost the chance for giddy group behavior when they entered formation. Just hearing someone say, "Hey, Barbara, we're going to try an Italian restaurant in Old Town for supper tonight. Want to come?" prompted a wonderful wild feeling of setting out on a high adventure. We discovered Pizza Spot, a family-owned restaurant that had sawdust on the floor and bowls of unshelled peanuts on the tables. I would sit at a table with my friends, sipping a Coke and eating pizza, and even if I was holding forth on the need for lay people to take part in the ritual of the Mass, the left-behind teenager in my head was saying, "Wow! This is what I never got to do in college."

Every so often there was a social gathering at the college that would include a band. The first night, I romped around the room as though I had never been to a dance in my life. The last dance of the evening was a Virginia reel and there must have been forty couples all lined up.

My partner was a priest named Dan. I had seen him around, but I had never met him because he was already in his fourth or fifth summer at Loyola, and he wasn't in any of my classes. He looked Irish, tall with startling blue eyes under thick worried eyebrows, with curly hair. When the reel was over our end of the line went out in a group to get something to eat.

Then Dan and I had a long getting-to-know-you conversation.

"Where are you from?"

"Oh yeah? Really? The Sisters of Notre Dame? I had the Saint Joe's in school myself."

"I have ten brothers and sisters."

"Oh my God, and me with only nine."

He actually was Irish. He was also funny, brooding, intense, and burdened by doubt. I started looking for him in the corridors, in the cafeteria, out on the benches along the campus walkways. And he started being there! Waiting for me after class.

"Hi, want some tea?" he would say, and we would go off and spend four hours talking over two glasses of iced tea.

"Hi, want to go to the movies?"

"Hi, can I walk you to the library?"

I couldn't figure out why I felt so peculiar, as though I had a kind of heavenly indigestion. And my behavior was odd too. I would rush out of class hoping to see him, and then when I did see him, I would just mumble, "Hello." Or else I would race up to him like some kind of Labrador retriever that had just been let off the leash in the woods.

One day Ellen said, "How's your friend doing?" and I realized she was teasing me. And then I realized why I had been feeling and acting so oddly. I was in love! Head over heels in love! This was it! Exactly like the songs!

And he seemed to love me! At least, he certainly wanted to be with me. We spent some very good times together that summer—laughing, talking, going out with our group of friends.

And then the summer ended, and it was over. ''This only happens here,'' he said, sorrowful, brooding, and so damned Irish. As though ''here'' was some kind of emotional free port before he went back to a life of denial.

Some of the students at Loyola during those summers fell in love and got married. Some fell in love and left their orders. And some fell in love and slept with each other. I just fell in love. Our passion went into warm hugs and conversation. If I hadn't been so awkward and innocent—if he hadn't had a painful love affair a couple of summers before—who knows what might have happened? In any case, it didn't. He is still a priest, and I hear he is still burdened by doubts. But I never heard from him again.

I was absolutely crushed when it ended. I couldn't imagine that such feelings would just go away. How could he just drop it? I wanted to talk about it at least, deal with it together with him. But I didn't have any idea how to handle such feelings. I was, for the first time in my adult life, unprotected and defenseless against my own emotions. When I left Chicago at the end of the summer I rode in the back of the car and cried all the way home. I had been in love, and someone had cared for me as a person, as an attractive woman. Not only was I miserable and confused and lonesome, I was also surprised. I had been—it sounds corny, but it's true—awakened. And I knew, even as I sobbed my way across the Middle West, that my experience was going to strengthen me as a nun.

Even if it was only holding hands and hugging, now I knew what I had given up when I took a vow of chastity. I had given up a unique source of connection, solace, and joy, *and* all the authentic emotions, from creative to despairing, that that connection can inspire. I hoped I would never again respond to people's most intimate problems with the ignorant certainties of a cardboard saint.

For the next four years I would have to choose, over and over again, to remain a nun. So many of my friends left the convent to get married. I envied them their babies, and I knew—as I had not known at eighteen—that I too could be happy as a wife and mother. But I was getting to know myself, redefining the boundaries of my life and reexamining my choices in the new world of post-Vatican II. And the Barbara I discovered still found her true identity as a Sister of Notre Dame. My responsibilities were to my community, and their responsibility was to me. I knew I had chosen, and was continuing to choose, the right family for me.

The paradox was that I needed freedom to make the choice in an adult way.

If I had not been able to go to Loyola . . . If I had not been able to fall in love . . . If I had not been able by 1974 to search for my own job in the church instead of accepting an assignment—well, I almost certainly would have left the order. Instead, I felt a tremendous sense of anticipation and clarity. I was sure the role of women in the church was going to broaden, and I would not have to leave the convent in order to live out God's plan for me.

I was definitely not going with the crowd. Many more women were leaving than were entering at that point. This seemed to the older nuns to be a catastrophic collapse that would leave them rejected, abandoned, and doomed to a destitute old age. Even in the seventies, every working Sister of Notre Dame was supporting two other, older members of the community.

As the average age of the members of religious orders rose—by 1988 the average age of the Sisters of Notre Dame was in the mid-sixties—new sources of money had to be found to support retirement homes. Enormous novitiate buildings were sold or rented to colleges. Rolling grounds around convents were developed into "Sienna Estates" and "Aquinas Acres."

Because we were forced to examine our resources, we noticed a glaring inequity—those of us who were paid were not being paid enough to live on. And the church showed no intention of stepping forward with support payments. The vow of poverty took on an entirely different perspective when I realized I was being exploited. Until then, "poverty" had meant living on fifty dollars or so a month for my personal needs, with all other bills paid from the central deposit. Now we began to experience "poverty" in its real meaning: exhaustion, overwork, and fear.

The old definition of a "nun" was disappearing. The great job was to imagine the new one. The women at Loyola had talked all the time about the next step.

"What do you see yourself doing?" a new friend of mine named Nora had asked me one evening.

"I would like to work in a parish as part of a team of priests and nuns," I said. "I want to use all the skills I have learned here. But in Boston the pastor of the parish I was in wouldn't even let me run for a place on the parish council."

Imagine how excited I was to hear her say, "In Tucson, where I work, a lot of the progressive parishes are organized with nuns and priests working as a team."

"Oh, how wonderful," I said. "I would love to be part of something like that."

A month later, after I had gone home to Boston, I got a letter from her saying there was a job opening at her parish in Tucson, and she had recommended me for it.

The job was exactly what I had hoped for. The divine plan seemed to be working right on schedule.

I should have remembered, being a nun, that the divine plan never turns out exactly as we hope.

Thirteen: Tucson

BARBARA

Tucson was a complete surprise to me. I had never imagined a place so free and open and fantastically beautiful. I had been so busy making sure I would get permission to go there, I had never really stopped to think about what it might be like to live in Arizona.

"This job will be a challenge," I argued, praying that my leadership group would agree with me. "It will open up new ministries for Sisters of Notre Dame."

"It would be good to have two sisters there," I was told. There wasn't another SND from Boston in the entire state of Arizona. We had provinces only in Connecticut, Massachusetts, Ohio, Maryland, and California. I knew they would never let me go alone. Happily another Boston SND decided to be a pioneer with me. A parish near mine in Tucson had an opening for a pastoral minister and she got the job. We both got permission to go and off we went.

I fell in love with everything. The church building was modern and round, with sunny meeting rooms and a wonderful circular worship space. There were two houses next to the church, one for the priests and the other, complete with a patio and a view of the mountains, for me and Nora, my friend from Loyola who had recommended me to the parish.

In the beginning, the job was everything I had hoped it would be. The first sign I had that I was truly in a less rigidly traditional place was the fact that there was no parochial school attached to the parish. People in the West didn't feel the anxiety and parochialism that the earlier generations of eastern Catholics did. In my parish in Tucson people were drawn together by the life and spirit and faith of the community, not by a stale compliance with old rules or a fear of slipping into mortal sin if they missed Sunday mass. At my parish they were creating a modern American Catholic church, as Vatican II had directed.

I had arrived at the best possible creative moment and I was thrilled to be a part of it. The parishioners did not think of me as a teacher—there was no school! They thought of me as one of the team of priests and nuns guiding the parish.

The team consisted of Father Tom, the pastor; two Jesuit priests, Tony and Francis, who were pastoral assistants; and Nora and me. Right away, I began to have the extraordinary experience of being a woman in a leadership position in a Roman Catholic parish. The freedom I was given was especially remarkable because there were more priests than nuns in the parish. I wasn't being included because there was no one else to do the job, but because the parish was honestly trying to practice consensus and equality.

We really *celebrated* the Mass. Our Sunday liturgies were community projects. Everyone became involved in choosing and playing the music. Even though Rome did not allow lay people or nuns to preach, we did it. And the church bulged on Sunday mornings. It bounced as our music echoed off the circular walls. People came because they found something there that gave some meaning to their everyday lives.

I was able to help in administering the sacraments of Baptism and Communal Penance. At times I was invited to concelebrate the Eucharist with the priests. I could say the prayers and touch the chalice and pass out the Host at Communion. Lightning did not strike me dead at the altar as I carried out these truly revolutionary acts. Instead, the parishioners were delighted. In fact, the pastor invited them to give out Communion as well. I felt the idea of the People of God was very alive in the parishioners.

I was embarrassed one day when I had to admit that their understanding of "church" was more inclusive than mine. I was sitting on a flowered, quilted couch in the family room of a parishioner's home where we were holding a women's adult religious education class. I can't remember what I said that prompted the hostess to speak up and set me straight. The hard truth is I was probably sitting there thinking I was doing just great while I was actually a hedgehog of nunny attitudes.

"Barbara, I am no different from you," snapped my colleague. "I have as many rights in this church as you do!"

I swallowed hard. "What?" I said, too startled to cover up

my furious response. "Why, I gave up everything. I gave up my chance to get married."

"Let's talk about this," she said. We did, but not to the extent we should have. I was not ready.

So much for my counseling skills when I needed to apply them to myself. Back in my counseling program at Loyola I had been a prize student. Observed, supervised, and sympathetically sharing, I was so impressive that my teachers had tried to persuade me to become a full-time therapist. But here I was, being really challenged, and I wouldn't talk. I liked being a leader, and I really resented seeing laywomen muscle in on my newly claimed territory.

That night I went home and cleaned the entire house, doorstep to patio, curtains to refrigerator drip tray. Convent training sometimes has its benefits. I was actually having an identity crisis, but I ended up with a clean house and a clearer mind. As much as I wanted the church to come alive, as much as I believed in equality, as much as I insisted that women must have the right to full participation in the church—I still had a head full of old tapes telling me I had special privileges because I was a nun.

I began to let go of a big part of my identity that night, the specialness-of-being-a-nun part. And I was left with a new, even more difficult confrontation with the same profound questions: What did it mean to be a nun, a Christian, a person of God? The answers began to come through the people in the parish.

Nothing was more rewarding and challenging to me than having people seek me out when they were in trouble. I hoped it meant that I was learning to be an effective woman minister, and I prayed all the time that I would do the right thing.

When Cheryl came to me I was pleased but not surprised. I had visited her at home several times, and gotten to know her family. Tony, one of the priests, and I had begun a young adult group in the parish, and Cheryl was an active member, a very thoughtful young woman of twenty-one. During our weekly meetings when we sat in a circle and shared problems, Cheryl had seen me responding to all kinds of questions about boyfriends and girlfriends, about parents and jobs and drugs. Apparently she decided she could trust me.

Tony and I were sitting in the parish house office when Cheryl came in, looking like Miss Western States in her blue jeans and cowgirl shirt. I remember I made some admiring remark about her boots. And then she said:

"Uh, is anyone else here?"

"No, just us. Did you want anyone else?" I said.

"No, no, I need to talk to you." She looked doubtfully at Tony, and then she seemed to decide it was all right if he stayed.

"What's wrong?" Tony and I asked together.

"I'm pregnant," she said, flatly.

"UmmHmm," said Tony, with a sympathetic dip on the "umm" that was perfect. An old-fashioned priest would have said, "I'll have to tell your parents," or "I won't give you absolution until you get married." Or worse things. But Tony and I were trained to help resolve moral dilemmas and human conflicts. Therefore, I was smart enough to know she had not come to tell us she wanted to get married.

"Are you sure?" I asked. She had just been elected president of her sorority. We had talked often about her plans for after college.

"I'm two months late, and I had the test. I'm pregnant."

"Weren't you using some sort of birth control?" I asked. It was an inane question, but I suddenly wanted to know the answer. True, the church preached against birth control, but the church also forbids sexual intercourse outside of marriage. I hoped Cheryl hadn't decided to dilute the sin of sex by avoiding the sin of birth control.

A new thought flashed into my head: The church's teachings on birth control and sex are really out of date.

"I can't take the pill," said Cheryl. "It gives me violent headaches."

"Oh," I said. This was no time for me to display my ignorance about birth control methods.

"Umm," said Tony, "have you thought about getting married?"

"It's not possible now," said Cheryl. "A baby isn't possible. We both have to finish school. And, well, we're not sure we want to be married. I'm going to have an abortion and I need your help."

At least she hadn't asked for our permission. She was a grown-up Catholic, exercising her own freedom of conscience. Cheryl wanted us to cover for her, to tell her parents, if they called looking for her, that she was away on a retreat with some girl-friends. She was positive her father would kill her if he found out. He hadn't seemed brutal or uncaring when I met him, but

Cheryl knew him better than I did. She wasn't a child. I couldn't think of any good purpose that would be served by telling her parents.

What could I do? I couldn't run away from her or refuse her. God would not walk away from someone who asked for help, whatever the help might be. I wasn't being asked to go to the clinic, but to "be with her" as her church, her spiritual support, during this most difficult time. Uneasily, I did tell her that I would not choose to have an abortion if I were pregnant.

During the day of the abortion, while Tony and I kept an anxious vigil by the telephone, I thought about what I had told Cheryl, and I realized it wasn't true.

Until then I had never asked myself what I would do, because I never thought I would face the problem. The only way I could get pregnant would be if I were raped. I sat there, watching a lizard skitter across the ceiling, and for the first time in my life I tried to imagine what it would be like to be raped, and then to discover I was pregnant.

In 1974, in Tucson, there were no rape crisis hot lines, and no rape victims had ever come to the parish for counseling. Women had not yet learned to speak out and fight back. All I had to work with were images: a man standing behind my bathroom door, grabbing me around the neck. Hurting me, humiliating me, threatening to come back. And then, weeks later, when I was still terrified and sickened, afraid to go out, afraid of the dark—to find myself pregnant.

The truth was that I couldn't imagine going through a pregnancy in that state of mind. My body would become so abhorrent to me that my mind would detach from my senses and I would never be whole again. As an adult Christian woman, I would be treating myself irresponsibly if I did not have an abortion. It would be the only moral choice.

Cheryl had made a moral decision, after much reflection and prayer. She was a faithful churchgoer, she believed God was alive in her life, and she believed she had to take responsibility for what happened in her life. It was not the right time for her to have a child. How could anyone else, *anyone* else, possibly claim the right to make that decision for her?

My thoughts ran on, following an inexorable logic. A "good" woman, making a conscious moral choice, is a sympathetic figure. What about the women who do not go to church, who live recklessly and care nothing about prayer and reflection? What about "bad" women? Should their choice be made for them?

Obviously not. Who would dare make such a judgment for someone else?

I began to think that there was something arrogant and repressive and morally indefensible about the Catholic church's attitude toward abortion—*and toward women.*

Unfortunately, I only *began* to think that afternoon. And as soon as I got that far, my thoughts veered away from my conclusion. After all, if I had fully understood what I was saying to myself, I would have had to leave right then, that afternoon. And I had nowhere to go. The church was my life. So for years to come I would try to make myself believe that as more and more women played a greater and greater role in the life of the church, the hierarchy would comprehend the injustice done to us. And in 1975 I was still fairly confident that the church, filled with the wisdom of the Holy Spirit, rededicated to peace and justice by Pope John XXIII, would amend the injustice within itself.

Instead, I discovered that my own little parish in Tucson, Arizona, despite its brave new rhetoric of equality and shared ministry and lay leadership, was still ruled absolutely by the whim of the male, hierarchical pastor.

I worked very closely with Tony, the pastoral assistant, in Tucson. One reason was because Nora, my friend who had urged me to come out and work with her, had stopped speaking to me not long after I arrived. For the first few weeks she had been warm and friendly. She kept talking about the great programs we would begin and how much she enjoyed having someone to work with who was really on her wavelength. But time and time again I would try to sit down with her to talk about neighborhood class schedules for religious education, or music choices for Sunday mass. And she either wouldn't show up for a meeting we had set only that morning at breakfast, or she would sit in the kitchen looking bored and finally say, "I don't want to talk about that now, Barbara." And go to her room! Eventually, I tried not to be in our house when Nora was there, which was very uncomfortable for me.

Even when a few parishioners congratulated me on being the first person in my job to last more than five months, I didn't get it. When I think of the time I wasted trying to figure out how I had offended Nora, it makes me grit my teeth. Because the source of the problem was right in front of me, and I never connected it to her behavior. There was a bottle of Scotch in the kitchen, and a bottle of Scotch in the living room, and a bottle of Scotch I had once seen on Nora's night table. And I somehow convinced myself that the reason these bottles were always half empty was because they were really the same bottle moving around the house.

In fact, it looked to me as though Nora drank nearly half a bottle of Scotch a day. Straight. And it never occurred to me she could be an alcoholic because I knew she only had one kidney!

Then one Thursday I reminded Nora that she had promised to lead a young adult group on Friday night.

"Don't be silly, Barbara," she snarled. "Father Tom and I are going on retreat this weekend."

"But you went on retreat two weeks ago," I blurted out.

Nora stamped out of the room. Tony and I led the Friday night group. Afterward the group always went out together to a Mexican restaurant for coffee. That night I just kept eating what was in front of me, and Tony could hardly help but notice.

"Are you upset about something, Barbara? Or are you afraid this place is going to close forever tomorrow?" he said.

I frowned. "I guess I just wish Nora had told me they were going on retreat again. I had to cancel a visit to see Mary so I could take her place this evening."

"Hmmm," he said (that therapeutic "hmmm" I admired so much). "I'll talk to you about that on the ride home."

"Why? What's going on? What aren't you telling me?" I demanded. I'm never very tactful, but the months living with Nora had made me hypersensitive to hidden secrets.

"Later, later," shushed Tony.

"Now!" I insisted.

Mark, a young man from the group, leaned across the table and said, "I think what he is trying to tell you, Barbara, is that Father Tom and Nora are probably on retreat in a motel room in Phoenix."

My jaw dropped. My eyes popped. Tony's eyes popped.

"You mean people in the parish know about this?" he asked Mark.

"Oh, sure," Mark said. "It would be hard to miss. My mother thinks they should either get married or stop screwing around." He coughed a little, and added, "Sorry."

We were never certain that Tom and Nora actually were sleeping together, but many of their actions certainly pointed to an intimate involvement with one another.

Driving back to our houses, I said, "The whole parish suspects something. You knew about it. And I didn't have a clue. No wonder Nora can scarcely stay in the same room with me."

"It's been driving Francis and me crazy," said Tony. "A love affair is one thing. I mean, it certainly isn't the first time such a thing has happened. But they're using parish funds to take their little pleasure jaunts."

Early the next morning after mass, Francis, Tony, and I decided we would have to confront Nora and Father Tom when they came back from "retreat." Now that we thought we knew why we had been working under so much stress, we would have to try to deal with it. After all, we were a team ministry. It was important to minister to each other.

How ghastly that encounter was! Monday at lunchtime found us all sitting around the kitchen table in the parish house. Very seriously and sympathetically, Tony explained that we were concerned about the effect of Nora and Father Tom's relationship on the community.

"And what about you, Tony?" snapped Nora.

"Huh?" he said.

"What about your relationship with Barbara?"

I was mortified. A blush burned across my face, and at the same time I could have strangled Nora. Tony was my best friend and my coworker. And, in fact, I was in love with him, but I was sure it didn't show. I had learned my lesson with Dan.

"What are you talking about?" I asked.

"Oh, don't give me that," Nora sneered. "You'd better make a date with your confessor."

"Why should I?" I said, furious and insulted and determined to be honest. "*I* haven't done anything wrong. So I love someone. What's wrong with that? But we aren't having a sexual relationship. And it seems *you are*!"

"I think it is time for you to remember your place, Sister Barbara," said Father Tom. I couldn't believe he had said it. So I laughed. He was making a joke, I thought, to ease the tension.

Quite cheerfully, I said, "You're right. I'm sorry, it isn't fair to be so personal. We support you in whatever you feel is right for you, but we are also worried about the effect on the parish."

"I am afraid, Barbara, that you have reason to be sorry," the pompous hypocrite said. "I think you had better go back to your own living quarters now."

As I went across the yard—or rather, as I stamped across the yard—I was worried. But then I started to giggle. The vision of a drunken Nora tumbling around in a motel room with Father Tom suddenly struck me as hilarious. I could remember a retreat I took during high school when we girls were solemnly informed that during every sex act three people were present: the man, the woman, and God. It occurred to me that sex was one proof that God has a sense of humor.

Two days later Father Tom informed me that I was no longer needed in the parish. In other words, I was fired. It was then the end of March, and I had to be gone by the beginning of May.

Tony and Francis were angry. The people I had worked with in the parish were angry. Some of the young adult group members actually asked Tony and me why we couldn't get married and stay. The idea seemed to make perfect sense to them, and I could see their point. We would have made a great team, living in a rectory with a white picket fence, doing God's work, supporting and loving each other.

"I don't think I'm the marrying kind, Barbara," Tony said gently. "But if I were, you would be the one." We, at least, parted as friends.

The older parishioners sent me notes of support, but when I talked to them, they said they couldn't risk challenging the pastor and bringing the whole scandal out in the open. If they did, they were afraid the bishop would replace him with a more conservative pastor. That kind of diocesan blackmail kept many parishes quiet in the seventies. What happened at my parish in Tucson was certainly not new. Father Tom and Nora were human beings, and far from the first consecrated individuals to find their lives were slipping out of control. The real problem was that the people in the parish were powerless to deal with it themselves. The participation they had valued turned out to be meaningless when it really counted. The parish council turned out to be a very useful new system for raising morale and therefore money, but it had absolutely no say about who would be paid with the money. No new structures existed to counteract the hierarchical church's natural repressive reflexes. Nor do they yet exist.

The day before I left Tucson for good, I preached the homily at mass. Drawing from my own life in Tucson, I spoke of my attachment to the people, the feeling of community, loving and living deeply and yet having to let go, not by choice but by force.

* * *

May 1975. I had two weeks to get back to Boston, find a job and a place to live, and then go to Chicago for the summer session at Loyola. I felt as though I was being put in a cage. "Good-bye canyons, hello clericalism," I muttered as I landed at Logan Airport.

The good news was that I could go home, to my parents' house, and be hugged. The bad news was that I was in a state of shock and didn't know it.

The Boston diocese told me about three job openings in three different parishes. None of them were for a pastoral worker. Women were not doing pastoral work in Boston. We were allowed to be religious education directors, a job that was becoming a full-time specialization now that the parochial schools were slowly disappearing—along with the priests and nuns.

I drove out to the towns around Boston to look into the jobs. At the first two parishes, the pastors put their fingertips together when they talked to me, like a little cathedral of the hands. And they called me "Sister."

When I got to Corpus Christi Parish in Auburndale, the last place on my list, the two priests waiting for me shook my hand and said, "Hello, Barbara." We sat outside on the grass under the trees and talked about the development of women in the Roman Catholic church. The pastor, Joe McGlone, seemed interested and sympathetic, so I decided to work in Auburndale. After I moved there I realized it was the parish of my great-aunt Margaret, who came from Italy with my grandmother De-Guglielmo and was a feminist. Aunt Margaret was now dead, but my uncle Rex, her husband, was still in the parish. I figured it was a good sign for the future.

Until about Christmas I just forged ahead, went to school in Chicago, came home, moved into an apartment in Needham with a group of Sisters of Notre Dame, and started working. And then one snowy day I went into my office in the rectory, and hung my wet coat over the radiator. The smell of wet, hot wool struck me as unbearably sad, as though a thousand ghosts of Christmas past and future were weeping on top of my desk. I decided lunch would make me feel better, and I went into the dining room where Joe and his nervous young curate were eating. Joe asked me a question about how we had involved the parishioners out in Tucson in preparing the Sunday liturgy. I was rattling on, glad he was interested, talking about how I led the congregation in prayer and I wished I could do it in Boston, when the curate interrupted.

"Could you talk about that stuff later, Barbara? Father McGlone and I have something *important* to talk about."

I put down my ham and cheese sandwich and took a little sip of water. And then I started to cry, slowly at first, just a little trickle down my cheeks. They didn't even notice. And I would not let them know, either. I left the room. Luckily, I had spent the last three summers studying counseling, and I was just barely able to realize that something was seriously wrong with me.

In those days I met once a month with a spiritual director, a Dominican sister. We reflected together on the links between our day-to-day lives and our spiritual life. She suggested that I see a counselor who was a former Jesuit. I made an appointment right away, and for the next six months we struggled together while I tried to make sense of my past—and my future.

Just being given the words to name my confusion was an incredible comfort. "Unresolved feelings." "Out of touch with my anger." Yes, yes, that's me.

I kept a little journal while I was in counseling, writing down problems to discuss, and occasionally scribbling long philosophical essays. As I look at it now, what surprises me is the pure fury—it was a healthy catalytic fury—I felt when I heard about yet another case of a priest being protected by his religious order when the woman he had been having an affair with became pregnant. The priest remained a priest, and the superior of the order discreetly arranged for the pregnant woman to receive support payments—or money for an abortion if she preferred! Somehow or other this hypocritical system was not my idea of the church I believed I was called to, nor was it the church I wanted to perpetuate.

What particularly disgusted and enraged me was the "boys will be boys" acceptance of men's behavior and the simultaneous callous disregard the church showed for the reality of women's lives.

Finally it struck me that my anger was not only a result of the fact that the church discriminated against "women." It was also the effect of the church's discrimination against *me*, a church woman.

By this time, feminism inside nundom had reached the same stage of discovery and determination as the secular feminist movement. My mailbox was stuffed every morning with newsletters from various nun's groups and organizations such as the Leadership Conference on Women Religious, the Women's Ordination Conference, and the National Assembly of Women Religious. Using skills honed to perfection by years of bending over hot mimeograph machines in parochial schools, we mailed off our thoughts, prayers, arguments, and exhortations written across pages, up and down margins, and even around address labels.

Whenever I read *Ms.* magazine or noticed the debates about the Equal Rights Amendment, I thought to myself, Great. Other women have noticed. I was very slow to realize that our struggle was part of a great worldwide struggle. Sometimes I would see articles about nuns in the feminist press, and they usually struck me as having been written by someone who thought we were ''good little sisters'' working for equality in our eccentric fringe area. I thought the Roman Catholic church was the very heart of the problem—and I still do.

On Thanksgiving Day, 1975, I gave up my favorite family holiday so that I could drive all day from Boston to Detroit. Four of us went, and when we arrived we were thrilled to find that more than one thousand other Catholic nuns and laywomen had also come to attend the first Women's Ordination Conference, ''Women in Future Priesthood Now: A Call to Action.'' Ordination for women (in every religion) had become a burning issue in theology schools—a not altogether surprising effect of the exploding population of female theology students. Was it possible? Was it desirable? Could women be ordained as priests?

The crucial importance of the conference was its result: we realized that the problem was not our sex but the Catholic church's *opinion* of our sex.

The one woman in that crowd I am sure I did not meet was Patricia Hussey. When our paths finally crossed in 1978, we spent hours and hours reliving that historic weekend in Detroit. She, it turned out, had not shared my exhilarating hope. I had wandered from one extraordinary session to another, listening, and thinking, My God, it may happen in my lifetime! Pat was thinking that if she were to be ordained, it would not be in order to follow the role model of most of the priests she had ever met.

As it turned out, the men sitting in Rome making the rules, the bishops and cardinals and Pope Paul VI, decided to deal with the pressure for change by forbidding it. In 1976 the Vatican published a ''Declaration on the Admission of Women to the Ministerial Priesthood.'' No, it said, ''. . . the Church, in fidelity to the example of the Lord, does not consider herself [*sic*] authorized to admit women to priestly ordination." The lengthy document, translated from church Latin into unctuous and intransigent Vaticanese, seems funny now, but it certainly didn't seem amusing then.

According to the Vatican declaration, ". . . we can never ignore the fact that Christ is a man." Women are not men. And so, unable to "image" Jesus in the priesthood, women are therefore disqualified by virtue of bodily parts. And anyway, men are the priests by "unbroken tradition"—a convenient obliteration of women's role in the early church. The Vatican's lengthy effort to write us back into obedient servitude concluded with "The Church desires that Christian women should become fully aware of the greatness of their mission"—in separate spheres of course!

The part of the Vatican statement that disturbed me the most read "It is sometimes said and written in books and periodicals that some women feel that they have a vocation to the priesthood. Such an attraction, however noble and understandable, still does not suffice for a genuine vocation . . . The priestly office cannot become the goal of social advancement; no merely human progress of society or of the individual can of itself give access to it: it is of another order." Not only did I feel a quite genuine "attraction" to the priesthood, but the Vatican, by dismissing the idea of human progress, seemed to be exempting itself from living out the message of Christ on earth. Worst of all, the Vatican was claiming that because God became *male*, males were godlike. That seemed a very unpersuasive argument to feminist theologians.

Feminists, nuns or not, experienced the seventies as a progression of consciousness from the personal to the political. And so it was for me. In Tucson, I had learned that my enthusiasm, my opinion, my skills, and even my vocation counted for nothing if I challenged the system. Apparently the church hierarchy and I had very different ideas of what it meant to be useful. I wanted to be useful to the people. The church wanted me to be useful to the priests, with no questions asked.

Back in Boston I began to pay attention to how my work was valued, or, as it turned out, not valued. One day I asked Joe, the pastor of Corpus Christi, how much a priest received as salary.

"It starts at six thousand dollars a year with an increment of seventy-five dollars for each year of being a priest," he said. He didn't mention the free room and board paid for by the people of the parish, whose financial donations supported the rectory. Nor did he include the cooking, cleaning, and care of Sister Rosetta, an elderly Sister of St. Joseph who was the rectory housekeeper.

Suddenly I understood the urgency of the phrase "equal pay for equal work." When I left my last full-time employment in the Catholic church, in 1978, my job consisted of directing the entire religious education program in a parish of about five hundred families. I was responsible for teaching the meaning and practice of the Catholic faith to all those people, from birth to death. I had also agreed, in fact I had eagerly volunteered, to expand and test my own role as a counselor and a leader of ritual celebrations in the parish. Truly, I was doing twice as much work as the priests.

And I was paid $4,000 a year. Without increments. I did have the use of a parish automobile for my work, and the Sisters of Notre Dame received money from the parish to pay for health insurance. But I was responsible for paying for my room and board, and when I went home after a full day's work, I went back to cooking, cleaning, and shopping.

Each of us, as nuns, took responsibility to share our resources and contribute to a general fund. When I was in school and not working full-time, other nuns were supporting me. As fewer and fewer women entered the community, and more and more left, those of us who stayed had to support the retired sisters. An important reason why so many of us began to take secular service jobs was that nuns who received decent salaries from secular institutions compensated for the inadequate salaries nuns received from church jobs.

Until 1972, nuns were not allowed to be a part of the Social Security program. The church took no responsibility for providing for retirement and was only shamed into helping when studies were released showing that elderly nuns qualified for welfare assistance. The financial condition of lay men and women who had spent their lives working for the church was also pitiful.

I had years of experience and a master's degree in pastoral studies. But, despite the fact that I was doing the work of the job described as "Director of Religious Education," the title itself was given to a young priest in the parish, who had no formal training in education. When I objected to the young curate, he said, quite casually it seemed to me, "Oh yeah, well, that is common practice in every parish."

"There are scarcely enough priests left in every parish to get the title, still less to do the job," I raged. "And still the church cannot admit that nuns are doing the important work. They won't even admit that we can do it."

I began to put different names to things. The church called my condition "poverty." I called it "exploitation." I had been trained in humility, but if I overlooked getting credit for the job I was doing it would be a disservice to my community as well as myself, because my education had been acquired at the cost of great sacrifice for the Sisters of Notre Dame. If the church refused to recognize the value of what we were doing in parishes, how could we continue to scrape together the resources we needed to train ourselves?

I felt that my life was being used up defending my place in the church. I think all women will identify with my experience the day I went to visit Frances in the hospital. This was my moment of truth.

Frances was dirty, poor, and severely alcoholic. Her husband was also alcoholic, and sometimes he knew when Frances was sick, and sometimes he didn't, or didn't care. They had a daughter named Kathy who was getting lost in the chaos, but she always turned up for my Confraternity of Christian Doctrine class. Some parishioners whom I had trained to be CCD teachers were very worried about her and urged me to check into her home situation. So I would drop in once in a while.

One day Kathy told me her mother was in the local hospital's intensive care unit again. I knew the priests had not been in touch with her situation, and Kathy said her father had disappeared. So I set out to make a pastoral visit. When I got there, the nurse told me Frances was hooked up to life support systems and could be visited only by her family and clergy. I peered through the window of the swinging door into the ICU. Frances was a faint shadow behind an oxygen tent, her bed surrounded by beeping machines. She seemed so frail. *Life* seemed so frail, as though with just a blink of my eyes all those beepers could stop. And I knew that I was the only friend she had left who might be able to be of some comfort if I could speak to her, or just touch her.

"I am her minister," I told the head nurse, "so I would like to go in and see her."

The nurse didn't even look up from her desk. "Only family and clergy," she repeated.

"I *am* her clergy," I insisted.

It was as if I was telling her I was from Mars. Embarrassed and furious, I left. When I got back to the rectory I ran upstairs to the second-floor study where the two priests I worked with sat.

"I can't believe this happened to me," I said, blurting out my story.

To my horror, they laughed. The young curate said, "Well, maybe if you were wearing your habit, you would have gotten in."

I turned on my heels and left the room. When I appealed to the hospital chaplain, he immediately put me on the list of visiting chaplains. But the joke in the rectory study wasn't funny anymore. It had been too hard to come so far over the past ten years as a nun and as a woman. It was time I was recognized for who I was, and not for what I wore.

If it had not been for the people of the parish, and the support of Joe the pastor, I would have been entirely discouraged. As I began to involve the lay people more in the life of the parish, they began to welcome me more into their lives. They didn't behave as though I should not be making visits because no nuns had ever done it before. They liked it, and most of my "work" was done on such informal occasions.

I remember one evening a man named Don showed up just as we were finishing a class for a group about to be confirmed. He wanted to talk to me and to the young priest I was working with about the church's position on artificial insemination. The priest shut down like a prairie dog jumping into its hole, and Don looked crestfallen. After the class I got in the car and drove over to his house. After all, he hadn't just dropped in on the spur of the moment to ask such a question. He must have had to get up the courage and to be sincerely seeking answers.

When I rang the bell, he opened the door and looked surprised and relieved. After he and his wife and I talked, I admitted I didn't know the answers to his questions, but I would get all the information I could and get back to him. As I was leaving, he said to me, "Why can't women like you be ordained? What is the Vatican's rationale? You do things for us that no old-fashioned cleric ever did."

I thanked him, and told them both how grateful I was for their support. As I drove home that night, I kept tapping on the steering wheel and repeating over and over, "What am I going to do? What am I going to do?" There were too many questions, and they didn't seem to be resolving themselves while I waited and prayed for guidance.

I knew I was a good minister. Would the church ever recognize it? Should I stay and keep chipping away at the patriarchal monolith by continuing as a role model for women religious? Should I leave and allow myself to grow without these painful restrictions? Why was I still a nun? Why stay? Why leave?

I couldn't seem to go any further forward, and I certainly couldn't go backward. If some of the parishioners asked me why I was still a nun, or why I couldn't be ordained, at least half of them asked me why I wasn't teaching in school, why didn't I wear a habit, what was I doing eating in the rectory with the priests?

By the time I left Auburndale in June of 1977 to go out to Chicago for the last semester of study for my master's degree in pastoral studies, I felt so alone I had begun to feel like an alien. And then a door opened to the next step.

My experience in the parishes in Tucson and Auburndale had convinced me that an area of parish life in which women were very badly needed was pastoral counseling. Most people seeking help with problems in their lives turn first to their church or synagogue. As a result, programs were being developed in theology schools to add the techniques of modern therapy to the traditional responses of sympathy, homily, and rules.

One of my professors at Loyola told me about a program leading to a doctorate in ministry offered by McCormick Presbyterian Seminary in Chicago. Not only did it seem to be just what I was looking for, but I seemed to be what McCormick was looking for. The director urged me to apply for a grant and I was awarded a full fellowship.

My provincial team in Boston was quite taken aback when I asked for a three-year leave of absence to go to school full-time. Probably they were not convinced of the value of the program I had chosen. At any rate, they said I couldn't go. I asked McCormick to hold my fellowship for a year, and, as I had hoped, I had worked it out by the next fall so I could accept it.

Once again I set out for Chicago. This time I felt I was on a clear road to the future. So far I had discovered that to begin to be considered equal to the clergy, I needed to work 150 percent harder than they did. I was going to become so well-qualified, so over-credentialed, that they would *have* to accept me. My Auburndale pastor had promised me I could return in the summers and try out what I would be learning in Chicago. He also assured me I could come back to the parish as a full-time minister, which meant doing almost everything but saying Mass. Someday, women would be ordained in the Roman Catholic church. If it happened in my lifetime, I planned to be ready.

Three nuns, Judy, Kathy, and I, set out early one morning in September of 1978, with all our worldly possessions packed into the smallest U-Haul trailer we could rent. We hadn't gone more than ten miles west on the Massachusetts turnpike when a state trooper stopped us. We smiled at him like the angelic nuns we were.

"Ladies, where are you going?"

"Chicago, officer," we chorused.

He stepped back and walked around our trailer, lifting a corner of the plastic tarpaulin we had tucked over the top of our books and records. He stared mournfully at my guitar and a couple of forlorn houseplants.

"You'll never make it," he said.

But we did. We tied down the tarpaulin, the weather stayed dry during the whole trip, and even the houseplants survived. I was in such good spirits that I insisted we stop for a real meal about halfway to Chicago. It was dark, and as we got out of the car I asked a group of men idling around under the lighted restaurant sign to stand guard.

"Watch the trailer for us, will you, while we're in getting our supper," I said. I must have used my Sister Charles Marie–voice because when we got inside, sat down, and looked back at them through the window, they were *watching*. Just sitting there on their motorcyles, in their leather jackets and their boots and tattoos, looking astonished, and watching.

We got to Chicago, dropped Kathy off at the convent where she would be living for the summer, and headed to the South Side to find my new home. The housing provided by the McCormick Presbyterian Seminary, where I would be studying, was for married ministers with families, or single graduate students. They had nothing available for a full-time female doctoral candidate. So I had arranged to live in an apartment belonging to the Jesuit School of Theology with two other women, one of them a lay student of theology and one of them a Sister of Notre Dame I had never met. It was a three-story, old-fashioned apartment building, and as I started up the stairs my heart lifted. There would be people in Chicago who shared my vision and my urgency. I needed to be with them. The answers I was looking for would come out of the wonderful months of thinking, just *thinking*, that lay ahead.

If things had gone exactly according to my plan, I might still be back in Auburndale, waiting for the day when women will be ordained. Instead, the unknown Sister of Notre Dame turned out to be Patricia Hussey.

She was away in Rome when I arrived. The first two weeks of my golden period of "just thinking" turned out to be two weeks of housecleaning and answering the doorbell to people who always looked disappointed and asked, "When is Pat coming home?"

When *I* rang the doorbell, that first expectant day, my other unknown roommate opened the door wearing a T-shirt which announced: "I Am Not a Nun."

"Uh-oh," I thought. "Here I go again, living with another crazy."

Fourteen: Rome

PAT

I was sitting on a stone wall overlooking a reservoir in the Berkshire Mountains. My eyes were closed, my deep breathing was going nicely, and I had just begun to achieve a relaxed meditative state when I heard a rustle and a hesitant voice whispering, "Patricia Hussey? There's a telephone call for you."

In a week I would be flying to Rome to attend the 1978 General Chapter Meeting of the Sisters of Notre Dame. It was the fifth chapter meeting of the series that had been going on every three years since the Vatican II council, and our order was coming closer to the end of redefining our mission and our future. Because I was one of only two young nuns invited to attend from the United States, so "new" that we had not yet taken our final vows, I wanted to get my soul well prepared for the task ahead. My way of doing that was to go away to an old farmhouse converted into a retreat house.

"Telephone," the whispering voice insisted.

I was furious. I didn't want to speak to anyone. And then I was frightened. The only reason someone would disturb me during a retreat would be in the case of a terrible emergency. I raced up the hill toward the phone, panting and praying nothing had happened to my family.

"Hello! What's wrong?" I gasped into the phone.

"Hi! I'm Barbara Ferraro," I heard. Whoever she was, she talked so fast I could barely understand her.

"What's wrong?" I shouted.

"Nothing is wrong," she said, with annoying cheerfulness.

"I'm your new roommate. I'm going out to Chicago. Can I bring along silverware or pots and pans? What do you need?"

And I thought, Oh, jeez, here we go again, another crazy.

Twelve years later I am willing to admit that Barbara's questions were not unreasonable. But in 1978 I was extremely wary about roommates. This would be my third year at the Jesuit School of Theology, and while the first year I had lived with two wonderful nuns, the second year's pair had left a lot to be desired in the compatibility department. There was friction between the two women. And one of them was still living there.

"What is the third roommate like?" chirped Barbara.

"I will leave you to make a judgment when you meet her," I said. I figured this Barbara person might get along with Claire Helene. Why should I mention her mood swings and the living habits of a stoat?

I went back to my stone wall, and then I went to Rome, and by the time I returned to Chicago I had almost forgotten about Barbara. As I let myself into the apartment, I felt the familiar sinking feeling—the sort of resignation Hercules must have felt when he entered the Augean stables. Then I noticed the place looked really nice. The layer of dead flies was gone from the bathroom windowsill, and the fragments of cockroaches that had decorated the kitchen shelves had been swept away.

It was a Saturday evening, and no one was home. I put down my suitcase and went across the building's entrance hall to the Jesuit common room. All the other residents in the building were Jesuit priests and Jesuit seminarians, and the apartment across from ours was where they ate. Michael and Jim, two of my friends from the year before, were in the kitchen, and we had a reunion, standing around with cups of coffee and doughnuts, talking about our summers.

The kitchen door of my apartment and the commons apartment both opened onto the same back steps. We had the door open, to enjoy the early evening sounds of the end of summer, and eventually I heard someone dancing up and down the steps and singing, "What I Did for Love."

Jim leaned out the door and said, "Hey, Barbara, Pat's here."

And in came Barbara Ferraro, a short little one-woman "Chorus Line," and she rushed across the kitchen and threw her arms around me and said, "Welcome to Chicago!"

Poor Barbara. Hugging me must have felt like hugging a mailbox. At that point in my life, I had decided that I was sick of having people hug and kiss me just because it was supposed to show warm feelings. I was particularly tired of Sisters of Notre Dame hugging me when I didn't feel they had any genuine warm feelings at all. It seemed like another layer of the habit, something they put on.

Unhappily for Barbara, at that point in her life she had just fully reclaimed her natural Italian exuberance. She hugged everybody, and she meant it. And to top it off, that particular afternoon she had actually been at the theatre seeing *A Chorus Line*.

Barbara sort of recoiled from my stolid response to her greeting (after I heard about Nora later, I could understand why). And for a minute we looked at each other.

Oh my God, one of the crazy nuns, I thought.

Oh my God, one of the nunny bunnies, she thought.

"How do you like the way the house looks?" Barbara demanded, as we headed back across the hall that night.

"Very nice," I said, grudgingly.

"Very *nice?*" she said. "I had to wash the kitchen walls with steel wool. I don't know how anyone could have lived here."

"Well, really really very nice," I relented. "Actually, I never could get Claire Helene even to empty a wastebasket. How did you get her to help?"

"I couldn't get her to help," said Barbara, a touch cautiously. "She spent all her time helping the Jesuits upstairs clean their apartment."

"Hmm," I said. "And did she greet you wearing her 'I Am Not a Nun' T-shirt?"

We started to laugh, and by the time we stopped, we both were sitting in Barbara's room. She had taken over the apartment's former living room and made it look as cozy as a fireplace on a February night. One corner was a study, another was a bedroom area, and another, facing the old front window, was a little sitting area.

"My gosh," I said, "I was always afraid to come in here last year. I was afraid I would find dead dogs under the bed, or bats in the closet."

We stayed up talking all night long. Normally, as I would learn, Barbara falls asleep promptly at nine in the evening, no matter where she is or what she is doing. But that night she was as bright as a button. I remember she was sitting in a little rocking chair, waving her arms and telling stories, her eyes getting bigger every minute. I was sitting in some kind of hideous secondhand stuffed chair that was marvelously comfortable, and the more excited Barbara got, the more relaxed I became. She told me about Tucson and Auburndale, about her family and why she was looking forward to studying at McCormick. I told her about Long Lane School and my family, about my failures as a grade-school teacher, and about the chapter meeting in Rome.

When the sun began to come up, we decided it was foolish to go to sleep. So Barbara put on the jogging shoes the parishioners in Auburndale had given her for a going-away present, and I rooted out my sneakers from my still packed suitcase, and we walked briskly east about eight blocks to the lakefront.

"Can't you just smell the salt air?" I joked, and then we started talking about our mutual love of the ocean. We finished up our marathon with an enormous breakfast at a restaurant called the Mellow Yellow. It was a small neighborhood place, with yellow checked curtains and daisy-patterned wallpaper, and for the rest of that academic year we would solve most of the world's problems over Mellow Yellow waffles. Our first breakfast together was spent on a preliminary discussion of new ways to understand the vows of poverty, chastity, and obedience.

"Oh, my," sighed Barbara, leaning back into the booth. "This is just wonderful. You think just like me!"

"I don't think I have ever lived with someone who would rather discuss justice issues than fight about who would clean the bathroom," I said.

"It's so refreshing to meet somebody so alive and so real," she burbled. "I don't have to waste time justifying myself to you. I'm so glad you turned out to be you!"

I felt my defenses begin to melt. Here was a new friend who was not only completely direct and honest about her feelings and her ideas—I could even *agree* with her feelings and ideas!

By the time Barbara and I met, she was thirty-five and I was twenty-nine. She had been a Sister of Notre Dame for sixteen years, and I had been one for eleven years. We had grown up less than ninety miles apart, and we had joined adjacent SND provinces. We were both members of an endangered species: relatively young women who had remained nuns. And yet, we had never met.

Plumbers and lawyers and breeders of Great Danes hold annual conventions, but the Sisters of Notre Dame had never thought to reinforce their sense of identity and unity with an annual jamboree. Even though there were only 1,500 of us in the United States in 1978, we didn't think it was especially important to know each other. The SNDs from other countries around the world were vague curiosities to us instead of potential collaborating agents of change.

A few times in the early seventies Barbara and I had attended the same education or social justice conferences, but we never met. It would not have occurred to either of us to put a sign on the message bulletin board saying, "All Sisters of Notre Dame meet in Room 412 at three o'clock." Even as the order was trying to democratize, to follow the dictates of Vatican II and get away from hierarchy and into the inclusiveness of the "people of God," we didn't really know how. Our leadership teams did meet to work out change and to bring the word back to the provinces, but Barbara and I were never selected to be on a leadership team.

Our loyalties and our identities as Sisters of Notre Dame were still tied to our provincial groups, an emotional bond carried over from the old cloistered days when communities of nuns were bound together by isolation, the repetition of prayer and hourly tasks, and by unquestioning obedience to authority.

For years before Barbara and I met, people had been asking us why we remained nuns. And for both of us, a great part of the reason was our strong sense of belonging to our provincial groups—no matter where we were actually living or working. Those nuns were our support groups, the people who shared a common mission with us, had the same goals, understood our problems. They cared for us, we cared for them.

We held on to our attachment and dependence on our provincial sisters for a long time—depending on it, insisting on it, trying to change them as we changed, trying to explain our lives to them long after the bonds had dissolved without our noticing. It was a little like a marriage that has faded but does not break until a crisis reveals it to be a hollow illusion.

The fact was, if we had put up a sign saying "All Sisters of Notre Dame meet in Room 412 at three o'clock," other SNDs might have come, but only because of a sociable curiosity. We no longer all shared the same visions and concerns as Sisters of Notre Dame, per se. By the late seventies, nuns had begun to rearrange themselves, crossing over into other religious communities seeking common goals and common missions. We began to unite with laywomen who shared our values. Even within our own order, Barbara and I, without really recognizing what was happening, had rejected the old idea that a "community" automatically exists because of a superimposed concept. Warm bodies within the same parish house did not automatically a convent make. We knew we had to live with people who shared our hard-won values, dreams, vision.

I don't think either of us were consciously aware of the transformation that was going on in our definitions of community. We thought all of us simply stood on different places on the same road, and neither Barbara nor I saw that we had already passed a crucial fork.

The first topic Barbara and I chewed over—along with our waffles—was the chapter meeting in Rome I had attended for six weeks just before we met.

"When I first saw the meeting room, I was overwhelmed," I said. The generalate and motherhouse of the Sisters of Notre Dame at that time was called the "Casa," and it had an enormous room where about a hundred of us all sat in two concentric circles. The delegates sat in the central circle, and those of us who were observers sat in a second circle behind them. I had walked to the Casa that morning from the Dominican Convent where I was staying, my first half mile *per pedes* on the soil of a foreign country.

"We had come from the whole world!" I told Barbara. "It was so moving to see us, black and white and yellow, young and old, conservative and liberal, in habit and out of habit. Almost everyone spoke a second language, and I felt very limited knowing only English."

At the same time, I had felt a breathless rush of hope and possibility. There we were, an international sisterhood, small in fact but large in purpose. Surely great things would come from this meeting. There would be so much to learn, so much to share, and by the end I was positive we would emerge a united force for social justice in the world.

I had just offered a quick prayer of thanks for being a part of such a tremendous enterprise when I heard the first order of business come up. I couldn't believe it. They wanted to discuss whether the young observers should have a vote as well as a voice. Sister Ann Monica from Ipswich, Massachusetts, expressed her disagreement with the process that had brought me to Rome. "My province has the largest number of young sisters who have not yet taken their final vows," complained Ann Monica, "so I feel one of my sisters should have been here instead."

The other "young" sister from the Boston province and I looked at each other and rolled our eyes. We had been chosen to represent young nuns in the United States. Delegates from all six American provinces had met in Washington, D.C., to discern who would be sent. "Discern" is a word nuns like to use to make a decision-making process sound holy. By now I think it sounds more like peering into the intestines of a sacrificial goat, but in 1978 I accepted the fact that in choosing me as a representative, my order had recognized that I was seriously trying to "discern" a relevant future mission for the Sisters of Notre Dame.

The process had involved months of work for dozens of nuns. I had even traveled from Chicago to Washington, D.C., to meet with the selection committee. Before I went into that meeting I murmured the prayer from Jeremiah: "I am but a youth, give me the words to speak," and I had been repeating it all the way to Rome. I hadn't expected that the first words I would need to speak would be to justify my presence.

"Would the young sisters like to address the question raised by Sister Ann Monica?" said Sister Marie Augusta, and Jeremiah gave me a nudge.

"Well, maybe we will have to discuss this later, Sister Ann Monica," I said, "but I want you to know I think you are wrong." And then I described the long and careful process that had gotten me there. Later, Ann Monica and I did discuss it, and she was kind enough to say that she could see why I had been chosen. "You have potential," she said. But much to my surprise another woman from the Ipswich province went to some trouble to ask me, "Why did you attack Ann Monica?"

I hadn't attacked her. I had disagreed, openly and honestly. Furthermore it wasn't anyone's business but Ann Monica's and mine. So I said so.

"But Patricia, dear. We do not express our disagreements on the chapter floor," said Ann Monica's champion.

"Then what on earth are we in Rome for?" I demanded.

"There is a time and a place for everything, dear," she said. "All questions should be resolved in an orderly, peaceful way *before* they come to the floor."

I thought that was the silliest thing I had ever heard.

Then it happened again. During another chapter session, Sister Marie Morris, a white nun who had been a superior in Africa for years, raised a very sore point. Quietly, reverently, but firmly, she said, "Sisters, we must examine our policies on missionaries. At times the women who have been sent out to work with me have been less than stable mentally. In some cases, nuns have been openly racist. Many times we have been sending our problems, not our best people, to Africa."

Not a single paper rustled as she concluded, "We must have nuns who respect the people and the culture."

Dolores Harrall, a black nun from my own province of Connecticut, spoke up. Dolores was a very powerful, compelling woman who died relatively young ten years later of cancer. I have always felt that the struggles she suffered as a black woman and a black nun ate her up. That day in Rome, she said, "Marie, I am deeply disturbed. I hope I am not hearing what I think you are saying."

"I wish I could tell you differently," said Marie. "But in fact, we have done an injustice to the people of Africa by some of the people we have sent. What I am saying is not popular, I am sure. But I beseech this group to make some strong statement. I am so sorry, Dolores."

The first general reaction from the delegates was denial. "It should be brought up in a private discussion, Marie," I heard. And, "It's not for everyone's ears, Marie." I was really shocked. Later, when I told Barbara about that reflex to hush up difficult topics, I was furious. "It must be because anger is not considered a healthy emotion for women," I fumed. "Everything is supposed to be joy and faith and hope and dreams, but we can't confront the harsher realities together. I mean, what could be worse than denying that we are running racist missions?!"

Now, looking back, I can see that I didn't appreciate the fact that I was watching an enormous change take place. Forever and ever, nuns had avoided the kind of real feelings which must be dealt with before people can take action as adults. They were, in fact, actually learning how to confront the harsher realities I was so fond of invoking. My own contribution was less that of a profound thinker (as I think I rather hoped) than that of a kind of unwitting catalytic converter.

In the end, the Chapter Acts of 1978, drawn up by the group meeting in Rome, was a mission statement I was intensely proud of having helped create. It would be sent out to all the 2,500 Sisters of Notre Dame for reflection and discussion as we moved closer to our goal of a new constitution based on the experiments of renewal following Vatican II. Years of struggle and discussion were still to come, but as far as I was concerned, that document defined what I was coming to understand as my mission. Its words are still an inspiration and a challenge to me.

We declared that we would "Deal concretely with the relationship of world hunger to the arms race; the global issue of racism and discrimination against women as it exists in church and society." And then, in a section titled "Toward a Further Understanding of Mission," we took up the challenge of the great Brazilian educator Paulo Freire in his book *Pedagogy of the Oppressed.*

"It is our task," we wrote, "to use conscientization (the process of raising consciences; learning to perceive social, political and economic contradictions and to take action against the oppressive elements of reality) as a process of education, especially directed to our mission among oppressed people, and that we encourage the process as a significant means of education and conversion of heart for our own membership."

After six weeks of exhausting, even harrowing daily meetings running for twelve hours at a stretch, our conscientization process was well begun.

After the meeting concluded, I was able to observe one of the great patriarchal rituals of the Roman Catholic church—the election of a new pope. Paul VI, whose serious error had been to repeat the church's initial mistake back in 1895 of banning birth control, had died on August 6, 1978.

All my life, as a Catholic girl, I had heard about the conclave of cardinals—the secret tallying of votes from inside the locked Sistine Chapel and the breathless crowd outside St. Peter's, watching for the signal of the smoke. Black smoke coming from the vent as the tallies are burned means "No decision." White smoke means *"Viva Il Papa."*

Most of the Sisters of Notre Dame still staying at the Casa had been driven down to St. Peter's at six in the morning so they would have a chance at finding places in the first row for the opening nine o'clock mass. Somehow, the excitement failed to hurry me. I didn't particularly want to be included in the "special but separate" ranks of the church's ladies' auxiliary. So by myself I caught a bus to the Vatican and got there about eight-thirty.

I walked into the crowd quite easily. It was actually kind of weird how I slipped through thousands of people, all fingering rosaries with one hand and pointing to notable cardinals with the other. I went right in to the basilica. Rows and rows and rows of old white men in lace dresses were watching the cardinals make their entry. A huge golden crucifix went by, and an endless parade of altar boys wreathed in incense. There was a nearly audible rustle of plot and counterplot, the pews whispered with the anxiety of factions. But for me, the lace and the incense and the music and the carved cherubs with feet as long as my arm had lost their charm. This was a political institution, a frail human institution, fully intent on the fundamental task of perpetuating itself.

The Mass started with the singing of the Kyrie Eleison, and I suddenly felt I had to get out of there. I couldn't stand the pageantry. I never had liked pageantry, and this particular spectacle seemed especially devoid of reverence or even dignity. I guess I was trying to get to a place where I would feel the presence of God, but I don't remember how I ended up in the crypt beneath the basilica. I walked around in the damp, chill air, and I came to the tomb of Pope John XXIII.

My hero. A man of God who did not fear change or challenge. A man who believed in the sacred within each human being. "John, if there really is a Holy Spirit," I prayed, "please inspire that gathering of men up there, because it truly looks overwhelming and hopeless to me." Two other women were also praying at John's tomb. When they looked at me and smiled, I realized I had been speaking to John out loud, and very sternly.

One of the women was old and crippled. None of us spoke a common language. We walked outside, two of us helping the crippled woman, and I remember thinking: This is what it is all about. This is what the church really is. It is people, not pomp and pageantry and make-believe piety.

On my way back to Chicago from Rome, I stopped in Springfield to see my parents. As my mother and I were doing the dishes, she asked me if I had heard that the pope had died. "Sure Mom, I was there when it happened," I said. "No, Pat," she said, "the new pope, John Paul the First, has died, and no one knows how." I waited for the punch line, and then I realized she was serious. This time, without the power of my on-location prayer, the cardinals elected John Paul II, a man known to be firm in his No's: no birth control, no married priests, no abortions, and definitely no women priests. Ever since, he has flown around the world posing as the defender of life, but he has in fact never failed to defend the deadly power of the status quo. He is the direct antithesis of the church I discovered that morning near Pope John's grave.

Fifteen: Chicago

BARBARA

"I don't know what happened to me in Rome," Pat said to me as she finished the story of her reaction to the conclave of cardinals, "but whatever it was, it was good."

"You had a full-fledged feminist moment of truth," I said. "One of those 'Aha!' moments that change your life."

"But I have been thinking as a feminist at least since 1975, since the Women's Ordination Conference," Pat objected.

"You had been intellectualizing since then," I said. "But when you saw all those men gathered together, claiming the right to define your life, you *felt* the truth of your ideas. Your personal became political, just as it did for me in Auburndale."

We were finishing breakfast in the Mellow Yellow Cafe. It was funny to be surrounded by so many daisies at such a solemn moment, but I was absolutely serious when I said to Pat, "What happened to you is a shattering experience. It can, just as you thought, be liberating. But life doesn't get any easier afterward. Do you remember the words of that song by Carol Etzler—'Sometimes I wish my eyes had never been opened'? Sometimes I do wish that. But there is no turning back."

"In that case," said Pat, "I think I'll have another cup of coffee.

We both attended the second Women's Ordination Conference, held in November 1978, at the Civic Center in Baltimore, a city chosen not only because Maryland was the seat of Catholicism's beginnings in the United States, but also because the state had voted to ratify the Equal Rights Amendment. Pat drove there from Chicago with some friends, and I flew there on a cheap ticket I had gotten months before. Imagine my astonishment when I discovered that we were part of a crowd of two thousand women attending.

Two years before, the Vatican declaration denying women the possibility of ordination had been issued. Most of us dismissed it as an ignorant statement with no theological substance. Most of the world's leading Catholic theologians had dismissed it too. But it had served one purpose. Now we had a clearer understanding of the irrationality and intractability of patriarchy.

In 1975 we had been asking to be let into the system. We were sure we could make a difference. And we would have—that's why they were so determined to keep us out.

From the outside, we were forced to examine the system and we found it ungodly. The discovery freed us to develop our own ministries out of our own faith experiences. By 1978 feminist religious women had begun to divide into two camps: one was the "we will change the system from within" camp, and the other was the "we must create a new system that is inclusive and just for all people" camp.

The banner strung across the auditorium at the Civic Center read, "New Woman, New Church, New Priestly Ministry." The conference opened with a liturgical service by the side of the Baltimore Harbor. The huge crowd of women was about evenly divided between nuns and laywomen. We wrapped ourselves in a gigantic gray plastic chain symbolizing the chains that oppress and bind us that we would transform into chains to link and free us. I later brought home about two feet from that chain, and I hung it on the bulletin board in the kitchen to remind us of our commitment to make the connections.

All of the discussion in Baltimore was of the connections: between racism, classism, and sexism. The most painful and most important revelation in all the discussion was the fact that we could not call for equality in society if we did not demand that same justice in our church for all people, no matter what their race, class, or sex. We were going to have to fight *for ourselves*, and it would take a while for us to get used to the radical implications of that realization. By the time the conference was over, I had moved beyond thinking of ordination as a central goal for me.

"Do you still want to be ordained, Barbara?" asked Pat, when we were back in Chicago.

"Oh, I *want* to be ordained. I am a Catholic minister. The proper job description for people like me is 'priest.' But even if

Rome would allow it, I couldn't join the present clerical caste structure of the church,'' I said.

The fun of living with Pat Hussey was that she was willing to sit at the kitchen table and talk about ''clerical caste structures.'' And we both knew just what the other meant by the phrase. We meant a Roman Catholic clergy of mostly white men, content to consider themselves superior to women, to blacks, to Hispanics. We meant clerical paternity funds and lavish life-styles and protected benefits and complete indifference even to the needs of other priests.

''One of the priests in my parish was alcoholic,'' I said to Pat. ''I told the other priests someone needed to see that he got help. They told me he was okay, he did his job in the daytime and got soused at night. And I told them in *my* community we at least felt concern for each other.''

''The nuns ran circles around the priests in the parish I worked in,'' Pat said, staring grimly into her cup of coffee. ''We worked longer hours, we had to provide and care for our own housing and meals . . . .''

''Well, dear,'' I said, in a mother-superior tone, ''after all, women know how to do those domestic things.''

''And,'' answered Pat, in an equally irritating sugary voice, ''if you were paid so much less than the priests, well, after all, men are men and they need their little comforts.''

''Like country club memberships!'' I burst out.

''Some of them have little comforts like a secret wife and children,'' laughed Pat.

''It's true!'' I shouted.

Only the day before, one of the young seminarians upstairs, having arisen from his daily nap, had said to me, ''Hey, this is great. All I have to do is put in three years, get my master of divinity degree, and I'll be ordained.'' I came home sputtering and raved at Pat for half an hour. There I was, working twenty hours a week doing typing at the Counseling Center, where I was doing my practicum for school, so I could send some money back to my community—even though I had a full fellowship. And I was so serious about the future role of women in the church that I was determined to be brilliant in every course. The women—nuns and laywomen—had struggled to get into these graduate schools even after years of experience. And the laywomen, without a community to back them up, had to work even harder than the nuns!

''What is wrong with this picture?'' I said. ''On the one hand, we have a group of women eager to learn and become more effective in their work for the Roman Catholic church. On the other, we have a group of boys who are flaking out and taking naps in the afternoon. Which ones get to be ordained?''

"So. You want to be ordained?'' asked Pat, again.

"I don't think so. I don't like the membership very much,'' I said. "So that leaves me with a big question. What *am* I going to do? What are *you* going to do next?''

"I think we need to work with grass-roots people. They need to believe they are church. I've been thinking a lot about liberation theology. If the church is to be meaningful, leadership must emerge from the *people*. They should be equally responsible for creating their church instead of being burdened by an imposed structure.''

"But when I tried to do that in Tucson, I got fired,'' I said.

"You'll have to think of something new,'' said Pat. "Isn't that why you wanted to spend three years studying theology?''

A good question.

I was the only woman, and the only Catholic, in my classes at McCormick Presbyterian Theological School. I had chosen McCormick not just so that I could pile up credentials and be ready to be ordained, but because it was the only theological school I could find that offered a practical course in what I knew I was good at—counseling and empowering people.

From the very beginning, I noticed that I was one of the people who needed empowering.

The ministers I was studying with were better educated than most of the priests I knew, but they were not as developed spiritually or emotionally as the women I knew in religious communities. It was pleasantly reassuring when my classmates urged me to become an Episcopalian or a Methodist. "We'll ordain you,'' they said. But I knew what a threat to them I would become if I switched. I could tell by their nervous responses to my approach to pastoral problems. My experience and perspective were feminist, and they didn't like it. I remember one class on organizing the community. Every one of the men produced a multi-planning program to impose on their congregation— albeit they planned to impose it with an upbeat "Everybody pull together now'' announcement. When I read my paper, which described a series of meetings at which I would gather people together and ask them what they would like to see happen in the parish, and what they felt they needed to see happen, I could tell by the ministers' smiles that they thought I was being sentimental.

At school I was the only person like me. And at home I was the only person who was not attending the Jesuit School of Theology. Not to mention that the five or six women students living in our apartment complex were rather obviously studying for a profession they would never be allowed to enter fully.

Worst of all, I was mortified to find myself intimidated by the theological language everyone used. "What do you make of the hermeneutics? Whose systematic theology are you speaking out of?" What was that supposed to mean?

Finally, I confessed to Pat that I felt I was way out of my depth. "I am drowning in theology, Pat," I said. "If I hear one more argument about High Christology and Low Christology, I am going to cry."

Bless Pat. She had already spent two years studying at the Jesuit School and she could toss words like hermeneutics and charism and androcentric around with the best of them.

"Relax, Barbara," she reassured me. "It's a professional language, like medical language or special education language. I remember when I first was in special education, and I was intimidated by people talking about EMRs and TMRs and EDs."

"Huh?" I said.

"Educable Mentally Retarded, Trainable Mentally Retarded and Emotionally Disturbed. But we turned it into a language precisely so that we would intimidate people. That's the chief aim of professions—to exclude people."

"But Pat, *I'm* the one being excluded here. How can I learn to talk sense to people if no one seems to be talking sense to me?"

"Barbara, remember who you are. Remember what you know. All the talk you are hearing is just an elaborate intellectualization of what you have been telling me all along."

I stared at her suspiciously. My future looked hopeless to me. I was afraid my brain had been stunted by the simplicities of the old Baltimore Catechism. Very patiently, Pat said:

"High Christology argues that it is more important that Jesus be God than that Jesus be a human being."

"Uh-huh," I said, intelligently.

"Do you remember when I went to see the *Messiah* and I left early because I suddenly hated the triumphal language? All those soaring phrases about Son of God, Lord of Hosts, Prince of

Princes. That is High Christology. And I myself have a very Low Christology. I believe the important thing is that Jesus was a human being, because I believe human beings are blessed with a God life within themselves. God trusted us as human beings to do good things in *this* world and therefore God became human in Jesus. God the Creator celebrates our humanity, as we must.''

"Well, sure," I said, "Jesus was a social justice person. He wanted to empower people here on earth. He wanted us to experience our divine potential."

"Now you've got it," said Pat, grinning.

"Gee, I've had a Low Christology all along," I said. It was a great moment. The language suddenly seemed merely a structure to organize and expand my thoughts. I wasn't dumb, I was just learning—literally learning at school—to make sense of all the knowledge I had acquired since I left the certainties of Emmanuel College behind.

"There is an awful lot going on in my head, Pat," I said.

"Maybe it would be good if you joined the women's group that meets at the Jesuit School of Theology," Pat suggested. "I'll introduce you to one of the wonderful women who brought us all together. She's a Dominican nun named Marjorie Tuite."

I didn't know what to make of Margie at first. She was larger than life, not only spiritually, but also physically. Margie Tuite was close to six feet tall, and she weighed over two hundred pounds. Her hands and fingers were long and strong like a professional basketball player's. Her laugh was a contagious heart-lifting roar, and it usually followed some terrific challenge she had made to someone else's conscience. People either loved her or hated her.

We loved her. Often either Pat or I still say, "Margie would have an idea," or "Margie should hear about this," or "Wouldn't it be wonderful if Margie were coming to visit?" But she died in June of 1986 and most of us who came to be known as the Vatican 24 blame the church. She was the strongest woman we ever knew, the mentor and goad and inspiration to our entire generation of progressive nuns. But the struggle with the church over abortion used her up and she had no strength left to fight cancer.

The blessing of Margie's life was that she doubled and tripled and quadrupled the strength of everyone who knew and loved her.

"What did you think about the Baltimore Conference?" she demanded the first time we met.

"I'm not sure I want to be ordained anymore," I said, fairly timidly for me.

"WHY NOT?" shouted Margie. Later I would discover that she was capable of making me analyze why I went to bed at nine o'clock at night, just for the fun of making sure I left no assumptions unexamined. But that day I just mumbled, "I feel it would be acquiescing in an unjust sytem."

"Ah!" she said. I perked up. "An interesting point of view." Thud. Imagine my surprise when Margie insisted, later, that I take her place on the continuing national committee of the Women's Ordination Conference so my "interesting" point of view would be represented. But that was Margie. You had to be careful what you said to her, because she would make you *do* it.

Margie was born in 1922 in New York City. In the 1950s she had worked in a parochial high school in Harlem, and she loved to talk about how she would go out at night in full habit to track down truants, climbing up fire escapes and jumping over rooftops. She marched with Martin Luther King, Jr., in the South during the most dangerous days of the civil rights movement.

From 1968 to 1973 she worked with Saul Alinsky, the radical organizer, at his National Urban Training Center in Chicago. One of the things she did to learn how to reach people was to spend four days and nights on the street with only a dollar in her pocket. That was how she discovered that the church buildings were all locked, and she had to walk back and forth from the bus station to all-night markets to keep warm.

In the late fall of 1971, Margie gathered together forty-seven American churchwomen in Washington, D.C., to discuss ways of responding to the 1967 encyclical on labor from Pope Paul VI called *Populorum Progressio* and nicknamed "The Eightieth Year Letter." It was written to celebrate the eightieth anniversary of Pope Leo XIII's encyclical *Rerum novarum*, which criticized the injustices of capitalism and called for rights for workers. Paul's letter concentrated on the need to assist the empowerment of the poor, and it urged Christians to involve themselves in the political process as a way to affect decisions that determine people's lives. The result of Margie's meeting was the founding of Network, the Catholic Social Justice Lobby Group in Washington.

In 1973 Margie was persuaded to come to the Jesuit School

of Theology in Chicago by its president, a Jesuit named Bill Guindon, who was himself something of a visionary. Her job was directing the social justice component of the school's program. People were already studying "Effective Pastoral Ministry" and "Counseling" and "Liturgy," but Margie made sure they *experienced* acting for social justice instead of just sitting pleasantly in a classroom talking about it. She, in effect, ran a practicum in making connections.

At the time there were three Jesuit Theology schools, one in Berkeley, California, one in Cambridge, Massachusetts, and one in Chicago. The school in Chicago—JSTC—was quite small, no more than about a hundred students at a time. Of those, perhaps one-half were women. About thirty of the women gathered weekly in a room in the basement of the JSTC faculty office building. In that circle of women I began my first systematic consciousness-raising.

We approached every issue by questioning domination, whether it be men over women, whites over blacks, First World over Third World. Some of us had walked in the civil rights, the Equal Rights Amendment, and the farmworkers movements. It was only natural that we would eventually make the connections with our own male-dominated church institutions.

Vatican II had opened windows, but the doors were being pried and pushed open by the feminist religious movement in the Roman Catholic church. We were trying to create a church responsible to women, a church that would share its power, a church which was sensitive to all powerless people.

Secular women's consciousness-raising (CR) groups transformed the isolation of individual women's experiences into a movement through discussions of very personal topics that revealed a powerful universality. My group did not discuss things such as sexuality, orgasm, friendship, housecleaning, and menstrual periods. It would probably have been very interesting if we had, but we didn't. Perhaps we all thought we had settled those issues for ourselves (and perhaps we really had). Our talks centered on topics such as our classes, jobs for poor women, and self-determination in Central America and South America. The results were the same as they were in every hardworking CR group. Over and over again, as we each spoke in turn, we recognized ourselves as members of the oppressed.

Margie's mission in life was to turn the patriarchal triangle into the sacred and human circle. "Here is the way it is now," she would say, drawing a huge triangle with her long hands. "A few men with power at the top, and almost everybody else at the bottom, powerless. Now why is that? Who has the power and who doesn't, and why? Always, always, ask yourselves: Who benefits?''

We all changed, in that room. As the discussions made great swooping connections between our studies, our spirituality, our experiences, the Roman Catholic church, and world events, we began to grow and to imagine new ministries. After the meetings we would go on talking, gathering again at a pizza palace called Giordano's.

Giordano's was the hangout for everyone at the JSTC. And it was at Giordano's that I realized one night that the men—our buddies, our pals, our comrades in the struggle—were not on our side. Jim, a man I really liked from the apartment compound, had just finished saying something particularly firm about the need for women's equality and the obsolescence of the church's institutional structures.

I finished shoving an embarrassingly large piece of pizza into my mouth, and I said, perfectly sincerely, ''Then why don't you refuse to be ordained until women can also be ordained?''

Many of the men at the table laughed.

''Well, why not?'' I demanded. ''How can you believe in social justice and become part of a system that denies justice to its own people?''

''Hey Barb, didn't you ever hear of changing the system from within?'' said Jim. And the men laughed again—nervously.

I was so mad I was speechless. Mad and surprised. A realization flashed through my mind: This jerk hasn't thought about the rights of women at all, and he's not going to. We are not important. He doesn't want us to be equal. None of them do. They are just using the words. I was just about to say all that aloud when I heard Pat's voice coming in low across the table.

''Barb, hey, Barb!'' she kept repeating.

''What?'' I snapped.

''You look like a woman who has just had a feminist moment of truth. One of those 'Aha!' moments that changes your life.''

Sixteen: Ready and Willing

BARBARA

Gradually, our women's group was becoming a little more forceful. We invented a blessing ceremony to mark the end of our studies, a kind of graduation celebrating our new ministries in which both men and women could participate. But when it was over, the men still went off and became ordained. So we held a ladylike prayer circle in the parking lot across the street from the church where the ordination ceremony was taking place. Proud parents of new priests walked by looking at us as though we were wearing pointed black hats and chewing on toads.

It was extremely *embarrassing* to be a feminist and to stand up for our own dignity. And we were learning there is no pain quite as numbing as the pain of feminists who must fight the very people they love.

Luckily, we had Margie Tuite. She came to our meetings, she showed up at our apartments, she goaded us on and challenged us. Her idea of "reflecting" was to shout, "How could you do that, Barbara? I saw you trying to justify your actions and sweet-talk John because you didn't want him to feel bad. The personal is political. You don't have to hate them, but you can't support them."

Pat finished her studies in the spring of 1979 and left Chicago. To my relief, Claire Helene moved on to happier hunting grounds in a housing complex full of men who had not taken a vow of celibacy. And I settled down for my last two years of work toward my doctorate in ministry, with two new roommates: Brenda, a nun, and Karen, a laywoman, who were also studying at JSTC.

* * *

Our women's group took courage for our own protests from the action of Sister Mary Teresa Kane. One of the most exciting mornings of my life had been October 7, 1979. I was only an observer, part of the national television audience, but because of the camera I got to see the action more clearly than Pat did, and she was there, an actor. What a moment it was! Pope John Paul II had been in office only a year, and he was just concluding his first visit to the United States. After a week of open-air masses, schoolchildren waving papal flags, ticker-tape parades, and meetings with priests and bishops, he was going to make a grand final appearance at a prayer service on Sunday morning at the National Shrine of the Immaculate Conception in Washington, D.C., followed by a farewell mass on the Mall.

Women had played almost no role in the pope's progression. But in Washington, because it is a Catholic center, there would be many, many nuns at the Shrine, both "new" nuns and traditional "house nuns." The Women's Ordination Conference had organized thirty laywomen to stand outside and demonstrate, and thirty nuns to make themselves visible inside by standing throughout the service, wearing blue arm bands. Pat was going to be one of the women inside.

I knew—we all knew—that Sister Mary Teresa Kane had been invited to speak a few words of welcome to the pope. She was the *only* woman asked to speak during his entire visit, but she was certainly an appropriate person to be asked. At the time she was the president of the Sisters of Mercy of the Union, and president of the Leadership Conference of Women Religious. On her own, with prayer and reflection, she chose the words which would fulfill the responsibility she felt to speak not only on behalf of nuns but of all women in the church. She did not submit her speech for approval from Vatican officials. As she continued past her opening greeting, I could scarcely believe the resolute dignity of her speech:

As I share this privileged moment with you, Your Holiness, I urge you to be mindful of the intense suffering and pain which is part of the life of many women in the United States. I call upon you to listen with compassion and to hear the call of women who comprise half of humankind. As women, we have heard the powerful messages of our church addressing the dignity and reverence for all persons. As women, we have pondered these words. Our contemplation leads us to state that the church in its struggle to be faithful to its call for reverence and dignity for all persons must respond by providing the possibility of women as persons being included in all ministries of our church. I urge you, Your Holiness, to be open to and respond to the voices coming from the women of this country who are desirous of serving in and through the church as fully participating members.

Tears came to my eyes. The women in the Shrine broke into thunderous applause. I saw Sister Teresa walk across the altar and greet the pope, kneeling for his blessing. Later, I learned that she had been instructed to bow from a distance and return to her seat, but she had spontaneously decided to behave as an adult human being. And then I saw Pat, wearing her blue arm band, one of thirty women standing in protest all over the church. I was so proud of them all.

From that moment forward, the JSTC women's group adopted blue arm bands as our symbol. As we cut up blue cotton cloth—Mary blue—we plotted our new strategy. We had decided we would move into the ceremony, inside the church, where we would stand and protest, following the example of the brave nuns in the Shrine.

The taking of Holy Orders is a sacrament in the Catholic church. The ceremony itself is inserted into the ritual of the Mass. The men waiting to be ordained lie facedown on the floor before the altar rail, and the bishop comes down from the altar and calls them forward.

"Joseph McGhee, come forth, you are called to be ordained," says the bishop. And the ordinate rises and replies, "I am ready and willing."

The first time we had tried our new protest, no one suspected anything. I guess they thought we had settled for symbols when they saw our arm bands. So they were surprised when, after the last man was called to be ordained, we began popping up, one after the other, all over the church, and calling out "I am ready and willing." Then we remained standing throughout the rest of the ceremony.

It doesn't sound earthshaking now, but at the time it was scary enough so that some of our group couldn't bring themselves to do it. They were afraid of offending the men. They didn't think it was right to disrupt a sacred ceremony. A few said they didn't want to risk blocking someone's view. Some of them had felt no qualm about lying in front of police cars during anti-Vietnam

War demonstrations, but they couldn't bring themselves to stand up for themselves in church. There were some very heated group meetings during which Margie tried to make us understand the concept of having internalized the rules of patriarchy.

I have to confess, I enjoyed those demonstrations. Ever since that scene in Giordano's pizza palace when the men laughed at my suggestion that they join us in our cause, I was indeed ready and willing. It was dreadful and humiliating to witness men being called forward when I, who was completely qualified for the priesthood in every respect except that I had been born with different body parts, could not be.

Eventually, a few men began wearing small blue ribbons pinned to their albs at their ordinations. Even that tiny gesture of solidarity so enraged the bishop that he passed the word ahead of time that he would turn away any man wearing a blue ribbon.

By 1981, we had become the scourge of the diocese, popping up at ordinations all over Chicago. We disrupted Franciscans, Benedictines, Jesuits, Dominicans, and parlor-variety diocesan priests. The Catholic church, even more than most authoritarian institutions, hates to be *disrupted*. John Cardinal Cody was not amused at the prospect of our presence at the ordination ceremony at Mundelein, the diocesan seminary in Chicago. Admission would be by ticket only, and any women seen handing out leaflets outside would be watched.

So we decided to change our strategy. Some of us would just try to get inside, however we could. And the rest would march around outside leafleting, wearing arm bands. When the day came, about fifteen of us drove out to Mundelein. Half of us headed for the entrance, and the minute the doorkeepers saw us they closed ranks. They kept asking for our tickets, and we kept pushing, and finally I squeezed under a burly arm and I darted up the aisle. When I looked behind the doors were being closed, and Donna and I were the only two that had gotten in. Donna is a Dominican nun, and she is almost as short as I am.

"Oh my God," I started whispering to Donna. "We have to do it." I was terrified.

"We're in here, so we have got to do it," agreed Donna.

"Right," I said, my teeth practically chattering, "I mean, no way we can get out of it. We'll do it. Right. Sure."

The cathedral was enormous. We had only gotten as far as the last couple of pews, and it looked as though a quarter of a mile stretched out before us to the altar.

"Okay, remember, there are fifteen ordinates. When the fifteenth name is called, then we do it,'' we kept repeating to each other. We sat in our places, and started counting.

Thirteen. Fourteen. We tensed. Fifteen. Up! We jumped on top of the kneeler and started yelling, ''I am ready and willing!''

And then from behind us came an echo. The rest of our group had crowded together and pushed the main doors slightly open. They were shouting, ''I am ready and willing! I am ready and willing! I am ready and willing!'' Can you imagine this mob of women—nuns and laywomen—screaming and interrupting the ceremony?

Cardinal Cody paused for a minute, and then he went on with the mass, and the doors were opened and the other women came in. We put on our arm bands, and got ready to stand for the rest of the mass. And then, all of a sudden, the mass stopped.

Cardinal Cody came to the pulpit, and very solemnly he said, ''It is unfortunate that I have to speak.''

Oh my God, I thought. They are going to drag us outside. Worse, he is going to tell us we are naughty girls.

And then he said, ''I have just learned that the pope has been shot in Rome.''

A lot of the people sitting around us looked at us as though we were personally responsible for shooting the pope.

All I could think of was that my parents were in Rome at that very moment. ''They were probably there,'' I whispered to Donna. It was absurd, but I found out later that they actually were there, about fifteen feet away from the pope when it happened. I suspect they would rather have been even closer to the pope than to have been in Chicago watching me shouting ''I am willing and ready.''

The church did not agree to ordain women. Instead, in 1981, the Jesuit School of Theology in Chicago was closed. The reason given was that Jesuits could no longer afford to run three theology schools. The number of male students was steadily declining—by the end of the 1980s there would be only 1,000 Jesuits left in the United States. But at the time it seemed obvious to our women's group meetings that the men were avoiding the school's heavy emphasis on social justice—and the pressure from the women students.

During my last year in Chicago I became involved with a group of women who were planning a feminist theology school. I remember taking the El to a room on the North Side of Chicago and meeting some of my heroines. Anne Carr was there and

Elisabeth Schüssler Fiorenza. Margie Tuite was there, of course, and Rosemary Radford Ruether. We had a wonderful vision of a place where women would be on the faculty and the theoretical curriculum would mesh with the practical. After more than a year of planning, the idea dissolved because the consortium of theology schools in Chicago would not accept our courses for credit.

At the same time, a similar program, the Women's Theological Center, was being developed by some women in Boston. It was successfully introduced and is still running. Helen Wright, a Sister of Notre Dame from the Boston province, came out to meet with our group to exchange ideas, and she asked me if I would come back and become the head of their new theology school. That made two job offers I had received before graduation. McCormick had asked me to become the assistant director of the doctorate of ministry program.

I was pleased to be offered those jobs. It was very satisfying to know that people in the academic world thought well of me. I liked teaching and I liked thinking. A bright career in religion beckoned. But there is a difference between a career and a ministry.

It had taken me years of study and work to name the difference. As I wrote my doctoral thesis during my last term in Chicago, everything I had learned during those years began to become clear on the page. My task was to explain, and ultimately to defend, what I had come to believe; my philosophy and theology of the human person, my understanding of ethics and morals, my struggle to synthesize present reality, scriptural tradition, and future hope. To my enormous relief, McCormick allowed me to choose Margie Tuite—feminist, Catholic, and mentor—as my thesis director.

I titled my work "Exile from Strangers," a phrase from Jeremiah which meant, to me, my sense of being exiled from the institutional church and its practices which had become as strangers to women's experiences. My subject was the Corpus Christi Parish in Auburndale and my experience working there from 1975 to 1980. Just as Pat had challenged me to do, I had tried to create an alternative model of parish life. I had used myself as part of the experiment, serving as an example of a woman minister, presenting an idea of a revitalized parish from a feminist perspective.

The most important work I had done was to try to involve lay-people in the life of the parish. In my thesis I carefully documented the questionnaires I had distributed asking what people wanted from their church, how they felt they could take part, what they understood by the ideas of faith and spirituality. Armed with their answers, I held a series of forums to begin a dialogue among the parishioners, and then we moved to form committees organized around such expressed interests as fund-raising, the parish newsletter, adult education classes, hospital visitation, parents' groups, and planning the liturgy.

Those groups were Auburndale's base communities, *lascomunidades, eclesiales de base* the circles of unity and respect and shared effort I had taken from my studies of the liberation theologians. I was happy with the results of my efforts and so were the parishioners. But, as I struggled to write my thesis, I found I was inexorably imagining a different future ministry for myself. The people in Auburndale had learned to take possession of their church, but I could be fired at any time at the whim of the diocese. I could go no further in Boston. And, as I wrote to them in my farewell letter, my experience with them had moved me to go beyond the parish, to stand with the powerless in

society. I didn't yet know where.

I had unfurled the banners of my faith and issued a challenge. I had an idea. God answered by sending me reality, exactly what I had imagined. Very soon, I would be in West Virginia . . . once again scrubbing floors.

Seventeen: Renewed Priestly Ministry

PAT

It was easy enough for me to tell Barbara Ferraro that she would have to think of a new way of doing grass-roots ministry. But what about me, Patricia Hussey? How was I going to put into practice the exciting new ideas I had learned to preach?

I wanted to move back into an urban community where I could live and work with the poor and be a real representative of what I felt God and Jesus and my religion were all about.

There is an old saying: if much is given you, of you much is expected. I felt that responsibility. I already had learned at Long Lane School the rewards of being able to help, of being *present* for people in need. Unfortunately, I didn't see enough of any of those things in the parishes where I lived. Instead, I saw a white priest telling drunken Irish jokes to parishioners he apparently had not noticed were black and poor. Another priest called hell-fire and brimstone down from the pulpit on anyone who practiced birth control, but his behavior with the altar boys caused such a scandal he had to be removed.

Most of all I hated homilies about how glorious the place in heaven will be for those who suffer on earth. I think God wants each life to be redeemed *on earth*, and God's church should be doing all it can to help instead of just preaching patience. I was astonished that anyone even showed up for mass when they were expected to sit in their pews and accept instructions to remain poor and overburdened and helpless. I thought they deserved better.

In the spring of 1979 I was officially declared a Master of Divinity. The men in my class were ordained, the women stood

151

and protested, and then I returned to Rhode Island to find work.
I wasn't looking forward to it. During the years in Chicago I
had been free to think and grow. I had loved being surrounded
by people who lived and breathed ideas of peace and justice. It
was hard to imagine not having a daily discussion with Barbara
about the best way to live out the Gospels. But she had two more
years to study, and I had to leave, still unsure of what I wanted
to do, or would be allowed to do. Barbara wanted to be ordained
a priest, and she ended up qualified to be a Protestant minister.
And I, who didn't want to be ordained, ended up with the right
degree for a priest.

I was packing up my books one day when Barbara walked
into my room carrying a list.

"I really think we should try to work together someday," she
said. "We have complementary skills. I've written them down."

I had to laugh. "Oh, Barbara, what will I do without your
lists? I'll probably forget to brush my teeth."

She rattled her list at me. "I am very direct," she said. "Very
serious, very task-oriented. Possibly too organized sometimes."

"And I am the poor slob who is indirect, disorganized,
and . . . ," I laughed.

"No, no, no, no," Barbara objected. "When I see something
that needs to be done, I wish it was done yesterday. You are
much lighter about things. If something goes wrong I turn it into
a lump in my stomach, and you just laugh, and then I laugh and
I loosen up."

"You think a decision has to be made immediately, and forever," I said.

"And you take forever to decide," crowed Barbara. "You
deliberate and consider and look at all sides of the issue while I
am seeing it in black and white and digging myself into a hole.
See? Aren't we a great team?"

"I'm shy, you love everybody," I said, joining in the catalogue. "I'm kinder, you are firmer. I am meaner in an argument
but you make so much noise you always get the blame. You're
right, Barbara, we would be a great team. But at what?"

"Don't worry," she said, "I've got two more years in Chicago, and by the time I finish we will have figured it out."

I believed her.

What could a thirty-year-old Sister of Notre Dame do in Providence, Rhode Island, in 1979? I felt I was a terrible teacher. I

didn't want to be a parish religious education instructor, and I wouldn't be allowed to do any of the parish ministry work I had so carefully learned in Chicago. The good news—in fact, the reason I had chosen to return to Providence—was that I would be living with a *small* group of SNDs, most of whom I liked and admired and had lived with in the early seventies. Two of them, Roberta and Catherine Frederica, I knew from grammar school. They were really good women, very down-to-earth, and they were models to me of post-Vatican II renewal.

What kind of nun is so picky about where she lives and who she lives with? My kind of nun, a new nun. If I had to spend all day offering up the discomforts of my environment, I would never have the strength to get on with the job of improving the environment for all of us. I had figured out that my job, or ministry, was to choose a manageable part of the things that need fixing and start improving them, without the frustration of living with nuns whose answer to every new idea was "What would the bishop say?"

I was asked to go and see about a job as director of religious education in Newport, the summer capital of the Gilded Age. The parish was rich, and opulent Newport was just disgusting. I walked along Bellevue Avenue and Cliff Walk looking at colossal monuments to greed called "The Elms," "The Breakers," and "Marble House." All I could think of was the people who had really paid for those excessive summer diversions: the coal miners in Pennsylvania crawling underground ten hours a day, and the immigrant Irish and Chinese digging out a railbed for one dollar a week.

How infinitely all those lives could have been improved if the wealth piled on wealth along the streets of Newport had gone instead into decent wages. I have never experienced anything as effective as Newport, Rhode Island, for making me want to put my ideas about living and standing with the poor into practice. There was one crucial experience I had never had—that of being a worker among workers. I decided I would get a job in a factory.

"In Rhode Island most of the people sitting in the pews are factory workers," I wrote to Barbara. "I don't know what life is like for people with day-to-day jobs. What does organized religion have to say to them? They still come to church on Sunday, but what does the church offer them in their daily problems with work and family and relationships? People rely on tradition and ritual to sustain them, but I wonder what more there could be for them, what more we could do to make God meaningful in their lives. At the very least they deserve priests and nuns who understand the issues they have to deal with. One of the major industries here is jewelry manufacturing. If I can get a job doing that, maybe I will find some answers.''

Eighteen: Vows

PAT

On September 13, 1980, I took my final vows as a Sister of Notre Dame. By coincidence, it was ten years to the day after Barbara had knelt at mass in her family's parish church and promised to live a life of poverty, chastity, and obedience. But what a difference there was in the ceremony!

For one thing, I didn't have a mass.

I had worked for months and months writing my vows. In fact, I had been working on them since 1978, when I came back from Rome and told Barbara how excited I had been to hear other young Sisters of Notre Dame talking about theologian Sandra Schneider's work on redefining the traditional vows.

"Isn't this one of the greatest ideas you ever heard?" I had enthused. "Try using the phrases 'responsible stewardship, responsible intimacy, and responsible decision-making' instead of 'poverty, chastity, and obedience.'"

"That sounds right," said Barbara. "Those words name our experiences as women. That's the way we've been trying to live." Then she looked crestfallen. "But your provincial team isn't going to go for it."

Luckily, a new provincial team had been elected by the time I presented my version of the vows, officially approved by a friend, Jim, who was a canon lawyer. So when the time came, I was able to say exactly what I meant, and mean exactly what I said. The hard part had been figuring out what I meant.

We lived simply, but we were not poor. No matter how carefully we referred to everything from shoes to books to shampoo as "ours"—meaning the community's—we were still not poor. I had seen enough poverty to know that we were comfortable—

and I had seen enough to know that I did not want to be poor. No one *wants* to be poor. But if everyone could behave as responsible stewards of the abundance God has provided, no one would be poor.

The vow of chastity is the renunciation that seemed, both to the secular world and certainly to the Vatican, to define us as nuns and priests. And yet, it had been carried to absurd lengths, a denial of all emotions and human attachments. It made even love suspect. The phrase "responsible intimacy" suggested to me a way to reclaim the emotions that make us all human, and to distance myself from the church's preoccupation with sex.

The very word "obedience" made me suspicious. It always made me think of Adolf Eichmann, who could try to defend himself for his part in the death of six million Jews by saying he was just following orders. It did not make sense to me, theologically, to promise to give up my will or my mind to anyone, not to a superior, not to a pope. Obedience, to me, means an honest effort to discern and to move toward God's will for me. By the time I came to take my vows, we had already moved very far from the submission of what was called "cadaver obedience." Consensus and common sense were the new guides to our decision-making.

As I look back, it seems odd to me that we all felt a need to add modifying words such as "responsible" to our directives to ourselves. The Chapter Acts had spoken of "*healthily* examining" and "*attentive* listening," of "forming *genuine* relationships." The adjectives now seem redundant, as though we might choose irresponsible stewardship if we were not reminded to do otherwise. They also seem arrogant, as though we were assuming other people might be incapable of "healthy" examination. Part of that language came naturally to nuns, who had been taught to make literal statements of intent. When we spoke, for example, of defining our mission, we really tried to define it from every direction. It was a habit of mind that would get Barbara and me into trouble.

But the repetition of "responsible" meant something more, something very important and liberating. The old vows implied a childlike irresponsibility. We were growing up. We would no longer accept the Vatican's view of women as being somehow deficient in moral reasoning and incapable of making moral decisions. And that idea, the idea of women as adults, would also get us into trouble.

* * *

By the time I made my final vows I was thirty-one years old. It was a great day, and a rare event by 1980. I was the only woman professing her vows, and I was able to design the ceremony exactly the way I wanted it, so that every single word and gesture would be meaningful—which is why I decided not to have a mass.

As fair warning, I sent out invitations with a letter saying that in view of the fact that sexism is alive in the church, and women are discriminated against, there would be no eucharistic ceremony. Instead, I would be having an inclusive blessing ceremony, with a man and a woman celebrating the liturgy. Some people were shocked and didn't come.

My family and childhood friends were there. As many of them as I could possibly fit in had a role to play. We all processed into the chapel at the Fairfield, Connecticut, provincial house, which I had first entered as a brash postulant thirteen years before. My brother Michael led the way carrying the cross. I walked up the aisle as part of the procession, a little embarrassed at being the center of attention, but so pleased to feel part of such a loving crowd.

Jim, a Jesuit with whom I had gone to school in Chicago, and Margaret Kilmartin, the only other woman from the group I had entered with who was still a nun, were the co-celebrants of the liturgy. Barbara did one of the readings.

During the middle of the ceremony I stood and faced the congregation and said my vows:

Yahweh, you are here and among your people. In their presence and in the presence of Sister Dorothy, who receives these vows in the name of the congregation, I dedicate my life to you forever. The Gospel inspires me, the call to create a world more justly loving challenges me, and the spirit of our foundress Julie continues to call me to commit myself to the cause of the poor and powerless.

I profess to live a life marked by a simple life-style, one which is chaste in love and for love of your people, and obedient to the Spirit who directs me toward justice as the Acts of the Sisters of Notre Dame express.

I am grateful to those here and distant who have called me into being and ever forward to be unafraid, and to you for your faithfulness which sustains me. In the everyday journey which continues with all life's promises, risks, doubts, and hopes, I ask for your help that I may remain faithful to you and your people. Amen.

My friend from Long Lane School, Ida Billingslea, and her wonderful husband, John, jointly proclaimed the Gospel according to Luke. We smiled at each other as they spoke—a black, Protestant, married couple standing with a white woman in my Catholic chapel:

The spirit of the Lord is upon me, because he has anointed me to preach good news to the poor. He has sent me to proclaim release to the captives and recovering of sight to the blind, to set at liberty those who are oppressed, to proclaim the acceptable year of the Lord.

Then John sat down, and Ida, in a long African gown, an Afro haircut, and earrings dangling to her shoulders, proclaimed what commitment was all about. Who better than Ida? She was the first person who taught me how to see God in every human being.

At the end, Margaret and Jim blessed some scented oil, and everyone in the congregation came forward to the altar rail. A small group of my friends, including my buddy from the fourth grade, Mary Ann Moran, went up and down the line, anointing people's hands with the oil and repeating Micah's words from the Old Testament: "Do justice, love kindness, and walk humbly with your God."

And then, for a grand finale, we all shared a fantastic covereddish supper laid out on tables on the lawn. Barbara's sister Jody and her two daughters, Danya and Jessica, brought some of the famous Ferraro family lasagna.

It took me a long time to make those vows, and when I did, I knew that they were "final" vows only with my awareness that nothing in life remains unchanged. I made them at that particular time because I had reached a deadline: I either had to become a professed Sister of Notre Dame or leave. And in facing the deadline, I realized I didn't want to leave. I was content with my life. It was both comfortable and challenging.

For me, and for Barbara too, that was a very happy time. We had survived the post-Vatican II revolution with our faith and our vocations strong and intact. We had been blessed with opportunities to explore what it meant to be a nun in modern times, and we had done the best we could to take advantage of those opportunities. Not many people are lucky enough to have the freedom to examine their lives and choose commitment to social justice. I tried to plan my celebration partly as thanks for that chance, and partly as a reaffirmation of my commitment.

Nearly ten years have passed since that day. I am still trying to live out my vows just as I wrote them. Only one thing changed. It turned out that the only way to keep my promise to God was to stop being a nun.

Nineteen: Worker Priests

PAT

My only requirement for a job was that I did not want to work in a place without windows. After a few days of walking the streets of Providence, Rhode Island, answering newspaper ads, I discovered that I had set a luxury standard for myself. Most of the places I saw were dark lofts, with boarded-up windows and no ventilation. I began to understand what Margie Tuite meant when she railed against sweatshop conditions. The next step was to start sweating.

The High Point Metal Company took up the second and third floors of an old manufacturing building in downtown Providence. It was a turn-of-the-century relic, but it had windows, and they opened, and most of the people working there spoke English and had been in Providence at least two generations.

I lived with four other Sisters of Notre Dame. We ate supper and had evening prayer together. Two worked for the diocese, one as a principal and one as a parish religious education director. I went to High Point to work as a stringer and racker. (It sounds like something out of the more alarming kind of personal ads, doesn't it?)

When the bell went off at eight in the morning, I would sit down at the first rack of the day. All the racks were two feet wide and three and a half feet tall, but some of them came with black bars running across in rows. Those were the racks for money clips, tie clips, earrings, necklaces, cameos, and lockets. The other racks were more complicated. They were simply a frame with copper pegs at the top. My job was to wind copper wire in rows from the top to the bottom while hanging pierced earrings with the wire. The work was so monotonous that I was sure I would have lots of time to think. Instead, I discovered I simply had monotonous thoughts: Gee, I wonder if I can fit thirty earrings on each peg? How tight can I wrap the copper? Will these star-shaped things go on this row if I move the Saint Anthony medals to the next row? Can I break yesterday's record?

The stuff to be strung, or racked, waited in cartons on tables at the side of the loft. The ten of us working in that particular section of High Point, almost all women, laughed and joked when we picked up our cartons. "Ah! Another rummage sale!" meant boxes full of medals and pins and clips all smashed together just as they had been scooped in from the stamping machines. "Quality!" meant exactly the same stuff, made of the same brass, but separated into little boxes with felt bottoms because they had designer logos stamped across their backs.

When I finished racking or stringing, the rack went off to Pasqual, the dipper. He dipped the racks into gold- or silver-plating solutions. The tanks he worked over were never covered, and he breathed in toxic fumes all day. He was a young man, married, with a couple of children, and I had never in my sheltered life heard language anything like the way he talked to the women he worked with. As he went through the room picking up full racks, his remarks made me feel as though we were the ones strung out and clipped up.

"Watcha got for me, sweetheart? Hey, get your sweet little ass moving. Your friend with the great jugs is way ahead of you. Donna, honey! What kinda sweater is that? Jeez, another minute around you and there'll be something else to hang those earrings on. Something good and stiff, you know what I mean? Heh, heh, heh. Whatcha thinkin' Pat? Sound good?"

"I'm thinking you are repulsive," I said. Pasqual looked delighted.

"Don't let him get you down, Pat," said Donna. "He's just teasing."

"He's trying to intimidate us. He's a creep. What gives him the right to come in here and verbally rape us?" I snapped. The other women looked at me as though I was crazy.

One day I saw Pasqual spitting blood into his handkerchief. He might be a creep, but leaning over those open plating tanks and cyanide stripping tanks all day was killing him.

We had a ten-minute break at ten in the morning, a half-hour lunch break, and then we were supposed to work until four-thirty—*if* they had the work. We were paid a minimum hourly

wage of $2.65, but what we earned depended on how much the
company was producing. Sometimes we went downstairs and
worked in a bigger section stamping out lockets, but sometimes
the work just ran out and that was that. After two years, the
minimum wage rose a few nickels and dimes, and I was making
something like $3.35 an hour. The most I was ever paid in one
week was $120, gross. There were no health benefits and no
pension funds. So the first thing I learned was that I, theoretically living under the vow of poverty, couldn't imagine how I
would live if I really had to depend on my job of racking and
stringing.

Nobody knew I was a nun. I hadn't worn a skirt in years,
much less a habit, and I showed up in grubby work pants and
sneakers just like everyone else. No lipstick, though. And definitely no eye shadow. I think the absence of eye shadow is what
finally gave me away.

The last thing I wanted was to reveal myself as one of the
good sisters before people got to know me. But *I* knew I was a
nun, and that meant I went home at night to a community that
had educated me and given me opportunities my coworkers could
never dream of. I could quit High Point at any time, and the
Sisters of Notre Dame would support me and provide health
benefits until I found a new job. The members of my small unit
of the larger community all helped with the cooking and cleaning. Most important of all, they were a constant source of encouragement and intellectual stimulation. They may have
thought it was a little odd for me to look for a blue-collar job
after getting a master's degree, but they were always ready to
hear about what I was learning.

Annamaria, on the other hand, went home at night to three
children, all the housework, and an Italian husband who was
receiving minimal disability payments. He didn't go to work,
but he didn't do anything at home, either. "What can I say? He's
Italian," she would shrug as we sat next to each other, racking
and stringing and talking. She was never late, she was careful
and quick, she was the primary support of her family—and she
didn't have a prayer of getting a better job. "Hey, I quit school
when I got married. And you tell me when I would ever find the
time to go back," she said.

I couldn't. I couldn't even figure out how her family was
surviving. One day we were both picking newly plated earrings
off the racks, wearing white gloves so we wouldn't leave any

nasty human fingerprints, and I said, "Is it nice having three kids?"

"Better than having four," she retorted, "not as good as having two."

There was no doubt that Annamaria was a Catholic. She wore a gold crucifix and five medals on chains around her neck, and a holy card of the Little Flower was stuck in the frame of the picture of her kids that she kept on her worktable. I must have glanced at the Little Flower, or maybe I just looked curious and she mistook it for disapproval.

"When those jerks down at the rectory start delivering groceries when I deliver the babies, then I might think about more. But I got caught with the first one when I was seventeen. I had big plans until then; I was going to nursing school. Then comes the second. You know how it is, you've got one kid, you think it needs a playmate. Then my mother-in-law and the priest and the doctor all carry on about how it's a sin to use birth control. I was twenty-two years old! What were we supposed to do? So along comes Angela. And of course she's the best one of all. Isn't that the way it always works out? But the next time it happened I took care of it. What does the pope know? Is he paying our doctor bills? Is he getting me a raise here?"

She changed racks. She straightened the picture of her children. And she nodded her head and said, "You do what you have to do."

"I can understand that," I said. I could.

A few days later Annamaria and I were talking about taking Angela to the dentist, and she wound up the story by asking, "Hey, Pat, you married? Or what?"

I wanted to answer "What." For months I had been ducking direct questions about my private life.

"No, I'm not married," I said, hoping that would satisfy Annamaria's sudden curiosity.

"How come?" she said.

I couldn't say "Gee, nobody ever asked me," or "I dunno." And I could tell she wasn't going to let me shrug it off. So I decided the moment had come.

"I'm a nun," I said.

"Sure you are," she laughed. "Hear that, girls? Pat is a nun."

Everybody laughed.

"Sure she is, anybody can see that. She's got the big white

bib under that pink sweater and the rosary beads in her blue jean pockets!'' shouted Donna.

"And she's got the veil all bunched up under that wig," said Jeannie from the end of the room.

Annamaria tugged playfully at my hair and said, "You are here because the pope sent you to make sure we don't drop any more pennies into the collection box, right?" It was amazing how well she could imitate Barbara in her Sister Charles Marie–mood.

They could *all* imitate Sister Charles Marie. Pretty soon the entire workroom sounded like a convention of dim-witted nuns.

"Nice girls don't do that, *dear*.''

"The husband is chosen by God to head the family, and it is a wife's duty to practice obedience."

"Birth control is a sin against nature."

"Nature is a sin against nature," chortled Donna. I laughed at that myself.

"I hate nuns," said Annamaria.

"That's not fair," I objected, suddenly indignant. So much for my fear that they would treat me too reverently if they knew I was a nun!

"Nuns today aren't like the nuns we had in school," I said. "Look at the nuns right here in Providence. Liz Morancy is a Sister of Mercy, and she's an elected state representative."

"Oh yeah, *those* kind of nuns. Those nuns are okay," she agreed.

"Well, I'm one of those nuns," I insisted.

"If you are a nun, why aren't you in a school somewhere, whacking my kids with a ruler? What are you doing stringing up earrings?" demanded Annamaria.

"Um, I'm getting in touch with the life of the parish," I said. That did it. I sounded nunny.

"Oh, jeez, you are a nun," said Annamaria.

For the next week, as word spread, people kept coming up from downstairs to stare at me. The most dramatic reaction came from Pasqual, the foul-mouthed dipper. Good Catholic boy that he was, when he found out, he stood ten feet away from me and could only mouth the words: "You're a nun?"

I nodded. He blushed bright red, shook his head, and walked away. I smiled demurely and went on stringing and racking. From then on we heard a lot less about great jugs.

Annamaria followed me to the rest room one day during our

morning break. "You remember what I said about not having more kids?" she said.

"Yeah, sure I do," I said.

"You have a problem with that?" she demanded.

I stood at the sink, crumpling up a paper towel. I had been thinking a lot about what she had told me. In particular I had been thinking about the teachings of the church on the matter of individual conscience. When Annamaria said to me, "You do what you have to do," she had been talking about making a choice as a morally responsible, adult, faithful woman.

"No, I don't have a problem with your experience," I said. "My problem is with a church run by celibate men who are afraid of sex and afraid of women and presume to insist that they know more about what God has in mind for women than we do ourselves."

"Jeez, Pat, I wouldn't go that far," said Annamaria.

After that, the conversations in the workroom returned to normal. The only difference was that occasionally some of the women would share a personal problem with me confidentially. They didn't say anything they wouldn't have said to a fairly responsive priest, but, as they often told me, one of their problems was finding a responsive priest.

None of the people who worked at High Point were members of unions, and the unions that were active in Rhode Island were going through a really rough time. The jewelry industry was in decline. The Reagan era of union-busting was beginning. I would never have imagined how difficult, and how dangerous, trying to organize a union is. I went to meetings, and listened, and came back and talked about what I had heard to the other women at work. They were very edgy when I brought up the subject, and I wondered why. "What's the harm of talking?" I demanded. "They can't fire us for just talking. Anyway, it's illegal to fire someone because of involvement with a union."

"That's how much you know, Pat," said Donna.

I found out what they meant in the next few months. A woman named Rosa who worked in another factory began to come to the union meetings. She was a single parent supporting two children, and she had been working as a stringer and racker for twenty years. One night I went to a meeting and a young woman organizer sat down next to me and said:

"Isn't it wonderful about Rosa?"

"What about her?" I asked.

"She was fired. She began holding meetings during lunch break, and the company told her they didn't have enough work for her. They blacklisted her. She can't find a job with anyone else. Isn't it great? We have really started something there," she said breathlessly.

The organizer was a college-educated woman, idealistic and hard-working, but she didn't seem to see the flaw in her argument.

"It sounds awfully irresponsible to me," I said. "What is going to be the responsibility of the union to this woman who is now unemployable?"

As it turned out, the less naive union leaders went to court to protect Rosa's job. The case is probably still in court. I, at least, had learned a lesson in the importance of thinking through the consequences of an action—including the consequences of urging other people to take action.

"Dear Barbara," I wrote one day after about a year of stringing and racking.

My friend Annamaria has been trying to go to school one night a week so she can get her high school equivalency degree. Her husband freaked out. His back was bad, she couldn't take the car because he needed to visit his mother—anything to keep her from going to school. Today she told me she asked Father Ryan—supposed to be the great liberal in the parish— to talk to her husband. And he told her that she should remember her first duty is to her husband's wishes!!!! Can you believe it? If he had ever had a real job as a cashier or a shoe clerk or a bowling alley attendant, he might have learned something. Forget about the horrible sexism in his answer. I'd settle if he knew something about what it is like to try to support a family on $3.10 an hour. If a priest can't figure out that a helpful response to Annamaria would be to tell her husband that he is committing the sin of envy against his wife and selfishness against his children who need the money she might earn—well, what good is he? What are the chances of his ever standing with the workers to improve these toxic work conditions? Is he ever going to speak out about the right to earn fair wages? No wonder fewer and fewer people show up for Sunday mass. There's no connection between their lives and their church.

"Dear Pat," Barbara wrote back.

So what else is new? I don't think priests necessarily have to work in bowling alleys to know what people deal with in their day-to-day lives. They could make a good start at connecting if they just *asked*. In Auburndale, when we began sending out questionnaires and holding meetings asking for feedback, people answered. They described ways they wanted to be involved in the life of the church, and when we made it possible, they showed up. They began to feel like church for each other.

I had to laugh at your letter. Forgive me, I know it isn't funny about Annamaria, but you sound so much like me in your response. I'm the one who would normally be furious and march right in and say to Father Ryan, "Get over there and tell that man he is sinning." So I will try to sound like you for a change.

What about the fact that Annamaria's husband's theology probably involves the idea of God giving him a wife to boss around? He can't help feeling threatened. What about the fact that dictating to him about "sin" would be as alienating as dictating to her about "duty"? It would be nice if Father Ryan, or anyone who takes on the job of being a religious leader, tried to help people to consensus and understanding and growth.

I'm beginning to think about my thesis, and I think it is probably going to be on the very point you brought up. Thank you, as usual, for making me think.

Margie Tuite dropped in last night and she stayed for supper. I let her read your letter, and she says when you come out to visit next month she will introduce us to some worker priests. No, they are not working in bowling alleys. They are day laborers.

The crocuses were just beginning to bloom when I arrived in Chicago for a week in the spring of 1980. I enjoyed a sort of renewal as I went around visiting friends and mentors.

Barbara, true to form, had typed up a schedule of times for the two of us to sit down and talk about what was happening in our lives. She wouldn't even adjourn to the Mellow Yellow Cafe until we had had at least an hour of serious discussion. So I sat down solemnly in her old stuffed chair, and scribbled things on her typed schedule: "Option for the poor." "Live with the people.'' ''Get involved in the community's efforts to organize around the issues oppressing them.'' We were beginning to have a picture of what those phrases might actually mean day-to-day.

''Visit priests with Margie,'' Barbara had put on her schedule. So one afternoon the three of us got on a bus and rode halfway around Chicago. It was a great trip. Barb and I were sitting together on a seat for two, with Margie sitting facing us, and we talked about the history of the worker-priest movement.

It began before World War II in France, where the working class had become almost entirely alienated from the church. During the war a few priests went in disguise to Germany to be with young Frenchmen forced into labor camps by the Nazis. Priests then joined the French Resistance and afterward went into factories and construction sites as workers, permanently sharing the life of the people. Inevitably, they became politically involved, and over the years the Vatican has tried to suppress and restrict what these missionaries to the modern cities see as their vocation.

We finally got off the bus in a neighborhood of shabby storefronts, small wooden houses, two- and three-story brick apartment buildings, and some struggling automobile repair shops. We climbed up the stairs to the top of one of the three-story buildings. Margie knocked on a door. A very slight man peeked out and said, ''Hello?'' Then he recognized Margie, his eyes lit up, and he threw open the door.

''Oh, Margie, come in,'' he said. ''It is so good to see you.''

''Andrew, here are my friends,'' said Margie, as she laughed and hugged him.

''King Kong meets Fay Wray,'' Barbara whispered. Margie sometimes reminded us of Falstaff on a good night, and the priest was really a *very* tiny man.

The four priests who lived in the apartment were just sitting down to dinner. It was only about two o'clock in the afternoon, but they got up at three in the morning to say mass and eat breakfast. By four or four-thirty they would be out at the places where day laborers stood hoping to be picked up for work.

We squeezed in around the table, and for the next four hours we compared experiences. They had been living in that neighborhood for five years, and they felt a tremendous commitment to the people.

''The physical work is awfully tedious and exhausting,'' admitted one of the priests, ''but at least we do believe that we have made a small difference in people's lives.''

They counted the painfully small signs of progress. At some of their work sites the men had organized to demand better conditions, things like overtime pay and toilet facilities and safety goggles. And in the neighborhood the people, who were mostly Hispanic, had begun to take up issues with their city council representatives.

"A cloud of filth from the recycling plant near here descended every afternoon. It was wonderful to see the people discover how to call up their city council member and demand action," said one of the priests.

"How do people feel about the fact that you are priests?" I asked.

"They don't know we are priests," said Andrew. "If they did, they would see us as from a separate class, a privileged class. The key to our mission is working *with* people, empowering them instead of leading them."

All the men around the table spoke passionately about their determination to stand in the circle, not at the top of the triangle.

"Our vision of Christianity is the faith and hope and love at work in the Latin American base communities, the *comunidades eclesiales de base*," they said. "The church too often stands on the wrong side, defending South American dictators, mine owners, oligarchies, the status quo. We don't want to be identified as people who support the status quo. Jesus stood with the poor."

"Well, you could avoid all that temptation to feel special by just leaving the priesthood," said Margie, never one to let an opportunity to challenge someone pass her by.

"I hope that never becomes necessary," said Andrew, gently. "We are trying to bear witness to Christ's message, not only to the people of our neighborhood, but to our religious order. We are taught, and in turn we teach. In a way, we are inventing a new meaning of 'priestly,' and we don't know what may come of it. In Latin America this kind of ministry is an invitation to martyrdom. But in Chicago probably the worst that can happen to us is that we lose our jobs."

"I am sure of one thing," Andrew added, very seriously. "Very soon nuns like you will face having to decide between your principles and the commands of the Vatican. This new Pope John Paul is deaf to women. Your movement is beyond his comprehension. And as for the Curia, every time they hear of a nun standing up and asking to be ordained, they cross themselves. Your ideas are too revolutionary for them even to appear to take you seriously. You reject their claim that they receive their authority from a male God because they are men. Where does that leave them? As mere Christians among Christians?''

A great, booming, joyous sound burst out from Margie's end of the table. Her laugh. ''Oh, Andrew, how wonderful it is to hear you talk. I think it is the first time I have ever heard a priest truly express feminist liberation theology. And no sooner do you understand it than you start lecturing us about it. But never mind, of course you are right. The Vatican will start trying to round the nuns up pretty soon. But it's too late. We are going to disperse them instead. The entire Curia will be scattered across Brazil, dropped one by one into base communities where they will *conscientização* and be happy as mere Christians among Christians. Won't it be grand?''

We all roared with laughter at the vision of the skies over Brazil raining cardinals in red coats. And then we said good night. I have never seen those priests again, but wherever they are working now, I am sure they know that Andrew's prediction—that someday we would have to choose between our principles and our vows—came true.

On the bus ride home we all sat brooding for a while.

''Well, what do you think?'' Margie finally asked. ''Is that the kind of work you have in mind?''

''I think so, something like that,'' said Barbara. ''It seems a meaningful way to live out the Gospel, to try to bring about justice in the world. I like the idea of *doing* instead of just preaching. It fits my vision of a prophetic church. But I have to admit, my family would think I am crazy, going to work in a factory with a brand-new doctorate.''

''What about you, Pat?'' asked Margie.

''I'm not sure,'' I said. ''What I have learned in the jewelry factory is that people deserve more than to have irrelevant God-talk dumped on them once a week. They deserve to live with an awareness of God within themselves. Don't laugh at me, Barbara, but if I could have one wish, if I could go around performing miracles, it would be to touch people and say 'Awake! Realize your glorious destiny!' And the damage done by poverty and lack of education and no respect would be healed.''

Barbara did laugh. I knew she would. ''You have a vocation to be Cinderella's fairy godmother,'' she said.

''Well, why not?'' said Margie. ''That is what Cinderella's fairy godmother did. It is also what Jesus did.''

"Exactly!" I said.

By that time we were back in Barbara's apartment, drinking cocoa. Margie was drinking Scotch, and she wasn't about to let us off the hook.

"How are you going to do it?" she insisted.

"I don't think I could last very long without admitting I am a nun," I said. "After all, I *am* a nun. I need my community. When all is said and done, the Sisters of Notre Dame are the circle that gives me strength."

"Me, too," said Barbara. "Being a Sister of Notre Dame is part of my identity."

"Something else is bothering you, Pat. What is it?" asked Margie.

I thought a minute more. "I was very shaken by what Andrew said about the possibility that sometime in the future our conscience might no longer allow us to remain as nuns," I said, slowly. "I have believed that after all these years of renewal, the church would keep moving forward. But I've been fooling myself, haven't I? The people of God and the Vatican are not necessarily on the same side."

"Hey, cheer up," Margie roared, throwing her arms around me. "You've forgotten who returned the church to the people of God. It was *Pope* John XXIII, remember? But it's a big, biiiig church, and it takes a while to get the whole thing turned around. Look how long it took them to admit the earth is not the center of the universe."

"But Margie," I said, "it wasn't any fun being Galileo."

"Sure it was fun," she insisted, bless her heart. "It's always fun changing things for the better."

Twenty: This Land Is Home to Me

PAT

Until the summer of 1981, while I waited for Barbara to come up with a plan for the future, I strung and racked and learned as much as I could in my post-graduate course on life. We had put together a one-page proposal describing our goals for the next few years. The time had come, we said, to live the gospel of justice, the social documents of the church, and the Acts of the Sisters of Notre Dame de Namur in a concrete way. We wanted to live a simple life-style, within our means as workers, and to identify and work with working-class people. We also wanted to be involved with others engaged in creating more just situations.

Very carefully, we defined some principles that we hoped would keep us constantly aware, challenged, and part of our communities. Once a week we would set aside time to reflect with each other about decisions that would affect our lives. We would regularly meet and reflect with other nuns involved in similar life-styles and work. And we would be equally careful to reflect with whatever social justice groups we became involved in about activities affecting us all.

We mailed copies of our proposal to people we knew who were doing community organizing. One response came from a Sister of Notre Dame working in South Carolina who had received a notice from some other SNDs working in southern West Virginia. It advertised a job in Charleston. A group called the Charleston Interdenominational Council on Social Concerns, representing fifteen churches and the Jewish temple, was looking for "a minister" to begin a new project. Covenant House, at that point, was an undefined, ecumenical venture that would involve both direct service with "people who fall between the cracks" and efforts to look at long-term changes required to improve those people's lives. (Covenant House is an independent, nonprofit organization and has never been connected to the Covenant House group of shelters for runaway and homeless teenagers which began in 1969 in New York City.)

"It looks like a good possibility," said Barbara, on the phone to me. "Listen to the last paragraph of their proposal":

Everyone working on the project is excited about the unlimited possibilities. Charleston is a focal point for this part of Appalachia. The city is the location of city, county and state government; is a center of industry and the focal point of work in the coal fields; and has all the problems associated with Appalachian displacement and colonization.

"Great," I said. "Let's give it a try."

We were invited to fly to Charleston for an interview. On Friday, February 13, 1981, Barbara left a blizzard in Chicago, and I left an ice storm in Providence, and we met in the warm sunshine of the Charleston airport. "Welcome to Wild, Wonderful West Virginia!" read a sign.

"My gosh, it sounds like Las Vegas," said Barbara.

"I think they mean the mountains and the deer and the rivers," I reassured her.

That Friday the thirteenth was a lucky day for us, and the beginning of a wonderful weekend. We were picked up and taken to stay with a group of families who had all spent time in a ministry in Africa and had brought their ideals back to Appalachia. They lived in a nearby town called Sod up on top of a mountain. They were just the kind of people we had hoped to meet: down-to-earth, open, cheerful, and committed to change. And Charleston was just the right size; not big enough to be overwhelming, but big enough so that we might really be able to make a difference.

Everyone we met seemed excited about the project, and yet they were very eager to hear how we thought it might be organized. No one had fixed ideas or solutions. They were warm and encouraging, and the only time we felt we were being tested was when we were asked on Saturday to serve at the soup kitchen called Manna Meal. We realized later that once the search committee decided we could talk to them, the question remained—

could we respond to the street people? Our credentials were excellent, but they wanted to know if we were all head, or were we also heart?

We were testing the committee too, of course, and we were impressed by the fact that they knew the names of the people coming in for the meal. There was no condescension, just welcome.

The house at 1109 Quarrier Street, soon to be Covenant House, was given rent-free to the project by one of the supporting churches. More than $100,000 in time, money, material, equipment, and furnishings was donated by the members of the new interfaith ministry. The first time we saw the place, prisoners on work release had just finished renovating the rooms in the front, but the apartment in the back was still a shambles. For once in our lives, we found a mess appealing. There was a kind of romanticism about being able to begin from scratch, to try to make the best of things without having to fit into anybody's shoes.

What most impressed us was that the people we would work with seemed genuinely determined to combine direct service to the poor, the elderly, the unemployed, and the street people *and* commitment to bringing about long-term change. Neither Barbara nor I wanted to spend all our energies Band-Aiding, as we called it, patching up the victims instead of rooting out the causes of the problems. We wanted to do both. This group seemed to share that goal and to mean what they said.

From its founding in 1977, the Charleston Interdenominational Council on Social Concerns (CICSC) had had a vision which they had written down as a mission statement. It included words we ourselves could have written.

> Together, across religious, social and economic boundaries, we need to address the common, human, social problems facing us all and attempt to respond to those needs. For through all our religious traditions, God is seen on the side of the poor, and the way we as human beings discover God is through the poor.

The Council's understanding of God was challenging and lifegiving: "It is clear that God through all our communal memories and different religious traditions has not been a comfortable God of the powerful, the aloof God of the elite nor a static and neutral God who blesses the status quo at the expense of those who have nothing.''

Those were, and still are, exciting beliefs that can shake up a lot of people and a lot of established religions if they are taken to heart. We wanted to be part of the effort.

We felt that the people we were meeting, both lay and clergy, had made a strong personal commitment to work together to discover God in one another and to bring forth the best from everyone in the effort to transform the city into a better place to live. And they did truly mean what they said. Over the years, their words and their actions have sustained us, guided us, and energized us.

By Sunday we had progressed to the point of discussing finances. We were having lunch in Wendy's, near the capitol building, and one of the ministers on the committee suggested that the Catholic bishop of West Virginia might be willing to provide a car for our use.

Uh-oh, I thought. "We need to let you know," I said, "that we have been very involved in the protests of the Women's Ordination Conference against discrimination in the Roman Catholic church, and we don't intend to change our political life. So if someone wants to donate a car, that's good, but let them donate it to the project, not to the nice little nuns.''

He looked a little flustered. After all, how could he have guessed how important it was to us not even to appear to be working for the local Catholic hierarchy? We were interested in *new* ministry. Good-bye parochial, hello interdenominational.

We definitely, definitely wanted the job. The committee told us they would let us know their decision on March 30.

"It is either going to be a very good day or a very bad day," said Barbara, as we separated at the airport.

When the day came, she was busy defending her doctoral thesis in Chicago, and I got the phone call we had been waiting for in Providence. As soon as I could, I reached Barbara.

"How did it go?" I asked her.

"Great," she said. "What's new?"

"Welcome to wild, wonderful West Virginia, Barb!" I whooped.

BARBARA

Pat was taking a long-planned vacation and my parents were celebrating their fortieth wedding anniversary that summer. My Ferraro siblings and I were giving them a surprise party, so Pat and I couldn't actually move to Charleston until late August. The last week of August, we put all our worldly possessions into the smallest U-Haul truck available. It wasn't quite as big as a small van and even so we had room left over. We had a trunk, a couple of suitcases, a box of books and records, and two impossible cornstalk plants that Pat had been mothering in Providence.

We were traveling with all the passports appropriate for two nuns. We had the blessings of our provincial governing teams in Boston and Connecticut. Our community had followed the rules of courtesy and protocol and notified the Bishop of Wheeling-Charleston, Joseph Hodges, that we were members in good standing.

The only thing we didn't have was a reservation for a motel room. After the tenth "No Vacancy" sign, we asked what was going on and were told that there were no rooms within a hundred-mile radius because of the annual county fair. We finally found one disgusting room in a motel that looked like the set for *Psycho II*. Luckily we had sense enough to run for our lives, and at the very next stop we found a perfectly nice place.

"I'm going to collapse," muttered Pat, staggering toward her bed.

"Me, too. I can't stay awake another minute," I said, stumbling toward mine.

Then we lay awake all night, tossing and turning, taking turns reassuring each other.

"Do we know what we're doing?" Pat would say.

"Sure, of course we do. It will be fun," I would answer.

And then, from me: "Will we feel at home in West Virginia?"

"We've already met some wonderful people," Pat would soothe.

Early the next morning we set out on the last leg of our journey. We took the long way around, over the mountains, coming into Charleston from the south on Route 60. The scenery was gorgeous. These hills and mountains don't roll, they rear and plunge. We began to talk about coming back to this or that spot and going camping. We had never gone camping in our lives but West Virginia was already putting its hold on us.

There is a passage in Eudora Welty's book *One Writer's Beginnings*, where she describes her elderly mother, who was born on a ridge in West Virginia, suddenly asking her daughter to play the song closest to her heart, the one she once sang around the house. Eudora sat down at the piano and played:

> O the West Virginia hills!
> How my heart with rapture thrills . . .
> O the hills! Beautiful hills . . .

Now I know what the song meant to her, and why the people born in those hills never want to leave, and always come back if they have to go to Detroit or Cleveland or Chicago to work. But even that morning I began to greet the towns along the route as though I had always lived there. Hello, Smithers, Boomer, and Belle. And then, up ahead, the capitol dome. Hello, Charleston.

And finally, hello, Covenant House. We got the key from the janitor at the church and walked in. Everything that would make the apartment a comfortable place to live was waiting for us, but the volunteers who had opened Covenant House a few months before had left the last details and the arranging to us. Actually, to be frank, they had left cleaning and window shades and door locks to us. Mushrooms were growing around the toilet, and at night I discovered enormous slugs creeping across the floor. I really freaked out. I don't like to be surprised by nature. An enormous dumpster full of garbage was steaming in the September humidity right next to our back door. Cars in the church parking lot regularly backed into our bedroom wall because there was no fence.

As we carried our things into the apartment, some of the people who presumably would be taking advantage of Covenant House's services peered in through the windows and offered helpful advice. "Window shades" went to the top of the rapidly growing list.

"Let's see what the front of the building looks like now," said Pat, pulling open the unlocked door between our apartment and Covenant House. "Oh, God," she said, stepping right back inside. There were people sitting on the floor, spilling coffee, smoking, sleeping off a drunk, milling around. Apparently Covenant House was open as a place to take shelter, but clearly it was waiting for us to get it organized. We would have to close it before we could open properly.

We met with the Covenant House board and suggested closing for a few weeks so we could scrub the place and also meet as many community service people as possible.

"When in doubt, clean," is always my motto. We scoured the bathrooms, scrubbed down the walls and windows, and shampooed the rugs. We got to be intimately acquainted with every nook and cranny in the building and in the process it became "ours."

Every day we tried to clean up ourselves enough to go out and meet some of the people we would be talking to so often in the months ahead at the Department of Human Services, especially at the Emergency Services Unit. They had heard "the nuns" would be coming to town, but we wanted to put faces on our label. We met people at the two other downtown agencies, the Salvation Army and the Mountain Mission, and the lawyers from the Legal Aid Society. Connie Kayser, who was a member of our board of directors and worked for a local social service agency, was an incredibly helpful new friend. She introduced us to all the resources in the community, pulling us along to meeting after meeting, introducing us over and over: "These are the nuns," "The nuns have arrived."

We are still introduced as "the nuns." Although one of the pleasures of moving to Charleston was the fact that everyone, once introduced, called us Barbara and Pat instead of Sister, they almost always had trouble attaching the right name to the right nun. I always point out that I am the older and wiser one.

By the time we were ready to reopen, we had a useful list of telephone numbers, and we had made ourselves a home.

Maybe all that doesn't seem like an enormous accomplishment. After all, what's the big deal about getting together a list of social service agencies in an area that has a population of only 64,000 people? And I will admit it shouldn't have been extraordinary for two grown women to buy some window shades and get our electricity turned on. But the fact is, no coordinated list had been in existence before. That lack was one of the reasons Covenant House was started.

Traditionally, each church building was supported by its congregation, and in turn the minister in charge of that building felt responsible only to the congregation. (Unfortunately, in most instances, the richer the church, the less responsive they were to outsiders in need.) The denomination usually had a charitable organization, but an individual church's response to a particular person turning up in need on the doorstep was unpredictable. They might be met at the door by a poorly informed secretary, or they might get to see a part-time volunteer outreach worker. The minister might be able to hand over twenty-five dollars and directions to the nearest shelter. At best, each church had its own emergency food pantry, or clothes closet, or petty cash.

When I worked in the parish in Auburndale I knew the pastor had an emergency fund, but I had no access to it and I was never told how it was allocated. I didn't even have a list of agencies to refer people to. Sometimes, if I couldn't serve someone who came to the door, they would go from church to church looking for help.

Most ministers can't, or won't, or don't keep up with available programs. I don't really blame them. Pat and I spend half our time trying to keep track of things like LIEAP (Low Income Energy Assistance Program) and FEMA (Federal Emergency Management Agency), not to mention housing and welfare and Medicaid regulations. Even the people who administer the programs often don't understand what they include. And the great unspoken rule of the system is, "Don't tell people what is available unless they ask." The system only works for people who know how to use it. Our job was to ask the questions, and teach people how to get answers and how to use the system.

People in trouble often turn first to their church, but the minister or rabbi or priest may not be able to respond appropriately, even to people in their own congregations. These religious leaders are not trained therapists or social workers. It is just not part of their professional training. In graduate school, Pat and I learned how to write sermons and how to get the folks in the pews working together, but we were never offered a course on making use of community services.

Pat always laughed about a "Communications" course she had taken called "Effective Pastoral Ministry." She called it her course in "When you, I feel, because." As in: "When you tell me to go to hell I feel angry because I am just trying to helpfully critique your attitude." It is a useful skill, of course, particularly if your entire congregation is angry because you want to turn the family chapel into a day-care center for poor children. But it is a different skill from the one needed when a woman comes in whose Social Security disability check has been cut off, along with her heat and electricity and Medicaid card, because the government's computer lost her record.

The practical goal of Covenant House was to develop a central resource center. But the idea of doing it by creating a cooperative ministry was new, something that was just beginning to be tried in various parts of the United States. And it represented an unprecedented willingness on the part of the churches each to abandon their own well-protected turf, which could provide only small solutions, and try to work together for big solutions.

In the mid-seventies, Charleston went through a stretch of fundamentalist attacks on school textbooks that they claimed were obscene, blasphemous, anti-American, and which promoted an atheistic religion called "secular humanism." The city's churches and temple came together to condemn censorship. Then, in about 1977, the pastor of St. John's Episcopal Church at the time, Jim Lewis, and a lay member of that church, Virginia Adams, encouraged the congregation to open their house of worship to Manna Meal. It was a painful decision for many. Most of the people who built St. John's, or whose parents built it, have long since moved away from the center of the city, up to the newer, richer neighborhoods in the hills overlooking Charleston. Many of them didn't believe their building should be shared. They didn't want to see "those people" in their church, and some of them have never come back to it.

But a new, deeper understanding of what it means to be a house of worship was growing in Charleston. In 1982, the pastor of the Ruffner Presbyterian Church, Don Steele, used the technique of "When you, I feel, because" to resolve opposition to the idea of using their basement gymnasium for a shelter for women and children. Some members insisted that their building was meant for those who contribute to paying the bills. Others argued for a commitment to those less fortunate. Don Steele asked each member of the community to talk with someone who disagreed with them on the issue. And after a few weeks, the community agreed to become the first church to open its doors for a women's and children's shelter.

The Interdenominational Council on Social Concerns grew out of those struggles, which were responses to the reality on the streets of Charleston. The coal industry was declining. The whole country was sliding into a recession, and there weren't even any jobs up north to migrate toward. As the cruel budget cuts of the Reagan era began to take effect, the poor were hit first and hardest. And Charleston is in the heart of Appalachia, one of the most economically depressed sections of the United States. More and more people were homeless, and the problem was getting worse.

And so the idea for Covenant House was born. Once it was open, it seemed an obvious solution. But it represented an entirely new way of thinking.

And what about us? Why were we so proud of ourselves? It is no big deal for grown women to have the electricity turned on. Except that we had never done it before. We had vowed to practice responsible decision-making, and for the first time, we had a chance to actually do it.

Until then we had always joined a household that was already established. We had never come to a work site where we knew no one, and where there were no other Sisters of Notre Dame. There were five other SNDs in West Virginia, representing four out of our five provinces, but the closest were an hour away in Sutton, where they were working in a parish and with women quilt-makers. Camille and Francine immediately became our friends, but we didn't see them very often.

It was exhilarating to be setting up something brand-new and sometimes it was funny. When I tried to open a bank account under the name Sisters of Notre Dame, they told me I couldn't. I had to explain that that was my name, financially speaking. After I explained, the person at the bank still looked baffled and said, "But what is this? Is this some kind of business?" It was wonderful to be away from the nunny culture of New England. Nobody gave us any special treatment. No deference and no discounts. No free tickets to the movies, no free parts for the furnace just because we were nuns.

I was being paid $10,000. Pat, part-time for the first year, was being paid $5,000, and also working in the check-out line at Foodland. We sent almost a quarter of our income back to our provincial houses as our contribution to the Sisters of Notre Dame. Covenant House sent monthly payments to our provinces to cover health insurance and retirement. Other than that, as part of our determination to live responsibly, we arranged to pay all our own bills. We even bought our own car. But I didn't open a checking account in my own name until I left the community.

Only 5 percent of West Virginia is Catholic, and the old suspicion of popery (very well justified as far as I am concerned) still lives in the other 95 percent. Some people were afraid we might proselytize. So I was horrified when we went to introduce ourselves to the pastor of one of Charleston's two Catholic churches and, after he had grilled us about our qualifications, he asked us how soon we would begin teaching his parish catechism classes. Our experience, our graduate degrees, didn't count. Nontraditional nuns were the last women he wanted to see in his parish. He wanted *nuns*—housenuns—the exploited labor force of the Catholic church.

PAT

The morning of the day we reopened Covenant House, Barbara shook out the dishtowel and said, "Now, let's go out the back door and walk outside to work."

"Why don't we just walk through the door into the front of the house?" I asked.

"Because the front of the house is work, and the back of the house is home, and I think it is really important that we have a little space between them," said Barbara.

So we locked the back door behind us, walked around the little one-story green house in the middle of downtown Charleston, West Virginia, and after experiencing a space of maybe one minute, we unlocked the front door and entered Covenant House—our work.

It was 8:00 A.M. on Monday, September 28, 1981. The first thing we did was lock the front door again, and look around inside to make sure everything was ready. The desk for the volunteer receptionist was just inside the front door. The sign-in book was open and waiting. The soap and the washing machine and dryer and ironing equipment were all set. The shower room was working, and the towels were in a neat pile. On the glassed-in front porch we had arranged a little circle of rocking chairs and easy chairs, with shelves for books and plants on the walls under the windows. In the main room, the one with the desk, two sofas faced each other on either side of the old green tiled gas fireplace. Off that room, beyond a Dutch door with a counter on top of the bottom half, there were offices for private consultations and record keeping. At the back, beyond the offices, was the door into our apartment.

On one wall we had hung a framed drawing of a rainbow surrounded with the passage from Genesis which explained why the name "Covenant House" had been chosen by its founders: "This is the sign of the Covenant which I make between me and you and every living creature that is with you for all future generations.'' Around the rainbow was written: ''When the bow is in the clouds, I will look upon it and remember the everlasting covenant between God and every living creature that is upon the earth.''

We were so proud of the place. It looked clean and welcoming. But would anyone show up? And if they did, would we have the courage to let them in?

The front of Covenant House has a bay window overlooking Quarrier Street. That day the windows were still warped shut, but we had hung net curtains over them. The room behind the window was the office where we planned to have our private meetings. We stood in the window, peeking through the curtains and jittering around.

''I'll unlock the front door,'' I said.

''No! Wait until eight-thirty,'' said Barbara.

''Right,'' I said. ''We don't want to set a precedent on the first day.''

''Almost time,'' said Barbara.

''Not yet,'' I said.

Our sentences were getting shorter.

''Will anyone come?'' wondered Barbara, twitching the curtain.

''What will we do if someone *does* come?'' I said.

''Well, it's eight-thirty,'' said Barbara, with a grim sort of smile. ''Let's find out. Open the door.''

By 8:35, Barbara looked like a little girl whose birthday party had been a flop.

''Nobody is coming,'' she wailed. ''Maybe they don't really need us here.''

''More likely they are afraid of us,'' I said. ''Didn't I tell you that the word is out on the street that The Nuns have arrived and things are going to be different?''

''How can they say that?'' she said, instantly indignant. ''We are open and friendly. We tell jokes.''

We were pretty nice, for nuns. But just in case, we had drawn up a list of rules and had run off a few copies to let people know what we expected. The rules included:

No coffee [we couldn't afford it, and people got too hyped-up on the caffeine].

No smoking [we didn't have any ventilation and the house is made of wood].

No showers longer than fifteen minutes.
No abusive language and no fighting.

When I look at that list of rules now I have to laugh. The very
first rule reads: "Each person using Covenant House will be
asked to meet with Barbara and Pat for an interview. What do
you want to do with your life? What ways can we work with
you?"

What do you want to do with your *life*?! What an intimidating
question for a first meeting! On the other hand, it's a good question and we still try to present it to everyone who comes in.
After all, the first step toward empowerment is the realization
that God has given to everyone the ability to make choices.

People did come. Slowly at first, and then faster. I can't remember the very first person who crossed our threshold. Probably it was just someone needing help getting food stamps or
some other routine problem. I'm sure it wasn't the full-blown
schizophrenic Barbara was expecting.

The work is exhausting, sometimes heartbreaking, and often
enraging, but the fact is, it is a lot more fun than it sounds. At
least, it is almost never boring.

Nowadays we see an average of ninety people a day. Some
are regulars who arrive every morning to sit in the front room
and read the paper. Some come one time and never return. In
the old days, our visitors would have been described as hillbil-
lies, bums, drunks, con men, nut cases, perverts, sickos, welfare
queens, pathetic geezers, coke heads, and weirdos. But Covenant
House thrives because some people in Charleston realized that
the poor do not choose to be poor. Now I really do believe that
there is more understanding of the reality of their lives and a
greater willingness to call them what they are: people of God.

One of the goals we set for ourselves was to do everything
we could to broaden that understanding. We see the miracle of
survival every day. Abused and battered bodies insist on life.
Spirits crushed by brutal personal catastrophes rise toward hope.
To Barbara and me, God is plainly revealed in such human
bravery. Nothing seems more callous and ignorant than when
the more fortunate people dismiss others by saying, "Anybody
who is homeless and therefore can't care for themselves should
be institutionalized or on a work farm." It is not true, and it is
certainly not helpful, to say, "Homeless people are limited in-
tellectually and are simply recycled in and out of the county
jail." I have heard perfectly nice people say, "Those people,

those retards, you know what they do to children." I hope my brother Michael never hears such an ignorant remark. Those kind of responses can finally break the human spirit.

"Those people"—the "not in my backyard" people—have names and faces, flesh and blood. They are not passive "clients" to be ground along on a bureaucratic treadmill. They have rights to food and shelter and clothing and health care. God is present in a woman struggling to find information about birth control. The man who comes into Covenant House to ask for a pair of shoelaces is sacred. I often think that God would appear on earth today as a poor person. In fact, God does.

We often speak at colleges and before high school and religious education groups, and we try to confront the myths: the "bootstrap" myth that anyone can pick themselves up; the "romantic hobo" myth that homelessness is chosen rather than endured; the "greater saintliness of the poor" myth, which is just an excuse to do nothing to help. We pass out worksheets, asking people to write down how much they spend on themselves a month. How much goes for videotapes and fast foods and makeup and jewelry and snacks? Then, when they have added it all up, we tell them what the welfare benefits are in the state of West Virginia.

It is amazing to me that we even have the nerve to call such payments "welfare benefits," as though it is something good for people. It is better than outright starvation I suppose, but not much better. When we first started working in West Virginia, a family of two received $164 a month, and a family of eight or more received a maximum of $360 a month. A month! Now it is $201 and $477, not much better.

After people have filled out our worksheets, we ask them to compare their numbers with what they would have to get by on if they were receiving welfare. Then we try to confront the welfare myths. The "once on welfare, always on welfare" myth. Not true: most people are off it within two years. The myth of "more children equals more money." In fact, the average size of a family on welfare in West Virginia is 2.5 people. All of those myths need to be—as the Acts of the Sisters of Notre Dame would say—healthily examined.

Listening is critical at Covenant House. Revelations come more often at the end of a phone conversation or over a scoop of laundry detergent going into the washer than they do sitting quietly in our private office. Darlene, in the beginning, wouldn't talk to anyone, anywhere. She came in, signed up for her turn at the washer, and that was it. She took no grief from anybody, and if anyone dared to look at her longer than she deemed appropriate, she would yell, "What's your problem?" The transgressor would melt into the woodwork. You didn't want her to ask "What's your problem?" twice!

Slowly Darlene warmed up to us. She didn't trust easily and for good reason. Her life had been pretty good until she was twelve. Then she discovered that her "mother" was her grandmother and her real mother was hospitalized. Darlene was the result of a rape in the mental institution. She told us she went crazy when she found out, running away, acting out, furious that she had been lied to all her life. She began being bounced around by the juvenile justice system and was hospitalized for observations.

"One day I didn't cooperate and I found myself tied to a pillar with bed sheets," she told us, "so I conformed. Who wants to be tied up? Animals were treated better than I was in that so-called hospital. Pumping me full of pills and Thorazine didn't help either. Finally I got out of there and was sent to a foster home. Both of them, the wife and her old man, jumped me. The social worker didn't believe me. She couldn't understand why I kept running away. Finally I turned eighteen and got loose of that system."

Darlene was like a dormant volcano, just waiting to erupt. When she could not express her frustration, she would finally explode after letting her feelings simmer for days on end. Often, we were her sounding board. At times, we must have gotten too close, because she would disappear for weeks at a time before she checked back again.

Finally, she picked a dramatic moment to show us she had really decided to trust us. We were sitting in the front office with three Sisters of Notre Dame, the Boston provincial team who had come to visit our work. Darlene came in and shoved a piece of paper in front of my nose, and as soon as I had read it she shoved it into Barbara's face. All I could tell was that it said she was pregnant. We had barely had time to exchange glances when Darlene shouted, as only she could, "Can you believe this? It only goes to prove that you only have to do it once and I didn't even like it!"

"Well," she went on, taking no notice of the three extra nuns who were arranging their faces into proper expressions of sympathetic concern, "I've thought about it and I'm not going to have a baby. I would be a rotten mother.'' It was a statement of fact, not a call for direction in her decision-making. Silent astonishment showed on the faces of the Boston team. Darlene was asking for our support and we stood with her, driving her to the Women's Health Center on the day of her abortion. Fortunately the anti-choice protestors were not at the Center that day. "If they get up in my face, I'll knock 'em down,'' she spouted. And no doubt, she would have.

Her story has a happy ending. Her farewell gift to us was to paint the whole interior of Covenant House. The last we heard from her she had returned home and had a full-time job. She ended her letter: "Thanks, you two.'' She even enclosed a donation.

Our days began to take on the rhythm we still follow. In time, as Covenant House expanded, we moved to an apartment in the old part of town near the capitol, and then we moved to a hilltop in the country. Every morning we go jogging, plan our day, and arrive at Covenant House before opening time. There are always a few people waiting on the steps outside. We spend the morning talking to the ones who want to see us, calling social service offices, passing out slips for things such as bus tickets, clothes from the supply kept in St. Mark's Church, food from the pantry stocked in the First Presbyterian Church, and visits to the free health clinic Covenant House started which now has its own building on Smith Street.

At noon we close and most people walk across the parking lot to the Manna Meal next door. Since we have been here, more women and children and old people go to what was once primarily a men's soup kitchen. At one o'clock we open again, and the whole cycle repeats itself until we shut at four o'clock. People go home, if they have one, or to an overnight shelter, or back to the street or the riverbank, or down Quarrier Street to a shabby room in the once elegant Holley Hotel.

Each of us tries to begin the day with a period of solitary meditation. Usually we end the day reflecting together and at least briefly try to think through some of the processes going on in our lives and work. Sometimes the reflection may be simply a short conversation, perhaps on the topic for the readings to be chosen for our Sunday worship service, but even that keeps us aware of the pattern and direction of our lives.

Usually we have some kind of meeting in the evening. We may, separately or together, need to plan travel arrangements for a group of advocates for the homeless and for people who have been or are homeless going to Washington, D.C., to demand solutions to homelessness. Or we may need to meet with our board, or such groups as the local AIDS Committee or the Rural Homelessness Advisory Committee. Once a year we take three weeks off. Barbara visits her family, and I go home to visit my brother Michael while my parents take a vacation. Until we stopped being nuns we each traveled once a year to our home provinces in Boston and Connecticut to take part in the reflections and decision-making of our communities.

When we first realized that part of our job would be to take part in the processes that determined the public policies directly affecting the people coming to Covenant House, we were very excited and nervous. For years we had been marching up and down outside trying to get the church to take us seriously, and suddenly we found ourselves before some open doors. Not church doors, but legislative doors.

I remember the first time we stepped before the microphone in a meeting at the Welfare Department. Barbara was going to speak, and I was going to "be present." We wanted to resolve a welfare regulation that in effect penalized people for coming to Covenant House or any other charitable agency. We had worked for hours and hours preparing her speech. Barbara took her seat with enough numbers and examples to critique the entire social services system of the state of West Virginia. She must have been persuasive, because that time our groups' efforts paid off and the regulation was changed. We weren't surprised that we succeeded, which shows how naive we were. But at least we were taken seriously.

Twenty-one: *¡Presente!*

BARBARA

We went to Nicaragua in March 1984. Like so many of the major events in our lives, Margie Tuite was responsible for this one too. She had founded the Women's Coalition Against United States Intervention in Latin America and the Caribbean. In time, she made thirteen trips to Nicaragua, Cuba, and El Salvador, taking groups of women from the United States with her to experience the reality of life in those countries, to be present— *¡presente!*—in their struggle.

Both Pat and I had been active in the Coalition in Solidarity with the People of Central America while we were studying in Chicago. Our lives as religious women trying to stand with the poor had been greatly influenced by the commitment to peace and justice and change expressed at the 1968 Medellín and 1979 Puebla conferences of the bishops of Latin America. Liberation theology was the basis of our understanding of *feminist* liberation theology—of our recognition of ourselves, as women, as oppressed and excluded. But it had taken the deaths of four women in El Salvador to make us begin to truly understand the connections between everything we had learned.

I will never forget December 4, 1980. I was still living in Chicago, and Pat was in Providence, when the news came that three nuns and a Roman Catholic lay worker were missing in El Salvador. Then came the word that they had been found, shot to death, in a common grave dug in a cow pasture. Three of them had been raped.

Pat had called me from Providence. "I met Maura Clarke," she said, her voice remote and slow with shock. "I met her last

189

year. Maura Clarke came to Providence to try to raise money for the Maryknolls. She spoke about how justice should live here on earth. I met her, Barb. I went up to thank her for her work. She had supper at our house. She was a woman in her fifties. Gentle. Soft-spoken. I can't believe it.''

I never wanted to go out to the missions. Pat was the one who joked about her romantic visions as a novice of going to distant lands and being thrown to the alligators in defense of her faith. That night I heard in her voice that the joke was over forever for her. We had been given new heroines, new prophetic models who had shown us what it really meant to live and die for faith.

Maura Clarke, Jean Donovan, Ita Ford, and Dorothy Kazel had been driving from the airport in San Salvador. Jean Donovan was a young laywoman who had been working with children. Maura Clarke and Ita Ford were Maryknoll nuns. Dorothy Kazel was an Ursuline nun. Who knows why they were murdered? Perhaps they were just in the wrong place at the wrong time.

Pat and I talked a long time that night. We called each other again, after we had each gone to memorial services. And just before Christmas, on my way home to visit my family, we went together to a celebration of those women's lives in the Providence cathedral. Friends of theirs spoke of the horror of their last hours, and of the miracle of their mission. All they had done was to live in small villages, helping people to take charge of their lives. They taught reading and worked in refugee camps, and they sat with the people in a circle and talked about scriptures and how they related to life in El Salvador, where an oligarchy steals their land and their dignity. And for that, the women were called Communist subversives.

To us, the most terrible perversion of their work came from Jeane Kirkpatrick, who was then the United States Ambassador to the United Nations. "The nuns were not nuns, they were political activists and we should be very clear about that," she was quoted in the papers as saying. I was so angry and so ashamed when I read that. My own United States government was supporting the people who had killed those four women, and tens of thousands of other innocent people.

"Theirs was a beautiful martyrdom," said the bishop during the celebration Pat and I attended in Providence. I felt her stiffen in the pew beside me.

"Idiot!" she hissed.

And I thought, If these women were now valued as martyrs,

why were they not valued enough to become priests? The Catholic church was no more willing to admit the dignity of women than the government in El Salvador was willing to admit the dignity of the peasants.

When we moved to Charleston, we joined the local Coalition on Central America. During one meeting of the Interdenominational Council that supported Covenant House, we asked if there was a church or a community in Charleston that might be interested in becoming a part of the network of sanctuaries organized all across the country to help Central American refugees. The Coalition arranged to bring a speaker from Washington, D.C., to a Council meeting. He spoke eloquently about the terror which people were escaping and of the dangers involved in helping them. Americans were going to jail for transporting refugees, for hiding them, and for refusing to cooperate with the Immigration Service. In 1983, the Unitarian Universalist Fellowship in Charleston declared itself a sanctuary.

Three other women friends of ours from Charleston joined us on our trip to Nicaragua in 1984. As we set about scraping together the money for the trip, we were very excited and very scared. We were going to be guests of AMNLAE, the association of women of Nicaragua named after Luisa Amanda Espinosa, the first woman to be killed in the revolution. Neither one of us had ever been to the Third World before, and it was wonderful to be going to visit a country in which both the church and women had been important in throwing out a dictator.

On the other hand, the United States was doing its best to destroy their new society. We had learned that the price of challenging the status quo could be death. And we might—even without making a challenge—have the bad luck to drive over a mine. I decided to deal with my own fear by not telling my parents where I was going—so *they* wouldn't worry.

The free health clinic we had started in Covenant House poked us full of shots, gave us bottles of pills for every possible ailment, and warned us not to eat anything fresh unless we peeled off the skins. We packed our knapsacks. And then, at the last moment, Pat broke down and phoned her parents.

"Mom, I'm going out of the country," Pat said.

"That's nice, dear," said her mother. "Where?"

"Nicaragua."

"When are you leaving?"

"In about an hour."

"Let me get your father," her mother said.

"Well, I didn't want you to hear it from the Red Cross in case anything happened," Pat said.

"We love you" were her dad's last words to her. "And call when you get back to the States."

About fifteen minutes before we left, Pat's mother called back in tears to say "I love you—in case anything happens." So I decided I had better tell my sister Mary where we were going. Consciences cleared, we left for Miami, where we stayed with a dear friend, Camille, another Sister of Notre Dame. She warned us not to tell anyone in Miami where we were going. "There are more contras in Miami than there are in Central America," she said.

We laughed, but when we got to the airport, the Nicaraguan plane was surrounded by armed guards—I think they were U.S. guards. Margie was there, and the fifteen other women we would be traveling with. As soon as we got to Nicaragua, we relaxed. Everything seemed slowed down to minus fifty miles an hour. I had never experienced the Latin American sense of time before, and I loved it. No place to rush, no deadlines to meet. I decided to take advantage of every single slow moment. Pat, I noticed, was finally living in a culture that moved to her natural tempo.

My Emmanuel College Spanish was not very useful in Nicaragua at first. Not only had I forgotten most of what I had learned, but my Boston accent made a mess of what I remembered. The evening we arrived, we sat down to a meal spread out on tables under the trees. I smiled at the Nicaraguan woman who was welcoming us to our end of the table.

"Are you hungry?" she asked.

"Oh, yes, thank you, thank you, I am *so* hungry," I said enthusiastically, mustering my version of Spanish.

She looked horrified.

"No, no," she said, raising her hands to her mouth. "Do you really?"

"Yes, yes, I *am* certainly hungry."

She looked even more upset.

Pat had an inspiration that saved me. "Barb," she hissed. "You think you are telling her you are very hungry, but you are actually telling her you want a man."

Dear Heaven! What a way to begin my career as an international traveler! Everybody blushed, and then everybody laughed. By the end of the week's trip, I had infinitely improved my

Spanish, and Pat and I had learned to share the deepest feelings of our hearts with the women of Nicaragua. The things they told us about peace and justice and faith were spoken in a language that needs no words.

People were so generous in their welcome. The rules we had been given about fresh fruit had to be abandoned right away when we saw that our first meal consisted of platters of fruit, salad, and beef. We were staying in a little hotel made of small cabins clustered together in a walled garden. Bravely encountering the Third World, I noted that there was no hot water, no screens on the windows, no air-conditioning. And the sound of gunshots popped all night in the distance.

Every morning we got up at dawn and boarded a bus to ride out and look at harbors, electric plants, and fuel tanks; economic targets attacked, damaged, or destroyed by the United States. Then, infinitely depressed, we would visit the women in various villages. It was extraordinary to meet the *madres*, the mothers of children who had disappeared or been killed by the contras, but who had no hostility toward us as Americans. "Go home and tell people what you have seen that Reagan has done," they repeated.

One night, when we were far out in the countryside of a northern province, we all attended church together. Afterward, our group split up and went home with various families. Pat and I were picked by a family of three women and two men with their children. We walked about two miles in the dark along a dirt road, and then the road ran straight into the front door of their house. It was a very small house, with a lean-to kitchen, but they had a television set, and the Walt Disney show—with Spanish dubbing—ran all the time we were trying to talk. I took the pencils and paper and balloons I had brought out of my knapsack and passed them around to the children. Then we had some melon and a piece of bread for dinner, and after that the entire family gestured for us to come along for a tour of their home.

The kitchen was full of parrots—flying around, sitting on the edges of the coffee cups, drinking from the water jug. I have always been afraid of dogs, but that night was the first time I realized I was also afraid of birds. Then we stepped out into the garden, where we were introduced to a flock of chickens and two deer named Bambi and Gandhi. I coped. But when we were shown to the other end of the house, in search of the outhouse, I stepped on a pig.

"Oink!" it said.

"Jesus Christ!" I said. (The family had no trouble understanding my English.)

The pig and our host family then escorted us to the privy. They pulled open the door, gestured to the two holes, handed us toilet paper, and then stood looking at us with great interest. Our modesty was further tested at bedtime. Everyone slept in one room, on boards. Obviously some people, perhaps the men, had been displaced because we had been given one little board at the end of the room. Like good North Americans we pulled off our clothes and put on the nightgowns we had packed in our knapsacks. The women stared with even greater fascination than they had at the outhouse.

All night long I heard roosters crowing. At four in the morning, when the women brought us coffee, I asked why their roosters crowed all night. And I learned that it had not been roosters, but the women in the neighborhood. Rosa, the oldest woman in our family, had been on vigilance duty that night. She crowed to give the signal that all was well, and then the women in the next block crowed, and then the next, every half hour.

When we left, Marta, the daughter of the house, gave us each a doily she had crocheted. They had nothing, and yet they gave us each a gift. We still treasure them in our home in West Virginia. As we turned to wave good-bye that morning, I saw the parrots drinking out of our coffee mugs, and suddenly I realized what the birds were saying. They were squawking: "*Sandino Vive*" and "*No Pasaran.*"

That day we traveled to a town on the border called San Francisco del Norte. A few years before, the contras had killed all the men in the town. One young man's heart had been ripped out of his body. But the women stayed, determined to rebuild their homes. Part of every trip Margie organized was a visit to a border town, to pray with the women and be present and show our support as North Americans.

For hours our group rode toward the border, standing up in two trucks. Men and women with rifles rode with us. Then the lead truck, in which Margie was riding, swerved over to the side of the road and we passed it. It didn't seem fair to leave Margie to be covered with the clouds of dust we were churning up, but it turned out that the roads had recently been mined, and the Nicaraguans wanted to make sure that if any truck got blown up, it wouldn't be Margie's.

It was unbelievably moving to meet with the mothers of San

Francisco del Norte. They were younger than we were, and they had already seen their children killed. And yet, they were staying, and even planting flowers in the ruins of their houses. They told us what we had heard so many times before, in the villages, in the factories, and meetings with government officials. "I am a Christian and a Sandinista and this is the church of my Christ. This is the revolution that my Christ would live. My God would want children to be fed and to learn to read." And these were the people our government were denouncing as atheistic Communists!

We met Fernando Cardenal, the minister of education, who was a Jesuit. Later, in December that year, Pope John Paul II forced him to leave the Jesuits because he would not abandon his post in the government.

One afternoon we met Nora Astorga, a heroine of the revolution, who had lured a notorious general of the Somoza government's National Guard to her house where he was killed by the Sandinistas. The United States refused to accept her as ambassador from Nicaragua—the general, of course, turned out to have been working for the C.I.A. But she was ambassador to the United Nations, before she died of cancer in 1988. She was a beautiful, strong woman, and she gave us an intricately carved gourd which we always keep in a special place.

The high point of our trip was the celebration of International Women's Day. Everywhere we went, men and women congratulated us for being women. That night, very late, we went to an amphitheater carved out of the inside of an extinct volcano. A huge crowd was watching women on the stage singing and dancing. As our little group came in, Margie walked down the long flight of steps, and people began applauding and calling out "*Compañera de la paz.*" It was wonderful.

Over and over again during our trip, women had said to us: "Go home and tell the truth of what you see." It seemed the very least we could do. We later spoke to church groups in Charleston, to the men's business club, to colleges, and to the Council on Agency Executives. Only a few people accused us of having been brainwashed by the Sandinistas. We were very happy when, a year later, the first Witness for Peace group of American citizens gathered in West Virginia and went to Nicaragua to be present on the border with Honduras to try to prevent contras from crossing on killing raids.

In Nicaragua, every Thursday morning at seven-thirty, Americans would gather in front of the U.S. Embassy to pray and speak and protest U.S. intervention. We stood with them when we were there, and when we came back to Charleston we stood in front of the federal building every Thursday morning, carrying signs and marching around with a little group. We did that for three years, until people began waving signs out of passing bus windows reading ''Please change your signs,'' and we figured everyone who might pay attention had noticed us already.

The most important thing we learned in Nicaragua is that the struggle there is really no different from the struggle in West Virginia. Here, as there, most of the people are poor. The land in Central America is owned by a few, and the people who depend upon it for life are kept without education or health care or alternatives. In West Virginia, most of the land is owned by giant corporations, who hold it for future mineral development. The poor people who live on that land, wherever they can find a nook or a hollow where they are allowed to live, have inadequate schools, no health clinics, and no opportunity. When they organize, they are accused of being subversive. And yet, we have met women living in those remote hollows who have borne a number of children by the time they are twenty, who carry water from their wells, and survive the winter eating squirrel they have caught, and vegetables and fruit they have grown and canned. And yet they still plant flowers. Like their sisters in Nicaragua and El Salvador and all over the world, they are noble and brave.

I don't think Pat and I ever spoke out loud what we had decided. We just agreed, without needing to speak, that we would do all we could, however we could, to help those women claim the dignity they deserve.

Twenty-two: Speaking Out

PAT

"A diversity of opinions regarding abortion exists among committed Catholics," read the opening of the statement Margie Tuite showed us in September of 1984.

"I can certainly agree with that," said Barbara, and she signed her name.

"Of course," I said, and down went my name. "Patricia Hussey, Sisters of Notre Dame."

It didn't seem to be a very big deal at the time.

Looking back, I believe Barbara and I signed that statement because we had finally realized that we, too, are *women*. That moment of recognition—"Aha! *I* am one of *them*"—is a crucial turning point. So many women I have known have tried so hard, so understandably hard, to avoid admitting that they are members of a group being denied justice. Each one tries to explain the riddle of her life by a "difference": poor or rich, single or married, white or black, gay or straight, smart or stupid. The "difference," in fact, is that we are all female.

I think that I was trying to choose a protective difference—to avoid being merely female—when I entered the convent. Becoming a nun made me special, and separate, and then I would never have to deal with the contradictions of being human and a female. None of that was conscious, of course. Nor do I regret my years as a nun. It was, indeed, my vocation. But it turned out that there is no way to avoid the contradictions. Certainly not inside the Catholic church.

The Aha! moment came for me when Barbara and I sat in the amphitheater inside an extinct volcano in Nicaragua and watched

197

our beloved Margie Tuite being applauded by the crowd. It was
International Women's Day, March 8, 1984, and I felt the power
of sisterhood. We are together, we all want the same thing, no
matter who we are or where, I thought. We want dignity, and
respect, and justice. I want it for these women. And I want it
for me.

It certainly took me a long time to reach that moment—years
of studying and discussion and acting and being pushed by
friends who had already acquired the courage to act for themselves. One big shove for both of us had come in 1982, when
we were still new in Charleston. Women from the local Wom-
en's Health Center and from the Charleston chapters of the
National Organization for Women and the National Abortion
Rights Action League asked us to testify against a bill before
the legislature which required girls under eighteen to have
parental permission for an abortion. It was called the Parental
Notification Bill.

We had never before been asked to take a public position
on a reproductive rights issue. We knew we would be asking
for trouble from the diocese. But I couldn't ignore what I had
learned about the reality of some teenage women's lives. What
if Elizabeth, from the Long Lane School, had had to get
permission from her vile father before she could have an
abortion? Parental devotion is a nice ideal, but it cannot be
legislated.

The West Virginia capitol is a fine building, full of long,
echoing marble corridors. As we walked through them that day,
we had to pass a gauntlet of right-to-life demonstrators. It wasn't
hard to pick them out. They all wore red roses on their lapels,
and little gold pins shaped like tiny baby feet or fetuses curled
up in the traditional fetal position. For some mysterious reason
they also chose severe white makeup and heavily rouged cheeks.
One woman, who was a dead ringer for Marcel Marceau, was
holding up a sign reading ''You were a fetus once.''

We testified in 1982 and again in 1983, speaking about what we
had seen in Covenant House. We asked the legislators to consider a fifteen-year-old girl who came to us when her mother
forced her into prostitution to earn money for her mother's drugs.
We talked about a fourteen-year-old girl who had run away and
had been living in an abandoned garage. Her father had been
sexually abusing her. If these women had become pregnant and

wanted an abortion, would it have helped them to have required that they ask their parents' permission?

"Are you aware," Barbara asked the legislators, "that in two years the Sexual Assault Information Center of Charleston counted forty-two cases of rape and incest reported on girls age one to ten, seventy-five on girls eleven to fifteen, and sixty-two on young women between sixteen and twenty?"

The legislature, 90 percent men, passed the Parental Notification Bill despite our appeals.

"I wonder how soon we will hear from the church?" I said to Barbara as we started work the day after our testimony. After all, parental notification bills were and are part of the harassing tactics being introduced by the right-to-life movement all across the country, and the Catholic church was and is coordinating the right-to-life movement.

Sure enough, the morning after we testified, the phone rang in Covenant House. It was a local pastor, the one who had wanted us to teach catechism classes. We had not heard from him since our introductory visit, even though he was theoretically part of the ecumenical council supporting Covenant House. (That financial support was withdrawn when we became publicly pro-choice, although they still send food.)

"What are you saying? What are you doing?" he demanded.

"I will be very happy to send our statement right over," I said.

The next thing we knew, he had informed his Sunday mass congregation that we had not been speaking for the church when we testified against the Parental Notification Bill. We knew that. We had been speaking as codirectors of Covenant House.

Oddly enough, we heard nothing more from the local diocese about our testimony until a year later, when we clashed with the bishop on an entirely different subject, but one about which the church feels equally passionate concern. I refer, of course, to real estate.

This time, we were not speaking as codirectors of Covenant House. We were speaking as nuns, as members of the discipleship of equals, as unwelcome disturbers of false peace and complacency.

Joseph Hodges was the bishop of the West Virginia diocese. He had, in 1975, strongly endorsed the pastoral letter on Appalachia, "This Land Is Home to Me," which had clearly set out the economic disparities in West Virginia. "We must LISTEN to the vast majority of plain people who would not be called poor, but who are not rich, and who increasingly share in the powerlessness of the poor,'' insisted the letter.

In 1982 Bishop Hodges, by then in his seventies, announced that he was going to go ahead with plans to build a $3.2 million pastoral center in the affluent Charleston suburb of South Hills. (It ended up costing $6 million.) There were already three retreat centers in West Virginia, a number so overly sufficient for the needs of the 5 percent of the state's population that is Catholic that people were booking into them for hunting and ski trips and small conventions.

At the same time, more and more people were coming into Covenant House every day. Things were particularly tough in Charleston. Unemployment in the state was the highest in the nation. Coal mines and steel mills were closing almost daily. In the counties surrounding Charleston, the statistics were horrifying. In Clay County, 32 percent of the entire population was living below the poverty line. In Mingo, Lincoln, and Logan counties there was almost no public transportation, certainly none to South Hills. In Lincoln County, the infant mortality rate had quadrupled in the previous four years. Surely, we thought, there had to be a better way to spend those millions than on a fancy building.

Barbara and I had been meeting every six weeks with some people we called our area church group. They were thirteen nuns, priests, and lay people from the southern counties of the state. All of us were working in some kind of ministry to the poor, and we met to discuss our continuing efforts to carry out the aims of the bishop's pastoral letter on Appalachia.

When we heard about the bishop's building plans, we stepped up our meeting schedule. A pamphlet was put together listing the critical needs of our area and asking the bishop to stop the project, at least until he had come to Charleston and listened to the people. We printed quotations drawn from the pastoral letter all over the pamphlet about the necessity of listening. And we said: ''We respectfully propose the beginning of a serious and open dialogue among the people of southern West Virginia and with the church hierarchy.''

No response.

A delegation went to Wheeling and asked the bishop to stop the process until he came and listened.

He refused.

Meeting after meeting was held, and things began to get a

little absurd. People who worked for the diocese were told they would be fired if they attended our meetings. One ordained minister who was a friend of the bishop lurked outside to see who might be going inside. This standoff went on for eight months.

So our group decided to stage a protest. We didn't work for the diocese and we couldn't be fired, so everyone got dressed for the event in our apartment in the back of Covenant House. A few people dressed up in clown costumes so they couldn't be identified. Also, it seemed a cheerful idea. Two Jesuit priests in our group, who were working in rural parishes, decided to disguise themselves. One put on a clown costume, and the other delighted us by appearing as Robin Hood.

It was a nice old-fashioned protest. About twenty of us stood along the highway, looking much more bedraggled than we felt, handing out pamphlets and a press release. We tied helium balloons snappily printed with "Human Needs, Not Buildings" onto the bulldozer. After a prayer and a song, we all went home, a day's work in the cause of justice well done.

Looking back, I can see that the press statement the group handed out might have caused Bishop Hodges some pain. We compared his stubbornness to a corrupt political machine. The group, we said, perceived him to be using a paternalistic, autocratic model of church. The money for the building was not his, it was *ours,* the people in the pews, we said. And we accused him of "a blatant attack on human rights" in his actions to stop our protests.

Not that we were wrong, but it is possible that we had failed to advance the dialogue in a sufficiently welcoming manner. By the time Bishop Hodges got to the last sentence of our press release—the sentence that was central to the pastoral letter and to our point—he might not have been open to the idea that "The people themselves must shape their own destiny."

The next morning, just as Barbara was cutting the picture of our clowns out of the local paper, the telephone rang. She picked it up and immediately started sputtering.

"I can't believe it, I just can't believe it," she kept repeating.

"What? What? What's happened?" I asked.

"Hodges has dismissed the Jesuits from the diocese," she said.

"I guess the Robin Hood costume was the last straw," I said.

"Don't you laugh, Patricia Hussey," snapped Barbara. "This is serious. What about our right to dissent? What about our right to express our conscience? We have to stand with the priests on this. It could happen to us!''

She turned out to be right. And, as usual, she bore the worst of the fight. Sometimes, it pays to be shy and quiet.

BARBARA

Pat is always seen as the reasonable and flexible one. I'm the one who makes the noise. One friend in Charleston, who supplied the balloons for our anti-building protest, once said that Pat makes the bullets and I shoot them. Maybe. But I've noticed that even when Pat does do the talking, I'm the one who gets the blame. We deal with it by making sure that no matter which one of us is talking, we both say the same thing.

Until the summer of 1983, we had never felt that we were speaking alone. Not only did we always reflect with each other and with our local church group before we took a position, we also consulted with our provincial groups. They were the people we turned to for support and understanding. That deep familial feeling is the reason that the six Sisters of Notre Dame who were part of our church group in West Virginia wrote to our provincial teams in Boston, Connecticut, Maryland, and California asking them to write to Bishop Hodges in support of the two Jesuits he had dismissed.

Elizabeth Michaels, who was one of the leadership persons in Rome at the time, happened to be visiting her home province in Boston and she saw the letter. She duly wrote to Bishop Hodges saying she hoped he would take another look at the situation.

The bishop wrote back to Elizabeth saying he had, in effect, made up his mind. Then he turned to the annoying problem of me: ''I want to share with you my concern about Sister Barbara Ferraro, a member of your congregation.'' I had been causing trouble by my criticism, he wrote, and furthermore (he suddenly thought it worth mentioning), he had a copy of my presentation on the Parental Notification Bill, which ''greatly disturbed the West Virginia Pro-Life Committee, Catholic Community Services, and the Social Ministry Department of the Diocese of Wheeling-Charleston.''

He concluded: ''In responding to your letter, I considered it important to inform you of my awareness, concern, and close observation of Sister Barbara's criticism and actions in the

Charleston area." In ecclesiastical language, this letter was one step short of a death threat.

No mention of Pat, you will notice. Even though she had done the actual speaking at our second appearance before the legislature on the same bill.

Bishop Hodges sent copies of that letter to diocesan officials and the offices of Catholic social services in West Virginia, but nothing was sent to me. The first I heard of it was when I got a phone call from one of my team leaders in Boston, Marna Rodgers, who said: "The team wants to see you when you come home. We've gotten a letter from the bishop we'd like to talk about."

"Gee," I said, "I'd like a copy of the letter."

"No," said Marna.

"Why not, if it concerns me? Duplicate letters have already been sent to everyone else in the whole world! And they have nothing to do with me."

"Well, you can't. It was sent to Elizabeth."

Finally, I managed to get a copy of the letter. Pat and I were livid when we read it! Why hadn't the bishop written to me? Did he think the good mothers would knock me back into line? It never occurred to me that he would succeed, that my progressive province—on the cutting edge of social justice issues—would be unnerved by a letter from a distant bishop.

I told the leadership team I would be very happy to talk about the letter. In fact, I *wanted* a meeting. Pat and I both knew we were at some kind of turning point and we needed challenging and healthy discussion.

"It is time to ask ourselves some questions," said Pat. "If we are going to continue to take our constitution seriously, we need to be ready for the consequences. It looks like this is a good moment to prepare."

We took time with each other, and with our area church group, and wrote down our thoughts. We had already sent our testimony on the Parental Notification Bill to our leadership groups, as we always did whenever we made an important and possibly controversial public statement. I remember writing a note at the time saying "This may be controversial and we want you to know what is going on." Now, before Pat and I left for our summer vacations, we sent to Boston a list of some of the questions I wanted to discuss at my meeting with the leadership.

Maybe we should not be involved in the abortion question?

What position should we be taking as Sisters of Notre Dame? Would they help me know whether I should be involved in the political aspects of the question? Isn't it important that we begin to discuss what can happen to nuns who continue to be public and disagree with the bishop or the church? It was already happening with the Sisters of Mercy. What about the Sisters of Notre Dame?

In bright August sunshine, I drove from my parents' house in Cambridge to my old school, Emmanuel College. I was excited to be going "home" and looking forward to my meeting.

I should have been warned that something was wrong when I arrived and was told that only one member of the team could be available to see me, Pat Johnson. But I hurried innocently on to her office.

"I know you're busy, but I am really interested in taking some time to discuss the questions I sent," I said.

"Well, Barbara," she answered, "the team is not interested in talking about them. We feel the problems you have with the bishop in West Virginia are questions of style and personality."

My jaw dropped and my eyes widened.

"What do you mean?" I asked.

What she meant, she told me, with the straightforward executioner's frankness unique to nuns, was that I was considered a violent woman. A woman seeking power. A woman who insisted that everyone else agree with her.

I burst into tears.

"How can you say this of me?" I protested. "You don't even know me. You have never worked with me. You have never lived with me. If I am seeking power, why am I living at Covenant House when I have a doctorate and I could be teaching in Chicago?"

"Even if I had never met you before today," she said, "I would make the same assessment. It's sort of like a gestalt moment."

Even though I couldn't stop crying, I was smart enough by that time of my life to know *I* wasn't the issue.

"You are personalizing this issue," I told her, "instead of dealing with it. I could accept your calling me energetic and involved and very committed. Yes, I am direct, and even hot-blooded. But I am not violent. And the real issue isn't Barbara

Ferraro, it is the work of all of us in the area church in West Virginia.''

No good. Nor did I get any support from the rest of the team. Over the weekend I asked the other team members, Marna Rodgers and Ginny Scally, if they agreed with Pat Johnson's description of me as a violent, power-driven woman. And they said Yes! I was devastated. Marna and I had entered together; she *did* know me.

Many months later I saw Pat Johnson, and she admitted that she *had* personalized the issue, that she just didn't like my style. But it still hurt. And it gave me no satisfaction, a year and a half later when the Vatican was threatening me with dismissal, to remind my province that I had asked for direction as a member of the community. If I had gotten a response on the issue in 1983, even if the province had asked me to avoid becoming involved in the politics of abortion until the community had established its position, I would have been open to their feelings. But all I heard was that I was a violent woman.

The next weekend was the annual assembly of my Boston province. Usually, it was my favorite meeting of the entire year, but this time I could barely hold up my head. Incredulous, I listened to Ginny speaking at the opening evening session. She was asking the Notre Dames to support Agnes Mary Mansour. A Sister of Mercy, Agnes Mary had been appointed head of the state Department of Social Services by Michigan's Governor James Blanchard. At first, her order and her local archbishop enthusiastically approved her new ministry. Yet, on the grounds that part of her department's budget was spent on Medicaid abortions (it was less than one percent of the total), conservative Catholics started a cruel campaign which eventually aroused the Vatican. Agnes Mary was forced to leave her community, sorrowfully noting that her vow of service to the poor, the sick, the uneducated, and the oppressed was finally more meaningful to her than her vow of obedience to a church that seemed more interested in control than in its Gospel calling.

Of course the Sisters of Notre Dame needed to support Agnes Mary. But her struggle was only going to be the beginning. The burning question of the assembly was how to protect *ourselves*. And that seems to be the hardest thing in the world for women to do.

One sister got the point. She stood up and asked: "What are we going to do if and when this happens to one of our sisters?"

They apparently did not know it already was happening to one of their sisters! Nobody said a word. I didn't say a word. How could I? I would have sounded violent, even power-hungry. I had been, for the time being, effectively silenced.

Worst of all, for the first time in twenty-one years, I felt outside the circle of my community.

Pat drove us back to Charleston, staring straight ahead, thinking and thinking and thinking. She was shocked by Boston's reaction. Her own province had been very supportive.

"Well," she finally said, "we know you are not the only nun caught between your conscience and the church hierarchy. We know the issue of abortion is not going to go away. And we know our provinces don't have the answers. So we will have to find some answers for all of us."

"Grumph," I said.

"Barb!" said Pat, suddenly inspired. "We're going to the Women-Church conference in Chicago next month. We'll be able to find out what is going on all over the country."

Women-Church groups are feminist base communities, small circles of women who share their stories and their faith, help each other to live in solidarity, and try to create rituals which reach back to the roots of our religious traditions. Three feminist theologians defined Women-Church with great clarity.

Rosemary Radford Ruether said it is "a feminist network of liturgical, home-based communities built on scripture and political practice."

Elisabeth Schüssler Fiorenza said Women-Church is "self-identified women and women-identified men in a discipleship of equals where women are no longer the 'other.' "

And Mary E. Hunt described it as a movement of "women who are religious agents (moral agents), justice-seeking friends moving in the direction of change."

Pat and I belong to a Women-Church group in Charleston. It blossomed spontaneously out of the seeking of several women of different faiths soon after we came back from the conference in Chicago. The circle of our Women-Church group sustains our faith in the word of God and it is where we feel closest to the Spirit. We are church to one another.

Nearly fourteen hundred women came together that November, 1983, to a conference titled "Woman Church Speaks."

They were seeking a vision of "church" that would speak to women's experience. The Women-Church movement had evolved from the insights of the Women's Ordination Conference, and had gained urgency after the complete rejection by the official church of our plea for full participation.

The conference made Pat and me feel that we had come out of exile and found a way to name and claim and celebrate our lives. Nearly all the women there were Roman Catholics, all on the same progressive wavelength, and most of them way ahead of us. Every moment was filled with spiritual affirmation and enrichment. And then we found a workshop addressing abortion—the issue we most needed help with.

Until then we had always faced the abortion issue on a case-by-case, situation-by-situation basis. At the workshop we attended that day, we began to understand that the ambiguities and "What ifs?" we had seen individual people struggling with were infinite. Every woman alive could, at some time, face a decision about whether to go through with a pregnancy. No woman's experience exactly duplicates another's. Eventually we would come to believe that no one except each individual woman is ultimately capable of deciding what she should do.

We listened to Frances Kissling, who had been the director of Catholics for a Free Choice since 1982. Founded in 1973 by four feisty Irish-Catholic women in New York City, Catholics for a Free Choice (CFFC) is a national educational organization. According to its mission statement, it is dedicated to supporting "the right to legal reproductive health care, especially to family planning and abortion. CFFC also works to reduce the incidence of abortion and to increase women's choices in child-bearing and child-rearing through advocacy of social and economic programs for women, families and children."

Frances Kissling is a large, jolly, brilliant woman. She often repeats what we heard her say that day: "The Catholic church, or hierarchy, has never been honest about its position on abortion." We did not guess how important she would become to our lives.

We listened to Marjorie Maguire, Doctor of Sacred Theology, speak of the wrenching personal experience that had motivated her and her husband, Dan, a professor of ethics at Marquette University, to write *Abortion: A Guide to Making Ethical Choices*. After watching their twelve-year-old son die a lingering death from a genetically transferred disease, they had decided that for them, if prenatal testing showed that a second pregnancy would also produce a doomed child, an abortion would be a moral choice.

Now we knew that wherever we stood on the issue of choice, we did not stand alone. And we knew that not all Catholics, not even all the most faithful and thoughtful Catholics, agree with the Vatican's teaching that abortion is always, in every case, an unspeakable crime.

Twenty-three: Going Public

BARBARA

"We need Margie," said Pat. We were driving back to Charleston from a meeting of our area church group. It had been an uncomfortable afternoon. The aftereffects of our protest against Bishop Hodges's multi-million-dollar Pastoral Center had divided us. It was midsummer of 1984 and we were still blaming each other for what had happened. Some of us felt it had been a bad idea altogether, some thought we had gone too far and cost the Jesuits their jobs. And some thought we hadn't gone far enough.

"Everybody in the group loves Margie. We all trust her. Maybe she would come down and help us work this out," Pat said.

Margie never turned down a plea for help. In mid-September we picked her up at the Charleston Airport. She was stopping off on what would prove to be an exhausting trip from Chicago to El Salvador, and she was so sick she should have been home in bed. The long hour's ride to Chapmanville was visibly hard on her. But the Spirit came back to us when she arrived.

Chapmanville is a little town in Logan County where another Sister of Notre Dame was pastor of St. Barbara's Parish. (There are many parishes in West Virginia run by women, a fact of modern Catholic life that the church covers up by sending in a visiting priest to perform the male magic of the Consecration on weekends.) Fifteen of us gathered in her house to dissect our feelings, conflicts, miseries, and strategies.

No one was better at the art of "When you, I feel, because"

than Margie, and by the end of the next day we all felt healed and happier than we had in months.

That night the two of us took Margie out to dinner at the Firehouse Restaurant in Charleston. We knew she was feeling better when she started thumping on the table and denouncing Archbishop John O'Connor of New York. (He was elevated to Cardinal O'Connor shortly after the election in which he played such a significant part.)

"Oh, he infuriates me," she fumed. "The hypocrisy! Claiming to revere the sanctity of life when he supports Reagan's deadly policies in Central America. He is a Republican. The nerve of him, using the weight of his office to influence the Catholic vote."

O'Connor, along with Boston conservative Bishop Bernard Law, had been carrying on an increasingly strident campaign against Geraldine Ferraro, the Democratic candidate for Vice President. Back in June, before the convention had even come to order in San Francisco, he had held a television news conference and declared, "I do not see how a Catholic in good conscience can vote for an individual expressing himself or herself as favoring abortion."

Geraldine Ferraro had been very clear about her position on abortion ever since she was first elected to the United States Congress from Queens, New York. "Personally I accept the church's doctrine that abortion is wrong, but I cannot impose my religious views on others," she often said. As a matter of conscience, she supported freedom of choice. The deciding factor, for her, had been the brutal cases of rape and incest and child abuse she had had to deal with in her time as head of the Special Victim's Bureau in the District Attorney's Office in Queens County. The principle of freedom of religion and conscience was important to her. That, plus the facts of her lived experiences, led her to disagree with the official church position.

"Her position is exactly the same as Edward Kennedy's and Mario Cuomo's," stormed Margie. "I've never heard them attacked by the church. Something tells me this has more to do with the fact that she is a woman and a feminist than it has to do with abortion."

Just a few days before Margie came to see us, O'Connor had spoken to a group of reporters. This time he accused Ferraro by name, saying she had made statements about Catholic teaching on abortion that were not true. It turned out later that he was talking about a two-year-old letter she had sent out with two other Catholic members of Congress inviting other Catholic representatives to a breakfast sponsored by Catholics for a Free Choice. "The Catholic position on abortion is not monolithic," it said. "There can be a range of personal and political responses to the issue"—the same true statement that was about to get us into trouble.

"I can imagine the pressure she must feel," said Pat. "I really admire her guts."

Geraldine Ferraro was the ideal Catholic woman, one who had once wanted to become a nun. Wife and mother, she went to mass, took Communion, was an active parishioner—she was Catholic to the core. Her family socialized with priests and nuns, and she regularly consulted with the Catholic charities bureaucracies about social welfare issues. She was part of the liberal Catholic establishment. And the conservative Catholic establishment was out to get her.

On Columbus Day she was scheduled to march in the Philadelphia parade. At the last minute she was forced out by John Cardinal Krol, a conservative who had delivered the invocation the night of Ronald Reagan's renomination. He threatened to pull all the Catholic school kids and bands out of the parade if she appeared, saying she was a disgrace to the Italian and Catholic communities.

Geraldine Ferraro was the first Italian-American ever to be nominated for a presidential ticket. And yet, the sons of Italy did not defend her. As a daughter of Italy, I was ashamed and furious and hurt for her.

It had been such a wonderful, wonderful moment when she was nominated! Of course I was delighted that her name was Ferraro. I even imagined I had found a way to make us very distant cousins. But the real joy was to see a woman up on that podium. Everything seemed possible; all the work of the past seemed worth it. I read somewhere that a woman delegate celebrating on the convention floor said, "It seems theological: this is the way the world is supposed to look."

"Instead, it's like a nightmare come true, isn't it?" said Pat. "The pope is dictating policy on American women's lives, and nobody seems to care."

Margie stopped in mid-swallow. "Oh, I almost forgot. I have this statement to show you." And she pulled something out of her bag. It was a piece of paper titled "A Diversity of Opinions Regarding Abortion Exists Among Committed Catholics." As we read it, Margie explained: "It was written in 1983 by Mar-

jorie and Daniel Maguire and Fran Kissling.'' We nodded.
''They circulated it to a number of other theologians and ethi-
cists for comment.''

She leaned forward, spreading out her long fingers on the
tabletop. ''Do you think you can sign it? It's a good, good statement. Geraldine needs to know there are Catholics out here who
support her. She shouldn't be subjected to this public flogging
by the bishops.''

I read the statement quickly, my eye taking in the key phrases:

''Abortion . . . can sometimes be a moral choice.''

''Only 11 percent of Catholics surveyed disapprove of abortion in all circumstances.''

''These opinions have been formed by familiarity with the
actual experiences that lead women to make a decision for abortion.''

''There is no common and constant teaching on ensoulment
in Church doctrine.''

''Therefore, it is necessary that the Catholic community encourage candid and respectful discussion on this diversity of
opinion within the Church . . .''

''. . . public dissent . . . should not be penalized by . . .
religious superiors, church employers or bishops.''

''We believe that Catholics should not seek the kind of
legislation that curtails the legitimate exercise of the freedom
of religion and conscience or discriminates against poor
women.''

The language of the statement seemed a little too churchy
to me, but it said what needed to be said. As far as I was
concerned, at the time, the statement was not supporting
abortion, it was simply calling for a dialogue on the issue.
''Dialogue,'' the way the word is used by the post-conciliar
church, does not mean a quiet chat over tea. The ''dialogue''
which produced the American Bishops' 1983 pastoral letter
on the immorality of nuclear war took three years and involved hundreds of hours of testimony and research and argument. The pastoral letter on the economy, which criticized
the sharp division between rich and poor, was the result of a
''dialogue'' of five years. Both had involved high-level international negotiations, and called forth fierce campaigns of
dissent from conservative American Catholics. But both had
been recognized as part of a necessary and healthy process.
A dialogue on abortion was long overdue.

Most of all, Pat and I signed the statement because, at that particular historical moment, we wanted to stand in sisterhood with Geraldine Ferraro.

Less than a month later, on October 7, 1984, at the height of the presidential campaign, the "Catholic Statement on Pluralism and Abortion" was published by Catholics for a Free Choice as a full-page advertisement in *The New York Times.* * There were ninety-seven signers, including two priests, two religious brothers, and twenty-six nuns from fourteen communities. An asterisk noted that it was only a partial listing. "This statement has been signed by many other Catholics. In addition seventy-five priests, religious and theologians have written that they agree with the Statement but cannot sign because they fear losing their jobs." Did those anonymous signers ever have foresight!

The first we saw of the ad was when it arrived in the mail. A friend had clipped it out of the paper, highlighting our names in yellow and applauding the statement and our courage.

"It is impressive looking, isn't it?" said Pat.

"For sure!" I said. We were very proud of it, carrying it around to meetings and showing it to friends. All the responses we got in the first few weeks were positive. I was particularly happy to get a note from Marna Rodgers. It had been a long, unhappy year since I had been so miserable in Boston, but we had all worked hard to mend the circle and I was grateful to read "Barbara, congratulations! I'm so proud of you and Pat. I saw the *New York Times* ad. It was powerful and so important."

The first response to the *Times* ad from the official hierarchy was a fairly innocuous *pro forma* grumble, printed in a Catholic journal, from John Quinn, the chair of the National Conference of Catholic Bishops. We shrugged our shoulders. "Not to worry," said Pat.

On December 11, at 7:45 in the morning, we heard the phone ringing as we walked through the front door to Covenant House. It was Margie, sniffing out information.

"What are you hearing, Barbara?" she said.

"Nothing," I said, suddenly worried. "Are we supposed to be hearing something?"

*See appendix for complete text.

PAT

Barbara motioned to me, pointing so I would pick up the other telephone.

"What's going on, Margie?" I asked, surprised by the tension in her voice as she greeted me.

"You both should know that the Vatican has issued letters reprimanding nuns for signing the ad," she said. Margie, of course, was a signer herself. "I don't have all the information, just what I've heard through the grapevine. So *please* call me if you hear *anything*. It is serious, Pat and Barbara. It is serious!"

We didn't have time to think about what she had said. Covenant House was open for the day, and the first dozen of the sixty or more people we would be seeing were already waiting in the front room.

As people signed in at the desk to take turns in the shower, wash clothes or see us about arranging payment of their utility bills or rent, we asked for help. "Would someone like to go and get the free newspaper?" "How about if someone puts on the Christmas tree and Hanukkah lights?"

Sally O'Farrell, one of our most valuable volunteers, came in right on time. She was carrying her usual bundle of goodies: sweaters, socks, and large bags for people's laundry. She also had a shopping bag full of Christmas candy and cookies, and makeup for the women. From her post at the front desk, Sally kept track of the laundry detergent, the appointment list, the telephone, and the mail that is delivered in care of us to our visitors.

"Hey, Pat!" I heard a woman named Loretta bellowing from the laundry room. "This dang washing machine isn't working."

"Forget it," I heard Carl, a regular, telling her. "The dryer don't work either."

"Oh great, just great," I said, annoyed. "It's only ten o'clock in the morning and the dryer is already overheated."

As I fiddled with the fuses, Harry, a severely arthritic former railroad worker, peeked through the door and said timidly, "Can I get a change of clothes and some warm gloves?"

I gave him a slip for the clothes closet at St. Mark's Church, but I didn't give him much of smile. The word "reprimand" was still floating uneasily somewhere in the back of my head.

Barbara and I looked out through the half door that separates our office from the main room. There were still a lot of people waiting to be seen, sitting on the unmatched chairs and tattered couch across from Sally's desk. Some more men were huddling just inside the front door, blowing on their hands to warm them from the cold. Christmas carols were playing softly on the radio. A few children sat at their mothers' feet, playing on the floor with blocks and puzzles from the toy box. The front door opened and closed, opened and closed, squeaking every time.

At noon we shut for lunch, and we spent the entire hour sitting in the front office staring silently into our cups of chicken soup. Every once in a while one of us would say, "Well, we shouldn't worry until we know what it is all about."

By mid-afternoon, the weather had turned colder and the atmosphere inside the house had changed. There was a familiar heaviness in the air which always signals some sort of crisis is about to erupt.

Another volunteer, Joe Hodgson, a retired judge, had come in to replace Sally at the front desk. Every seat was filled. I was in the front office with a twenty-year-old man we had never seen before. He was hunched over on the couch, wringing his hands and avoiding my eyes. "I'm all mixed up," he whispered. Tears ran down his face. He wiped them off with the back of his sleeve, and then he sat without speaking for several minutes. I was trying to be present for him, trying to wait for him to be comfortable, but I had both fists clenched in my lap. Some kind of extraordinary chaos seemed to have erupted in the front room.

"My parents were both killed in an accident by a drunk driver," my poor young man sobbed. "I don't know if I want to live or die. My world has crashed in."

Barbara tiptoed in and made a heroic effort to whisper quietly, "I think you'd better come with me." I had never known her to interrupt a counseling session, so I assumed it was extremely important.

"I'll be right back, I'm sorry to leave, everything will be all right," I said, sounding like an idiot, and I turned the hall corner into the main room.

In the middle of the room sat two mentally retarded children. The boy was playing with toys. His sister was sitting next to him, rocking back and forth. As I looked at her, she let out a strangled scream and burst into tears. Abruptly, she stopped screaming and began to pull on tufts of her hair. Tufts were all she had left.

"She's going to chew on her hands next," said Barbara. "She

keeps repeating the same actions." Sure enough, the pathetic girl started gnawing on her fingers.

"Her brother doesn't seem to think much about it," said Joe. "And look at her arms. She's covered with scars. Maybe she isn't just upset. Maybe this is normal."

"But how did they get here?" I asked. We all looked around and Barbara noticed a woman in the sunroom, sitting very still on a rickety chair. "Something's wrong," said Barbara, heading toward her.

"You doin' okay?" asked Barb.

The woman, whose name turned out to be Drema, was ashen and sweating.

"I come in from Huntington with the kids," she said, gasping. "Could you help me find a place to stay?"

"How did you get here?" said Barb.

"We walked the back roads," said Drema. "We was two days at it."

Barbara and I looked at each other, horrified. Huntington is forty miles from Charleston.

"My husband gets drunk and beats up on me and the kids. You know what I'm saying? I had to get away. He don't know where we are." She looked pitiful. "You won't tell him, will ya?"

"No," said Barbara. "We don't tell anyone where people are."

Drema gave a big sigh and shifted a little. "I'm not feeling all that well, either. My heart's bad and I run out of my medicine."

"What are you feeling?" asked Barbara.

"I feel like someone's been standing on my chest all afternoon."

We had become really handy with a blood pressure gauge but we weren't too good with heart attacks. Barbara stayed with Drema, patting her hand, while Joe called an ambulance, and I went to see what was going on in the laundry room.

"Give me that!"

"No. It's mine."

Two men were about to kill each other, if I didn't kill them first.

"What's the problem?" I snarled.

"He took my comb."

"Hell I did, it's mine, he took it out of my coat pocket."

The patient minister to God's people did not care that people who have very few possessions can be desolated by the loss of a comb. "Quit it, just quit it right now!" I shouted. "That's enough! Get another comb at the desk and quiet down!"

They departed, muttering as they fled out the front door: "Hey, if *Pat*'s mad, we better come back tomorrow." A few people followed them. I never get mad, or rarely, but even so, I don't think I was any more terrifying than the girl pulling out her hair under the Christmas tree.

The ambulance came. Drema kept insisting, "I don't care to go to the hospital." Barbara kept reassuring her, "We'll make sure your children are taken care of," and she sent me a desperate look meaning "How are we going to deal with this?"

And just at that precise moment, Joe said, "Pat, I hate to disturb you, but you have a telephone call from Rome."

Wonderful. Just what we needed.

"Hello," I said.

"This is Sister Catherine Hughes. Whom am I speaking to?" said a distant voice. Catherine Hughes was the general superior of the Sisters of Notre Dame at our international center in Rome.

"This is Pat, Catherine."

"Is it possible to talk with you and Barbara right now?"

Well, it couldn't get any worse. And I didn't want to have to call back to Rome on our phone bill.

I covered up the speaker with my hand and yelled to Barbara, "Pick up the phone, it's Catherine Hughes in Rome. Come on, I'm not joking. I'm dead serious."

So there we were, each on an extension phone, twenty feet from life, death, and anarchy in our front room.

"Are you both all right?" said Catherine, pleasantly. I had met her at the 1978 Chapter Meeting.

"Yes," we said. Merry as elves.

"Well, I know this is not the best time or way to give you this news, but I feel it is important for you to know directly," she said. "The Congregation for Religious and Secular Institutes has issued a letter to our congregation. It is a rather *harsh* letter. I am sending a copy immediately to you in the mail."

We knew the letter would be about our signatures on the *New York Times* ad. Catherine told us it asked us to retract or we would face dismissal from our communities.

It was nice of her to warn us. It would have been even nicer if the Vatican had sent *us* the letter. But that's not the way hierarchy works.

"Both of your provincial teams have been contacted. They will follow through with you in the States," Catherine concluded. "I am leaving for Africa but I'll be in the States in March. We will talk then. Take care of yourselves."

We said thank you and hung up. The ambulance drivers wheeled Drema out the door. We walked the children, Rheba and Billy Joe, across the street to the shelter where a protective service worker would take them to temporary foster homes.

I walked back into the front office. The young man who had just lost his parents was still there, looking at me hopefully.

"I guess we are both in big trouble now," I said.

Twenty-four: The Vatican 24

BARBARA

A few days after the telephone call from Catherine Hughes, Pat and I received Xeroxed copies of the letter in the mail. *Sacra Congregatio pro Religiosis et Institutis Saecularibus* said the letterhead, which was also adorned with the seal of the Vatican. The Sacred Congregation for Religious and Secular Institutes, or CRIS, is the Vatican office that validates religious communities of men and women. It has the authority to approve or disapprove of a congregation's mission and goals as stated in a constitution. By extension, CRIS claims the authority to approve or disapprove of a congregation's members—whatever the congregation may think.

It was an extremely harsh document: peremptory, authoritarian, absolute, and deliberately threatening. But the most unnerving thing about it was that it was addressed not to us, but to Catherine Hughes, in Rome.

Dear Sister,

In the Sunday, October 7, 1984, edition of *The New York Times* there appeared on page E7 a full page advertisement, entitled "A Diversity of Opinions Regarding Abortion Exists Among Committed Catholics." Among the misleading and erroneous statements of the ad is the following: "Statements of recent Popes and of the Catholic hierarchy have condemned the direct termination of pre-natal life as morally wrong in all circumstances. There is the mistaken belief in American society that this is the only legitimate Catholic position."

This attitude in respect to the Magisterium is in contradiction

219

to the teaching of the Church (cf. *Dogmatic Constitution of the Church, 25*). The signers of the ad are, therefore, seriously lacking in "religious submission of will and mind" to the Magisterium.

Moreover, the Second Vatican Council, recalling to mind the constant teaching of the Church, affirmed that abortion is "an unspeakable crime" (cf. *Pastoral Constitution on the Church in the Modern World, 51*). The Revised Code of Canon Law punishes abortion as "an offense against human life" and declares that "a person who procures a successful abortion incurs an automatic (*latae sententiae*) excommunication" (Can. 1398).

On the basis of what has just been said, you well understand that "the pernicious upholding or spreading of doctrines condemned by the Magisterium of the Church," especially on an issue of such gravity, is a flagrant scandal and is sufficient cause for the dismissal of a religious guilty of such conduct (cf. Can. 698,1).

I request you, therefore, to direct Sr. Barbara Ferraro and Sr. Patricia Hussey, members of your Institute, who undersigned the declaration in the above mentioned newspaper to make a public retraction. A notification of the retraction shall be sent to this Congregation for Religious and Secular Institutes.

In the event that the religious refuse and in fact do not make a public retraction, you are to proceed in accordance with Canon 696.1 and as directed by Canon 697 to warn the religious with an explicit threat of dismissal from the Institute. It will be necessary to arrive at this step—even though to our mutual regret—if the religious remain obstinately disobedient to the Church and to you, the Superior.

With sentiments of deep concern for the well-being of religious life and of gratitude for your cooperation in this serious and sensitive matter, I remain,

Sincerely yours in Christ.

The letter was signed by Archbishop Jean Jerome Hamer (now a cardinal), Pope John Paul II's personal choice for the job of enforcing discipline on canonical orders, and by the second in command, Archbishop Vincenzo Fagiolo. We remembered, with a chill, that Hamer had signed the Vatican declaration on the impossibility of ordaining women.

Pat was ominously silent. She was staring at me, but she wasn't seeing me. I looked down at my own hands, holding my copy of the letter. Everything in the room seemed weirdly remote and insubstantial. The part of me that is a trained therapist must have switched on in self-defense because a voice in my head said, Barbara, what are you feeling right now?

I am feeling small, and bewildered, and foolish, I thought.

Do those feelings remind you of anything? prodded my professional self.

I sat there, trying to catch hold of my feelings and name them. Embarrassment . . . Humiliation . . . Caught out in something naughty . . . What ever made me think Covenant House was so important? . . .

And then the source of those feelings began to come back to me in haunting voices: "We don't ask questions, Barbara, dear . . . You must mortify your curiosity" . . . "Sister Mary Kevin, may I ask forgiveness for speaking on the stairs?" . . . "It is not possible for you to major in mathematics, Barbara, dear."

I felt like a novice. A pre-Vatican II novice. I was *supposed* to feel that way. That is the kind of nun the Vatican thought I should be.

And how do you feel now? I asked myself.

I am not a novice, I answered myself. I am forty-one years old. I have spent all the years of my adult life trying to discern God's will for me and to act on it. That is why I signed the ad.

Try to remember those years in the days ahead, myself warned myself.

Pat was still staring.

"Pat," I said, "what are your feelings right now?"

She blinked. "My feelings?" she said. "You mean how do I feel about reading a letter that dismisses my conscience and my intelligence as 'lack of submission'? How do I feel about knowing that a man in Rome can threaten to take away my work and my vocation and my community without even having the common decency to write to me personally?"

"How do you feel?" I repeated.

"I feel insulted," Pat said.

* * *

The two priests and two religious brothers who had signed the ad quickly "regularized" their relationship with the Vatican and were never heard from again. The sixty-seven distinguished lay Catholic signers received no letters from the Vatican demanding that they recant (although they did suffer other reprisals). If the real issue had been the Catholic church's insistence on the sanctity of fetal life, surely all the signers would have been threatened with wholesale excommunication. But the real issue for the Vatican, it was already becoming clear, was not moral principle, but obedience to the patriarchal hierarchy.

Of the twenty-six nuns who had signed the ad, one was never identified, and one was Sister Rose Dominic Trapasso, a Maryknoll whose order fell under the jurisdiction of the Congregation for the Evangelization of Peoples. She eventually received a letter from her superiors but the issue somehow quietly disappeared.

Twenty-four nuns were left: the Vatican 24.

Since our call for dialogue with the Vatican had been so emphatically rejected, we would have to dialogue with each other to plan our next step. On December 18, lay signers and nun signers from all over the country flew to Washington, D.C., for a meeting.

December is the busiest, saddest month at Covenant House. The merrier the holiday, the more people we see suffering from extreme depression, loneliness, and loss. The last thing Pat and I wanted to do was to abandon everybody and try to find a seat on a flight to Washington.

"If the Vatican had done it on purpose, they couldn't have found a worse time of the year to threaten the nun signers," I complained as we drove to the airport.

"Well, at least we know the Vatican isn't being cruel on purpose," said Pat.

"What makes you so sure?" I said.

"Because the Vatican doesn't know who we are, or what kind of work we do, or what kind of people depend on us," said Pat. "We are just nuns, to be seen in 'religious garb' and never heard."

Early that morning I had gotten up as usual, finished some packing, and spent time meditating. By seven o'clock there was still no sign of Pat. I decided she probably needed some extra sleep, but by seven-thirty I thought I'd better wake her up. Just as I headed toward her door she emerged in her bathrobe and slippers, carrying a pencil and paper in her hand.

"You okay?" I asked.

"I've been lying in bed thinking," she said.

She tapped the piece of paper with the pencil. "One last time," she said, "let's be as clear as we possibly can about where we stand before we get into this meeting. And let's write it down."

First, we agreed we would not sign anything, because whatever we might sign would be misinterpreted for its own purposes by the Vatican.

Second, there was no possibility of our agreeing to recant, because we had done nothing to recant from. How could we recant from a call for dialogue?

And finally, were we willing to face the worst?

"There is a very good chance that at the end of this we will no longer be nuns," said Pat.

We looked at each other. No longer nuns? What would that mean? Who would we be? What would happen to us?

Finally, I said, "I don't really see that we have a choice anymore."

"Neither do I," said Pat. "So, let's go to Washington."

When I saw who had come together in that meeting room in Washington, my first thought was "Oh! This is *wonderful*! We can take this on and win."

Pat and I, arriving from the hills of West Virginia with our knapsacks, were tiny minnows in a group of very impressive marlin. We knew personally very few of the eighteen nun signers who were present but we knew *of* almost everyone. We knew them from their talks at Women's Ordination Conferences and at Women-Church meetings; from their work on peace and human rights issues around the globe, particularly in South Africa and Central America. We knew their writings on feminist theology and ethics. We had studied their examinations of justice issues within the Roman Catholic church and society.

First, I saw Margie Tuite. She pulled Pat and me over to a corner of the room and said: "I have a gift for you." She pulled a package out of her bag. Wrapped inside were two hand-carved mahogany crosses she had brought back from El Salvador. They hang in our bedrooms in Charleston today. We couldn't have guessed that day how precious they would become to us, and we teased her.

"Are you feeling guilty, Margie, because you made us sign the ad?" we asked.

"No, no, no," she said. But she didn't laugh.

Next I saw old friends and colleagues from the women's group Margie had organized in Chicago. Judith Vaughan, a Sister of St. Joseph, had come from Los Angeles where she ran a shelter for women and children. Donna Quinn, a Dominican, had served a term as president of the National Coalition of American Nuns (NCAN). So much experience, of so many kinds, was present that day. In 1982, Ann Patrick Ware, a Sister of Loretto, had been one of the leaders of the National Coalition of American Nuns' public opposition to the proposed Human Life Amendment (known as the Hatch Amendment after its principal sponsor, Senator Orrin Hatch of Utah) to the United States Constitution. The National Conference of Catholic Bishops supported the amendment, but Ann Patrick had appeared on the "Donahue" show to publicize NCAN's opposition along with Donna Quinn and another signer, Margaret Ellen Traxler.

Margaret Farley, a Sister of Mercy and a tenured professor of ethics at the Yale Divinity School, was there, and so was Anne Carr, a nun of the Presentation of the Blessed Virgin Mary and a professor of systematic theology at the University of Chicago. Maureen Fiedler, another Loretto, who is codirector of the Quixote Center, a social justice organization in Washington, D.C., would turn out to be a consistently clear thinker as well as a person with a gift of laughter.

I looked around the room, eager to hear what each one would say, and I felt a tremendous wave of relief and confidence. I would not have to fight this battle alone. I could stand firm in my small place in the circle, supported by the convictions of some of the most articulate and outspoken nuns in the United States. Together, we represented hundreds of years of commitment to the Roman Catholic church.

As Pat and I took our places at the round conference table, we both felt we were taking part in an awesome moment. It was an honor for the two of us to be there.

Slowly and cautiously the process of reflecting together began. Each woman spoke of her experiences to that point. We each explained why we had signed the ad in *The New York Times*, what our feelings were about the Vatican's response, and what we hoped to see next.

Anger, shock, and anxiety flowed around the room. But there was also laughter. Mary Ann Cunningham, another Loretto who was working at the time in Denver, told us that when she heard of the letter from CRIS she decided they should know something about her before they threw her out. She sent a letter to Rome describing her work, and included a picture so they would know what she looked like. The letter was returned, with a note attached advising her to "Communicate through your superiors."

Mary Ann is tall and was heavy at the time, and she declared, "If they come to throw me out of my congregation, they are going to have to send two very hefty friars, because I intend to be nonviolent and I will go limp on them."

Some of the nun signers, more accustomed than Pat and I were to maneuvering through the labyrinth of Vatican politics, spoke of "handling" the demand that we recant. Some others felt very sincerely that the Vatican had interfered with the autonomy of our communities and denied our freedom of conscience, and therefore the most appropriate response was no response at all.

I wanted every one of the Vatican 24, and every one of the presidents of our orders, to write a collective letter to Archbishop Hamer. "Thank you for your concern and that of the Vatican, but you will not tell us what sensitive issues we can or cannot discuss. As a matter of fact, we encourage dialogue, especially on the most sensitive of issues, and those issues include abortion." What an impact that would have had, coming from a group drawn from fourteen religious orders!

Everyone at the meeting understood the importance of standing together. The issue was not just our right to dissent, big as that issue was. Nor was it just a challenge to the Vatican's rigidity on abortion, huge as that issue was. It was also a matter of resisting, perhaps once and for all, the Vatican's reactionary redefinition of the meaning of religious life for women.

A pattern emerged as we shared our concerns. American nuns had been experiencing something worse than interference under Pope John Paul II's "restoration." We were experiencing outright repression.

Not that we were the only targets. The Vatican had repeatedly attacked and even attempted to silence the great liberation theologians, Father Gustavo Gutierrez in Peru and Father Leonardo Boff in Brazil. Their arguments for a more democratic church, like those of liberal European theologians, were attacked as "Neo-Marxists." So too was Fernando Cardenal Martinez, the Jesuit in Nicaragua who had refused to resign from his job as Education Minister in the Sandinista government. All around the world, John Paul was busy reestablishing a pre-Vatican II Catholic church, elevating conservative cardinals and bishops, disciplining male religious orders, trying to force the spiritual yearnings of 900 million people back into the authoritarian Roman mold.

All over the world (except perhaps in Vatican City), there are twice as many Catholic nuns as there are priests. In the United States, the nuns are far better educated, harder working, more experienced, and have broader ministries than the priests. Without us, and without the volunteer services of Catholic laywomen, there would be scarcely anyone to actually run the parishes. And yet, to the Vatican, we were not a pastoral resource but a test of obedience. Even before the ad in *The New York Times* appeared, Vatican insiders had been pursing their lips and talking about the need for "a real housecleaning." Joseph Cardinal Ratzinger, the prefect of the Congregation for the Doctrine of the Faith—a job that is the twentieth century's version of the Grand Inquisitor—let it be known that he thought American nuns had been damaged by their contact with the outside world. They had, he said, been contaminated by the "feminist mentality."

In fact, in the Vatican's eyes, there were two problems. The nuns they had were too independent. And the kind of nuns they wanted were too few. The Vatican's idea of a solution to both problems appeared in 1983, when CRIS issued a document called "Essential Elements in the Church's Teaching on Religious Life," which directed nuns to return to separate convents, to live only with members of their own order under the rule of superiors, and to put on recognizably religious garb. "Religious life cannot be lived in the world," said CRIS. This example of Vatican wish-fulfillment was so at odds with my belief that the way to live out the Gospel was *in* the world that I ignored it. Pat said at the time that it was a warning, and she was right.

Even as we sat in the meeting in Washington, the National Conference of Catholic Bishops was working on a pastoral letter on the role of women in the church—without inviting more than a few token women to participate. Eventually, women successfully demanded a series of hearings before the first draft of the letter was published in 1988 (and a second, *more* conservative draft in 1990!), but the bishops, despite a few words about the need for equality, never seemed to realize that sexism is the problem, not women.

"And look what happened to the Mercies!" one after another of the nun signers repeated as we went around the table. Until the *New York Times* ad, the Sisters of Mercy had been the target of most of the Vatican's displeasure with American nuns. The Mercies had taken seriously Vatican II's call to stand with the poor, and they had laboriously put themselves through a process of discovering ministries relevant to contemporary American society. Sister Teresa Kane, heroine of the confrontation with the Holy Father in the Shrine of the Immaculate Conception, is a Mercy and was then president. The Mercy Hospitals are the second-largest not-for-profit health care network in the United States, and in 1977 the order decided that their responsibility to patients obliged them to provide post-partum tubal ligations under certain circumstances. They were forced to drop their plan when the Vatican threatened to replace their executive team unless all procedures that might control reproduction were banned in their hospitals.

In early 1983, Agnes Mary Mansour, a Sister of Mercy for thirty years and director of social services of the state of Michigan, had resigned from her order under pressure from local conservative Catholic groups and the Vatican. Early in 1984, another Mercy, Sister Arlene Violet, was forced to choose between resigning from her order or dropping out of her campaign for Attorney General of the State of Rhode Island. She resigned, unwillingly. In March of that year, Sister Elizabeth Morancy, another Rhode Island Mercy and a member of the state legislature since 1978, was told that she could not run for reelection. The new canon law prohibited nuns from seeking elected or appointed civil power, and although the bishop—who had just publicly praised her work for the poor—had the power to grant her an exemption, he refused. She, and the Mercies, put up a stiff fight, but eventually she also was forced to choose her legislative seat over remaining a nun.

I was sure the Vatican 24 would stand firm. The moment had finally come for us to demonstrate what we had learned in twenty years of consciousness-raising. We had talked about sisterhood and tried to reach out to laywomen. We had tried to exchange the oppression of the hierarchical pyramid for the strength and dignity of the circle. We said that we stood with the poor and for freedom of individual conscience. Now we had a chance to *do it*.

My moment of exhilaration lasted until I tried to catch Margie's eye and share it. She was shaking her head and frowning, as though she was trying to focus.

"I know I am not being as clear in this struggle as I have been in all the others," she said, "but this time it is *my* life. I have been a Dominican for forty-four years, since I was sixteen years old.''

She looked around the table, smiling a little at Pat, who at age thirty-five was the youngest woman there. "Some of us are not spring chickens," Margie said. "What is at stake here is our status as nuns, our job security, our homes, and our retirement. We could lose everything."

But Margie, more than anyone else at the table, understood what else was at stake. She was the one who had challenged us over the years on every issue, demanding over and over again that we "make the connections among forms of oppression." "Clarify," "Choose sides," and "Act in solidarity, especially with people who are poor and struggling to survive," she said. We all recognized our alternatives. We could stand with each other, with women, with the church we believed in as a community of the people of God—and risk losing everything. Or we could submit—and deny the truth of everything we had learned and experienced in the last twenty years.

There was only one word, finally, to describe our feelings, and we used it in the press statement we released after the meeting. The word was "anguish."

PAT

"I think it went pretty well," said Barbara, as we left the meeting.

"You do?" I replied, glumly.

"Well, yeah, I do," she said. "Not one of the signers talked about retracting. And none of them have been asked to retract by their orders.''

"Umm," I said.

"I felt really great, until I noticed that Margie is worried," Barbara admitted.

"Exactly," I said. "And how come the representatives of all the orders' leadership groups met separately yesterday? Why weren't we all meeting together? Doesn't this concern all of us?"

Four members of the leadership group had reported the results of their meeting to the signers' meeting. I didn't feel very encouraged when we were told that each superior would meet with her signer or signers, that they were simply going to acknowledge receipts of the Hamer letter, and that they would meet again in January.

"I also think it is a bad sign that we are suddenly talking about 'superiors' when we have spent the past twenty-five years trying to create collegial government," Barbara said.

"The really bad sign is that some of those superiors—the representatives of our elected leadership groups—have asked their nun signers not to attend tomorrow's meeting with the lay signers. And some of us have agreed to stay away."

We both knew what was happening. The leadership group wanted to make sure the soon-to-be-dubbed Vatican 24 stayed away from the lay signers' press conference. We were all fairly adept politically, and many of us were used to being public figures. There wasn't much chance that we would pour oil on troubled waters, and that was exactly what the leadership group hoped to do by being quiet, avoiding publicity, and playing for time.

And so, armed with that naive hope, they cut themselves and some of the nun signers off from the strength of the entire circle from the very beginning.

Now that it is all over, I sometimes wonder what I would have done if I had been one of those leadership nuns. Their position was not an easy one. If they simply refused to "direct" us to retract, or failed to dismiss us if we refused, as the Vatican demanded, then they themselves would be guilty of disobedience—in the Vatican's opinion. Even if they were willing to go that far, the dangers to the entire order were real. The Vatican might put their own men in charge, as they had done in the case of the election of the head of the Jesuit order in Los Angeles.

Almost every order of nuns involved in our controversy was already embroiled in a struggle to have their new constitution approved by CRIS. The period of experimentation and renewal called for by Vatican II had ended with the publication of a revised canon law in 1983. The results of those experiments had been laboriously translated into new constitutions which, because we were canonical orders subject to canon law, had to be approved by the Vatican.

More accurately, our constitutions had to be approved by a series of totally anonymous, overlapping, and contradictory judges within the Vatican bureaucracy. Whoever they were, the "Vatican" showed every sign of ignoring the results of our years of experience and imposing their "Essentials of Religious Life." Without the canonical status those constitutions provided, there was a chance the orders could lose their property and their meager resources.

For example, most of the Sisters of Notre Dame were still teaching school. Very few SNDs were involved in the kind of ministry Barbara and I had found, a ministry the Vatican did not look on kindly as supporting their idea of who or what nuns ought to be. So without a constitution validating the SNDs as a religious order, the sisters could simply be dismissed from their schools. I can understand that no leader would want to risk placing such a burden on an entire community, especially when many members of the community did not agree with the ad's position.

I don't think it would ever have come to the point of wholesale housecleaning. I agree with Barbara that if we had all stood together, the Vatican would have found a way to back down.

And I also believe that if the issue had been anything other than abortion, the nun signers would have responded differently. If, for example, they had been told, "The meeting on Central America you are thinking of attending is a somewhat delicate matter because the group that has asked you is involved in armed struggle, so we don't want you to go," the response would have been, "We're going." But abortion is the issue where we claim ourselves as adult human beings responsible for our own moral choices, and that is the most difficult gesture any woman ever makes—especially a woman who is a nun trained to obey.

The joint meeting at the St. Charles Hotel the next day, January 19, was something to behold. Some of the finest minds in the Roman Catholic church were present, eager to help, to reflect with us and offer support—theologians Elisabeth Schüssler Fiorenza, Rosemary Radford Ruether, Kevin Gordon, and Joseph Fahey. Frances Kissling of Catholics for a Free Choice was there, of course, along with Mary Hunt and Diann Neu of WATER (Women's Alliance on Theology, Ethics and Ritual), and Maureen Reiff and Dolly Pomerleau, two women who were very active in the Women-Church movement.

"This is tragic," Barbara wailed. "Why aren't we all here, superiors as well, to hear one another and work together?"

Barbara and I, at least, were tremendously refreshed and energized after that meeting. The lay signers felt much freer to express their anger at the Vatican's continued assault on human rights within the church, and they didn't hesitate to state it publicly. The part of their press release that we found especially poignant, because it placed our action in the context of the entire struggle going on in the church, read:

> This seems to be another attempt by the Vatican to silence public discussion in the church whether voiced by theologians of the First or Third worlds, bishops, clergy and religious holding public office, especially women in the church. The current Vatican action requires women to comply with the directives of a patriarchal system in which they have no real voice nor power. This seems to us contrary to the spirit and teaching of Vatican II which says . . . ''let there be unity in what is necessary, freedom in what is unsettled, and charity in any case.''

There was never any chance that the leadership group could succeed in keeping the story from the press. But the first leak didn't come from us. In the middle of the nun signers' meeting, a staff person came into the room and said,

''Press calls are coming in for a number of different signers.''

Press? How did they find us? How did they find out? Very quickly we discovered that the U.S. Catholic Conference of Bishops and the Vatican had each released press statements announcing that we had been threatened with dismissal unless we retracted our ''published statement asserting that Roman Catholics hold diverse views on abortion.'' The Vatican's statement concluded: ''Vatican officials said the congregation's (CRIS) order amounts to 'severe admonishment' of the nuns for taking an unauthorized public stand.''

We felt betrayed! We had been asked when we first heard the news not to go to the press, and we had not. Quickly, we nun signers put together our own statement. Naively, we expected to be described as faithful dissenters, but of course the press named us ''The Abortion Nuns,'' and the Vatican became even more scandalized.

Barbara and I were dismayed to discover that we had a large pile of messages from press people. Apparently we had been among the nun signers immediately identified by reporters who took the trouble to read the original ad. We thought they would be satisfied by the group's press release, but the next day, as we left the St. Charles Hotel, a mob of reporters stood outside waiting to pounce on anyone who looked like a nun.

I guess our knapsacks disqualified us, because no one tried

to stop us. We slipped through and marched straight to the nearest ice cream store.

"I don't think it is appropriate for us to say anything to the national press," said Barbara, licking her double-dip chocolate chip cone.

"Neither do I," I said, digging into a hot fudge sundae. "In fact, the whole idea terrifies me. But I do think we'd better answer the call from the reporter for *The Charleston Gazette*."

When we got to the airport to catch our flight home, we called the Charleston paper, which quoted us the next day as saying:

> The question is not about the abortion issue but whether as Catholics we have a right to question or dissent from what the church is saying. It was important that we issued the October 7 statement in a heightened political context. Catholic women are clearly being targeted today by some hierarchy. We have never been publicly pro-choice, but we think that other Catholic voices clearly need to be raised.

We were quoted accurately at the time. It is funny, sort of, to look back and see that we too were evading the issue. In the beginning we felt it was important to stay with a call to dialogue, as the ad had asked. But eventually, as we were pressured to state adherence to the church's teaching on abortion, we were forced to confront our own beliefs, and finally to state publicly that we were pro-choice.

The really big question on both our minds was "What are our parents going to think?" We had to warn them and reassure them that we were in good physical and mental health. From two pay phones in the middle of Washington's National Airport, each of us called home. Our parents already knew about the Vatican's press release, but they assumed that since they hadn't heard from us we were not in trouble (for a change). As soon as they heard our voices they knew we were indeed embroiled in the controversy and it wasn't going to end overnight. They listened to us intently, and both sets urged us to get rested and keep smiling.

My father took the news very seriously. "You know, Pat," he said, "if you continue in this fight with the Vatican you won't win. The Vatican is a giant and unless you succumb to their demands, you know they'll follow through on their threats."

"I know, Dad," I said. "But in the long run, even if I am kicked out, the Vatican will not win."

My mother was very upset. "How can they do this to you?" she said. "You've all given up your life to God in this church."

"This has nothing to do with God," I said, "and everything to do with church politics."

Twenty-five:
No Turning Back

BARBARA

Pat and I welcomed the new year of 1985 by jogging three miles and answering the phone. We had mixed feelings about the calls from reporters. On the one hand, we were glad to have a chance to tell our side of the story. But at the same time, the attention was terrifying and invasive. Even unflappable Pat confessed that she was afraid she would suddenly burst into tears or start shouting in the middle of an interview. I felt harassed, unable to plan, unable to put five minutes together to get my work done.

Work seemed more rewarding than ever, especially since the people at Covenant House were so tickled by our new notoriety. "We are so-o-o glad that for a change it's ya'll that are in trouble and not us!" they teased.

Six or seven times a day, one of us would get a call from a friend or a relative. "How are you?" they asked. "What are you going to do?"

We only knew what we *weren't* going to do. We would not retract, and we would not leave nundom.

Many of the people who called were confused about our actions. Even some of our relatives and friends who were very up-to-date on Vatican II were puzzled.

"I'm embarrassed to admit this, Barb," one friend said when she called, "but I don't understand how you can disagree with the church's teaching."

"Linda!" I said. "How can I agree when I think the church is wrong? And I certainly do think the church is wrong when it denies that women have the capacity to make moral choices about their own reproduction." I drew a breath and went on: "Furthermore, the pope is not the entire church, the people of God are also church, and . . ."

"Hold it, Barb," interrupted Linda. "I can understand the lay people signing. I would have signed myself if I had had the chance. But you are a nun."

"So?" I said.

"Don't get mad at me, Barbara, I'm trying to understand," Linda said. "As a nun aren't you supposed to obey?"

"I didn't become a moral zombie when I took those vows," I said. "And I'm pretty tired of being told nuns are spokeswomen for the church. Until we can be ordained we are no more official than any layperson, and the most we can hope for is to have a little more clout when it comes to speaking *to* the church."

"But Barbara, wouldn't it have been better if the nun signers had spoken to the church less publicly?"

I sighed. "Would you say the same thing to someone who blows the whistle at the Defense Department, or at a local judiciary system, when hundreds or thousands of people are being injured by their policies?"

"Okay," Linda said. But then she added, "Shouldn't you leave the convent if you don't want to play by their rules?"

I put my head on my desk and held the telephone up in air. When we had called for dialogue, we didn't know the starting point for many people would be in the Middle Ages. Poor Linda, she was one of the first of many, many people to put both of us through this conversation.

"Linda, this is my church and being a nun is my life and I have a right to dissent and I have a right to try to change the church. Those are *my* rules."

"Okay, go for it," she said. We laughed. Then she suddenly sounded worried: "But what if they force you out?"

"Pat and I think that is a real possibility," I answered her. "But we have decided that we are willing to risk it."

"But, Barb," said Linda, "you two love your life. Have you thought about what losing it would be like?"

We had thought of very little else ever since the meeting in Washington, and so far the only picture we could imagine of life after nundom was winter at the bottom of a cliff. But we had at least imagined the worst possible consequences of not compromising. Amazingly, once we faced the bleak reality we felt much clearer about what we had to do.

Of course, we never came close to imagining how hard it would turn out to be. As we struggled over drafts of a letter to our provinces in Boston and Connecticut and tried to make arrangements to fly to Chicago for the next signers' meeting, we would never have predicted that we would be writing the same kind of letters and making the same kind of travel plans for the next three and a half years.

On January 1, we mailed a lengthy letter to our provinces explaining our reasons for signing the ad in *The New York Times*. Every member of our provinces received a duplicate copy. We shared our thoughts about women's concepts of participatory government and about our understanding of mission and the practice of responsible obedience. We acknowledged our awareness that many of our sisters had serious concerns about our action, and we tried to analyze what was happening not just to the two of us, but to all of the women in the church. "The letter from CRIS is counter to any way or process out of which we operate as Sisters of Notre Dame," we wrote. The Vatican approach—shut up or get out—was a violation of our collegial method. In fact, the Vatican's decree was a violent act.

Hoping to return to the rational discourse of our own process, we asked: "What should our response to such a letter be?"

We concluded: "What is occurring now has serious ramifications for all of us in religious life, not simply the two of us as Sisters of Notre Dame. The present atmosphere of repression will neither subside nor disappear. The question is: what can we do as a congregation and congregations united together to address the present situation?"

A few days after we mailed the letter we telephoned our provinces to request open meetings with all the members. We asked that all our communications with the governing teams be open and available to everyone. We needed to hear their answers to our questions.

On January 18 it was twenty-seven degrees below zero in Chicago. Twenty nun signers and about twenty lay signers gathered at the Cenacle Retreat house on Fullerton Avenue. We were very touched to see some new faces added to those of the people who had attended the Washington meeting. Marjorie Maguire was there, and so was novelist Mary Gordon, who had left her small children at home and come to offer her help.

Most of the nun signers would have their expenses paid for by their communities (Pat and I paid for our trips ourselves except when we had been summoned by the Vatican). But many of the lay signers joined us at great financial cost, their contribution to the cause of bringing about justice within the church.

It was, therefore, really insulting when the leadership group, which was staying in frozen seclusion at a convent in the suburbs with some representatives from the Leadership Conference of Women Religious, again refused to meet with the lay signers. Some of the finest feminist theologians and writers in the world had come to Chicago to offer their support to the Leadership Conference and to the nun signers, and the superiors wouldn't even enter the same room with them. By the end of the weekend the lay signers finally, in desperation, hand-delivered a letter to the superiors across town, urging them to stand firm not only for the sake of their sisters, but also for the future of the American Catholic church.

Looking back, I don't really think the leadership group knew how to handle a struggle that required forging links with fourteen different communities to be successful. They had never before been faced with the necessity of presenting a common front, and they began to fall back into the old nunny habits of mind, thinking We'll deal with our own and My group is different from that group and What do those laywomen know about our situation? Instead of concentrating on their common problem, they began to focus on the trivia that divided them—which order had a motherhouse in Rome and therefore was different from an order with diocesan rules, and so forth. And as for cooperating with the lay signers—well, clearly that was beyond their imagination, despite all those years of feminist rhetoric. The message Pat and I got from our own general government group was that they were worried that the signers would coalesce, and we would *not* be able to work alone! And so the stage was set for the Vatican to divide and conquer, to impose "submission of will and mind" on American religious women.

At the moment, I was not demonstrating any very great understanding of the situation myself. I had no realistic idea of the time and intricacy and patience required for true dialogue. Nor did I realize how painful it would feel to actually *be* the agent of change, instead of merely a voice arguing for change. I wanted it all settled and understood immediately.

"And you are not even giving credit where credit is due," Pat warned me, when my complaining got to be too much for her. She always understood the meaning of process far better than I. "You won't even admit that it is brave of our governing groups to be replying to the Vatican that they find no cause to dismiss us. No one is being asked by their leadership to retract, and no one is planning to retract."

True enough. The fault lines that would divide the nun signers later were not really visible at the Chicago meeting. Immediately afterward, newspapers across the country were full of extraordinarily strong quotes from nun signers. "How can we retract the truth?" asked Donna Quinn, pointing out that the ad referred to the fact that a diversity of opinions on abortion exists among Catholics.

"The notion that someone not in that community can call on my superior to put me out is so demeaning and thankless," Ann Patrick Ware was quoted in *The New York Times.* "If dissent is not tolerated in the church, it's difficult to see how it is different from a totalitarian state where you can't speak your mind for fear of sanctions."

"I am not willing to abandon the field to the least—the least humane, the least open, the least thoughtful," Kathryn Bissell, a sister of the Congregation of Humility of Mary and an analyst for the Nuclear Regulatory Commission told *Vogue* magazine. "They, in the name of humanity, victimize the one person who is a victim. I am appalled; they don't have the intellect to make such judgments."

"This is like using snow shovels to kill butterflies," Margaret Traxler, a School Sister of Notre Dame, told a reporter. "We have been gang-raped by the Vatican," one of the signers was anonymously quoted as saying, which gave us all a chance to repeat the line.

No priests raised their voices in our support, but apparently we could defend ourselves. The Vatican must have been astonished. We were American nuns, educated and professional, and they had vastly underestimated us.

The most challenging words Pat and I heard all weekend came during the joint meeting of nun signers and lay signers. Feminist theologian Mary Jo Weaver made a statement which haunted us in the months to come. She read a summary of the lay signers' meeting, repeating the goals and the strategies we had agreed on, and noting that we had all affirmed ourselves as church to one another. Then she paused, and concluded: "This is a moment in history. We can either capitulate to an already dying institution or let what has been die and give birth to something new. The dying, as we all know, will not be easy nor will it be done without much grief."

The room was silent. Pat and I looked at each other, and I whispered: "No turning back!"

We came away from Chicago with enough courage to accept an invitation to appear on the "Donahue" show. Many of the nun signers had already spoken to the national media, and we felt a responsibility to add our voices so the Vatican would know we all stood together. Also, we wanted to stand with the lay signers, who were already beginning to suffer reprisals. Lectures and teaching jobs were being canceled. Not only were they being silenced, but their livelihood was threatened.

First we made sure that we wouldn't have to confront someone like Cardinal O'Connor on the show. We said "maybe" after they assured us that the other guests would be Margie Tuite and Judy Vaughan, my old colleague from the women's ordination protests in Chicago. At the time, Judy was running a shelter for women and children, the only one in Los Angeles that would take pregnant women over twenty-five with children, and the local church had forbidden Catholic Charities to send people to her after she had signed the ad.

Like the good women religious that we were, we reflected about appearing on the show with our area church group. With their support, we said "Yes." On January 27 we would fly to New York and appear live the next day.

The Saturday before we left I came home from a meeting about five o'clock in the afternoon and found Pat sitting in the living room looking a bit stunned.

"You may not believe this, but I just had a call from South Africa," she said. "It was from Peggy Loftus." Peggy was one of the members of the Sisters of Notre Dame General Government Group (the "Gs" as we always called them) in Rome. She had telephoned us from Johannesburg to ask: "Is it my understanding that you are going on the 'Donahue' show?"

"My first thought was Oh, was it advertised on South African television?" said Pat. "And when I said yes, it was true, she said, 'Well, you understand you are no match for the likes of Phil Donahue.' "

Pat explained that we had given great consideration to our decision, and we felt it was important for people to hear directly from the four of us what was happening.

"And then," said Pat, "she said she hoped we would gaze into one another's eyes and change our minds. If not, she said there could be serious consequences."

"Like what?" I asked.

"I asked her that," said Pat. "She said we would talk about that when she gets to the United States in two months."

So we gazed into each other's eyes and then we said: "We are going on!"

The next few days the phone never stopped ringing. Sisters of Notre Dame from Connecticut and Boston kept calling to warn us to be cautious. Margie called to plan what we would say on the show. We wanted to avoid the topic of abortion. At that point we still believed that our main argument with the Vatican was about power and control and our right to dissent.

We were very naive.

The last phone call before we left for New York was from a friend in Charleston who wanted us to know that Bishop Joseph Hodges had died that morning of lung cancer. As the plane took off, I was surprised to find myself praying that my old adversary, Bishop Hodges, would discover that his building project had won even less favor in heaven than it had on earth.

We spent the evening in the Drake Hotel, guests of the "Donahue" show, picking at our delicious complimentary dinners and grilling each other with possible questions. Until midnight the phone in our room rang and rang and rang. It seemed that every nun in the Boston SND province wanted to warn me about something. The final straw was when someone said, "If you say anything contrary to what the church teaches, you could be out of the community tomorrow." And then, to make it even worse, Margie arrived, very nervous and agitated and saying she wouldn't be able to answer most of the questions.

"In the fashion of the prophet Jeremiah," said Pat, "we will pray that we will be given the words to speak."

Morning, and a limousine, arrived. At the studio we were greeted, shown around, given a bit of makeup. About five minutes before the show began, we met Phil Donahue, who tried to put us at ease, knowing that we were appearing at what we thought was a great risk. He kidded us about his own history with parochial school nuns and said he was glad to be in charge at last. Margie let out one of her contagious laughs, and then announced that she was going to faint.

A man crouched beneath a camera (the one with the red light on top is the one that is on, they warned us) held out his hand, counting down the seconds with his hand. Three. Two. One. Go!

Of course, as soon as the red light went on, Margie took command. "Forty years a Dominican nun and now the Vatican wants me out," she said. She spoke of the great harm Archbishops O'Connor and Law had done to Geraldine Ferraro during the presidential campaign. The audience responded with warm applause. To us, it seemed like thunderous applause. Somehow, of all the things that we had thought might happen, we had never imagined that the audience might be with us. But they were! All my tension dissolved in that first brief moment of applause. I felt tears welling up in my eyes, and I thought, Oh no, not here.

"The world is watching," we had been told. And it was all right. Over and over again we said that we were simply calling for a *dialogue* on abortion. We sounded mild and thoughtful and Phil Donahue carefully fielded questions that might get us into even more trouble, such as one on women's ordination. "We did it!" we said as we hugged each other in farewell. "We did it *well*!"

Back in Charleston, a huge bouquet of flowers was waiting on our dining table, with a note from a group of wonderful women friends: "We are so proud of you. You have helped the cause of women today by your courage, more than you'll ever know."

In the days that followed we received letters and Mailgrams from women all over the United States thanking us for giving voice to their own experience. We were surprised, and touched, and encouraged. And we were so grateful, so very grateful, that we had not allowed ourselves to be silenced.

We had called for dialogue, and we got it. Pages and pages of it. The letters poured in.

Sometimes, when we opened an envelope, a piece of paper would fall out with the word MURDERER! written in big red letters. And sometimes we would get long handwritten notes on pink floral stationery asking how could we question the Holy Father and how could we support aborting the human race. But twenty to one we got letters urging us to stand firm.

"I left the Catholic Church because of its opposition to birth control."

"It's time someone took on this pope. Sister Teresa Kane spoke for me when she asked that women be allowed to be priests, and your group speaks for me in asking for respect for women.''

> I am a faithful Catholic. For years I sat in the pew and ignored the sermons denouncing birth control. I watched my diocese organize anti-abortion marches, and I tried to keep on believing that there was God's Church and it was not the same as this temporal, political American Catholic Church. But when I read about the Vatican 24 I realized I am not willing to be a hypocrite any more. I will no longer sit silently in the pew with my daughters and be told by a male celibate priest that it will be a sin unless we sign up to march outside a local abortion clinic—that it will be a sin for them to control their own reproduction—that it will be a sin if one of my girls grows up to be a lesbian. I worked in my state for the Equal Rights Amendment and now you have made me realize that if God is to be truly present in my children's lives I will have to work for equality in the Church.

Pat and I were planning to fly to Springfield, Massachusetts, on February 9 to meet with our leadership teams and the members of both our provinces. We copied some of the letters we had been getting to take with us. Not many of our provincial sisters had worked as closely with women, especially poor women, as we had, and we hoped the letters would convey the kinds of experiences we had witnessed better than we alone could.

We both felt an enormous responsibility to explain our position as clearly as possible to our communities. As we began to plan what to say we made lists of important points. A chronology of events so far. Why we had signed the ad. The right to dissent. The primacy of informed conscience. The political implications for women religious of the Vatican's continuing attempts to interfere in the internal lives of religious communities. The issue of power and control.

"We have to know more about the abortion issue," Pat said. "Up to now we have been arguing from instinct. We have seen women choose abortion and we have believed their choice could be morally right. But we need to go further than that. We need to study the history of the church's position on abortion. I want to know why the Vatican feels so strongly on this issue," she said.

"The truth is, I need to clarify why *I* feel so strongly on this issue," I said.

And so we began a year of study and argument, discussion and confrontation, prayer and pain. By March of 1986 we were no longer calling for dialogue. We were publicly, urgently, demanding recognition of women's right to choose.

Twenty-six: The Aha! Year

BARBARA

A diversity of opinions regarding abortion exists among committed Catholics. . . . These opinions have been formed by:

- familiarity with the actual experiences that lead women to make a decision for abortion.
- a recognition that there is no common and constant teaching on ensoulment in Church doctrine, nor has abortion always been treated as murder in canonical history.
- an adherence to principles of moral theology, such as probabilism, religious liberty, and the centrality of informed conscience; and
- an awareness of the acceptance of abortion as a moral choice by official statements and respected theologians of other faith groups.

—from the advertisement in *The New York Times* Understanding is like inspiration. It seems to strike all at once, with a click. The tumblers slide into place, the door opens, the light flashes on. "Aha!" we say. "I see!" And the answers flow out. It seems immediate, but in fact that swift and irreversible moment has been ripening slowly, gathering behind a thousand questions. "Aha!" is a cry of victory that sounds only after a long struggle with puzzlement.

Pat and I called the year from February of 1985 to March of 1986 our Aha! year. It was a year of continuous struggle, when our questions seemed to be answered only by more questions. We met with our governing teams or members of our leadership six times, with our entire provincial communities two times, and once more with the other nun signers of *The New York Times*. We wrote four lengthy letters of explanation and analysis to the Sisters of Notre Dame. We studied ten letters to us from our government group. We made countless long-distance telephone calls to other SNDs and to other nun signers of the ad in *The New York Times*. And, at the same time, we read everything we could find on the history of abortion, on the ethics of abortion, and on the history of the Catholic church's position on abortion and human sexuality.

In a way, the Vatican did us a favor. Without its inquisitorial demand that we publicly disavow what we privately believed, we might never have gone on asking, "Why? Why? Why?" And if we hadn't, we would never have been able to say:

"Aha! I see! The problem is that we are women. The Vatican considers us to be less than men. Therefore, they can deny our experience, our connection to God, and our sacred dignity as human beings."

Painful though that realization was, eventually it freed us to join the great circle of women determined to define ourselves as whole in God's eyes.

There was certainly no doubt that "a diversity of opinions regarding abortion exists among committed Catholics." Pat and I had been listening to that diversity for decades. National polls backed up our experience. In 1989, 83 percent of the American public polled felt that abortion should be legal under certain circumstances, and 82 percent of Catholics felt the same way.

The great majority—79 percent, according to a 1985 poll—of Catholics believe that they can be considered "good" Catholics even if they disagree with the church on abortion, birth control, and divorce. Even back in 1970, only 29 percent of all American *priests* agreed with the 1968 papal encyclical condemning all forms of artificial birth control. Today, 91 percent of Catholics say the church should approve birth control.

Why, we asked ourselves, does the church hierarchy stubbornly, even obsessively, preach against birth control? Surely a reliable means of birth control is the most reasonable way for a woman to avoid the necessity of having an abortion. Yet the church continues to allow only the least reliable method of all, a biological game of Russian roulette called the rhythm method.

Nothing in the Old or the New Testament supports a ban on contraception. The church has always disapproved of sex, but its "tradition" against birth control is quite recent—as recent as the invention of reliable methods. The first time the Vatican specifically denounced birth control was in an encyclical from Pius XI published in 1930—just about the time public attitudes in general were changing in favor of contraception. The tone of that encyclical was set in its first sentence: "How great is the dignity of chaste wedlock . . . ."

Casti Connubii, as that encyclical was known, was generally agreed, by the deep thinkers in the church, to be a mistake. For decades, as good Catholic women struggled to reconcile reality with the admonitions they heard in the confessional, the men in charge of theory prepared their arguments in favor of greater individual control of procreation. They lost. The Vatican was not willing to admit it had made a mistake. In 1968, Paul VI, ignoring the opinions of theologians, bishops, and even his own papal commission, published *Humanae Vitae*, which insisted, "Each and every marriage act must remain open to the transmission of life."

And then, precisely because the argument against contraception was so dubious, the hierarchy was forced to shore it up by turning compliance into a test of faith.

Millions of Catholics have been alienated from the hierarchical church because of its hypocritical and cruel position on birth control. The most shocking, and saddest, result is this: according to the Alan Guttmacher Institute, Catholic women are 30 percent more likely than their Protestant sisters to have abortions. Why? Obviously, the Catholic church's irrational preaching against all artificial birth control results in a higher rate of unmanageable pregnancies among Catholic women. They practice birth control, but they choose the least reliable methods instead of such autonomous means as sterilization and the pill.

The damage the church has inflicted on itself is nothing compared to the damage it has done to all the world's women, Catholic or not. Of the 1.6 million legal abortions performed just in the United States each year, one half, or 800,000, are the result of contraceptive failure. But, partly because of lawsuits against contraceptive industries, partly because of FDA approval policies, and partly because of the American Catholic church's political opposition to public funding for research, the United States is decades behind Europe in the development of safe and effective contraception. Internationally, the church has blocked funds for family planning programs—thus denying millions and millions of women the ability to choose.

"The church really hates the idea of people having sex for the fun of it," Pat said one day.

I laughed. "What else is new?"

"But Barb," she said, "there is something prurient and dishonest about the church's loathing for the body. It is almost a denial of the sacredness of God's creation."

"Read this," I said, handing her a copy of comments by Christine Gudorf, a professor of theology at Xavier University in Dayton, Ohio.

The area of sexual ethics is a wasteland in the Catholic Church. Rome [lacks] the possibility of speaking with authority to the people of God concerning those issues which are at the heart of most people's experience—issues of sexual identity and behavior, issues of fertility and birth, issues around the end of life or the end of marital love. An institution which fails to understand a people's experience of life's beginning and end, of love and sex, cannot ever hope to authoritatively articulate for the people norms for the socio-politico-economic structuring of human society.

"I can agree with that," said Pat, when she had read it. "But I still can't understand how the Vatican could have become so isolated from human experience."

"It is their job to deny human experience," I said. "The pope bases his authority on being male and celibate. If he can't persuade us that sex is bad, and women are inferior, then what is he? What are priests? They are just ordinary folks in the circle of the people of God."

"Aha!" said Pat.

Obviously the true issue the Vatican 24 had challenged when we signed the ad in *The New York Times* was the authority of the Vatican. One particular sentence really set off the alarm bells in the hierarchy.

Statements of recent Popes and of the Catholic hierarchy have condemned the direct termination of prenatal life as morally wrong in all instances. *There is the mistaken belief in American society that this is the only legitimate Catholic position.*

Pat and I entirely agree that the church has a right and responsibility to teach, but we believe that the teaching church is made up of the pope—*and* bishops, theologians, and the people. We also believe that we have a right and a responsibility to dissent when, in good conscience, we think the church is wrong. Freedom of individual conscience was one of the most important affirmations of the Second Vatican Council.

After all, the official church has been wrong many, many times over the centuries. It was wrong to condemn and sentence Galileo to imprisonment as a heretic because he insisted that the earth was not the fixed center of the universe. It had to back down, but not until this century, on its teaching that only Catholics would go to heaven. It raised only weak protests in the face of the Holocaust, the most horrifying moral catastrophe of our century.

In 1718, Lady Mary Wortley Montagu returned to London from the British Embassy in Constantinople with the method of vaccination against smallpox, one of the greatest scientific discoveries of modern times. The church's reaction, as usual, was to resist change. One hundred years later, long after vaccination had overcome the initial public suspicion, the Catholic pope was still denouncing it as a sin, a flying in the face of God's scourge. And so, in the name of "natural law," thousands of people went on dying in smallpox epidemics.

In every age, as science broadened understanding of God's creation and education deepened trust in individual human morality, people have challenged the church. It is not surprising that in this century, when science has at last discovered safe means for women to control our own reproductive lives, that the church resists. The hierarchical church has always been limited, able to imagine only the means to control what *is*. Christ, on the other hand, imagined what *might be*.

The church is not infallible. The popes did not claim to speak infallibly until 1870, when the First Vatican Council invented the doctrine to fortify a centralized authority. But even the modern popes do not claim to speak the truth at all times, on all subjects. Papal encyclicals do not claim to speak infallibly. A pope must figuratively ascend the chair of authority and announce *ex cathedra* that he is about to define a dogma of faith. Then, and only at that moment, is the Pope infallible. Neither John XXIII, Paul VI, John Paul I, nor (so far) John Paul II ever spoke infallibly.

There have been infallible pronouncements on such obscure matters of Catholic doctrine as the bodily assumption of the

Blessed Virgin Mary into heaven. *But no pope has ever spoken infallibly on abortion.*

Indeed, Marjorie and Daniel Maguire, in the pamphlet *Abortion: A Guide to Making Ethical Choices*, say: "Most moral theologians in the Church agree that no Pope has ever issued an infallible teaching on any specific area of morality. Many even say that it would be almost impossible for him to do so because morality involves circumstances and no one can know all the circumstances of each and every person in the world."

"Aha!" I said. "Now I see why the letters from CRIS to the nun signers keep insisting that we state our adherence to the church's 'clear and constant' teaching on abortion. The Vatican claims a kind of de facto infallibility for any opinion that has been around for a while."

"But the church's position on abortion has never been clear. Or constant!" said Pat. "Do they think we cannot read? Do they think we know nothing about church history?"

"You ought to realize by this time, Pat," I said, "they are not interested in discerning the truth. They are interested in power and control."

"Isn't it odd, Barb," said Pat, "that whenever the Vatican feels its control slipping, it marches right into the bedroom?"

One Sunday morning during our Aha! year I was visiting my family in Massachusetts. We went to mass, and I had to sit through a sermon on abortion.

"Abortion is wrong in all circumstances. It is murder. This has always been the church teaching. Rome has spoken, the case is closed!" pronounced the priest.

He was not telling us the truth, although he may not have known it wasn't true. For the first time in years, I wished I could be a parish priest. Instead of sitting in a pew, fuming, I would be able to preach on the true history of the issue, and to invite the congregation to participate in a dialogue on the morality of abortion in the present time.

By the time I heard that sermon, Pat and I had spent months studying the intellectual underpinning of the church's attitude on abortion and the always related subjects of sexuality and procreation. I knew by then that the "clear and constant" teaching of the church was in fact fragmentary, a record of conflict and argument, of ambiguity and inconsistency reflecting historical events and church politics and levels of scientific knowledge.

Abortion itself has always been a problem—or a solution. Men have discussed it, and women resorted to it, throughout history. From the earliest centuries of the Christian era, the church has considered abortion taboo, but the reasons given for it being wrong, and the severity assigned to the sin, have varied. In the early centuries the church fathers, who were far more preoccupied with sexual sins than they were with abortion, worried that abortion might be used to conceal evidence of a woman's adultery and fornication, and if so, it was bad. Augustine, who lived from 354 to 430, was violently phobic about sex, but even he did not believe abortion was homicide in all cases, since it was unclear at what point an embryo becomes a human person—a debate which continues to the present time.

By the Middle Ages, the anti-sex, pro-celibacy faction of the church began to win the upper hand. They argued that *any* kind of sex that avoided fertilization, and contraception and sterilization as well as abortion, was the equivalent of homicide. Even so, from the fifteenth to the sixteenth centuries, the church accepted abortion if the mother's life was at risk. Given the state of medical practice at the time, an abortion itself could put the mother's life at risk, and concern for women's health was at least part of the church's general opposition.

During the next three centuries theologians occasionally developed more sophisticated arguments for the exceptions that would permit abortion. Thomas Sánchez, a seventeenth-century Jesuit theologian, said that the fetus, at times, could be considered an "unjust aggressor," a term developed in Christian ethics to justify killing in war.

Never, in all those centuries, was the issue of abortion a central concern to the church. Discussion was erratic, even indifferent. Women and children were never considered really exciting subjects for theological power plays. As Beverly Wildung Harrison, professor of Christian ethics at Union Theological Seminary in New York, writes in *Our Right to Choose*, her brilliant and comprehensive study of the history of Christian teaching and tradition on women's nature, procreation, and abortion:

Neither a recognition of the intrinsic value of fetal life, children, or women nor a concrete concern for improving the lot of women and children has been a major hallmark of Christianity over the centuries. Dominant Christian groups have been concerned more with control of sexuality and the social order and the preservation of male prerogatives.

Pat and I began to understand that the church's present, twentieth-century preoccupation with condemning abortion is really a continuation of that drive to preserve male prerogatives.

"It seems to me that the Vatican is becoming a little illogical on this issue," I said to Pat one day. "According to the new canon law, a person having an abortion can be excommunicated. But if someone kills a newborn baby, commits rape, tortures and kills another human being, or even drops a nuclear bomb on civilization—they are not considered sinners worthy of excommunication! Where is the logic or justice in this?"

Pat laughed. All during our Aha! year, and for several years afterward, we swung between laughter and tears, rage and disbelief. That particular day Pat was taking the long view.

"Look, Barbara, over here, by the orange juice," she said, pointing to the breakfast table. "We have the Vatican. Rigid, centralized, patriarchal. Think of them as the dinosaurs. And over there, by the newspaper, we have today's women. For the first time in human history we are released by legal abortion and contraception from the church's definition of us as a kind of lumpen reproductive class. Women are the future!"

I had to laugh myself. "Aha!" I said. "Could it be the *legality* of abortion that offends the Vatican? In 1973, the *Roe v. Wade* Supreme Court decision decriminalized abortion in the United States. Only a year later, in 1974, the Sacred Congregation for the Doctrine of the Faith came out with its Declaration on Abortion."

In that declaration, the Vatican abandoned the old Catholic traditional opening for individual conscience: *ubi dubium, ibi libertas*—where there is doubt, there is freedom. The declaration states that it "leaves aside the question of the moment when the spiritual soul is infused. There is not a unanimous tradition on this point and the authors are as yet in disagreement." Nevertheless, the document then makes the leap of logic that the fetus is a full human *being* from the moment of conception, and is entitled to the "right to life."

I copied a paragraph out of Beverly Harrison's *Our Right to Choose* and pasted it on top of the first page of my Xerox of the Vatican's declaration on abortion. It read:

From the patristic period onward, the selective perceptions operative in the historical judgments of Christian teaching on abortion are skewed, because women's well-being is not perceived as a central moral issue and women's experience and reality are not understood as relevant to a moral analysis of abortion.

The Vatican declaration seemed to me to be the inevitable result of two thousand years of dismissing women as irrelevant to a moral analysis of abortion. It elevates the fetus, the zygote, to a status the church denies women—full personhood.

One day, as we were sitting in our living room surrounded by research, Pat looked at me sorrowfully and said, "Barbara, you are the devil's gateway."

"Who said so?" I asked.

"Tertullian, third century," said Pat.

"Oh, well, he was famous for his misogyny," I said.

"Maybe you prefer the sentimental kind of misogynist?" she replied. "How about Pope Paul VI, who said 'equality makes woman virile and depersonalized: it does violence to that which is profound in her.'"

"John Paul II laments the loss of *kenosis*, or sense of abnegation in nuns," I retorted.

"I'll just bet he does," said Pat, crossly. "But Thomas Aquinas is my favorite. He, by the way, was not accepted as the master of Catholic theologians until a hundred years after his death in 1274. During his lifetime he was considered a heretic. For the time, he was not particularly hostile toward women, and he didn't have much to say on abortion except to defend a 'formed fetus.' But he did view women as inferior by nature. He agreed with other theologians on the old Aristotelian idea that 'hominization' or ensoulment took place forty days after conception *for a male*. A female took longer, perhaps eighty days, because females were never quite properly finished. Of course, they also thought the entire baby was contained in the sperm and just nested in the womb. A female baby was misbegotten, the result of a defective seed. One of the topics the male theologians liked to discuss back then was whether a female had a rational soul."

How lengthily they have discussed us over the centuries! And always using the Latin words for "male," even when they were talking about things that could only apply to women. I can almost see them, debating, wearing that smug smile of superior knowledge I have seen a thousand times on the faces of priests, from the Vatican representatives Pat and I would finally face, to the most callow male seminarian. Women's rights, our bodies, and our lives are an intellectual problem (a minor problem) to them. They spin scholastic arguments like long decorative ribbons curling out from a presumption false at its core. But it has never mattered to them that they do not know what they are talking about, because the ribbons were in fact about the issues they have *really* cared about: against the Gnostics, against a previous pope, against (in the case of *Casti Connubii* in 1930) the Church of England.

However elegantly reasoned and seductively phrased, their arguments have always been beside the point. Not one has ever been relevant to the decisions faced by the actual women we see at Covenant House.

"I still don't get it," said Pat, after almost a year of trying. "There is something irrational about the Vatican's position."

"How many times have we said that before?" I laughed.

"Well, we keep trying to see their logic," she said. "I wake up at night trying to put all the pieces together. But even if I accepted the idea that human life begins at the moment of conception—which I am not sure I do—it is life, but not a *person*. And even if I agree that human life is absolutely sacred and must be protected at all cost—which I do—it still doesn't make sense. Women's lives have value, surely more value than a potential life. I don't promote abortion. I think everything should be done to avoid having one. But . . ."

"But the only way we could believe that abortion is always wrong would be to believe that the woman's life doesn't count," I finished her thought.

"We would have to believe that all women's lives are without value," Pat said, hesitantly, "or are valuable only as a means of reproducing."

"We would have to believe that women cannot be trusted to have children."

"But it is women who care for children, who nurse and nourish and sustain life," Pat said. "Women make the heroic choice to accept responsibility for a child when they can."

"And yet," I said, "the church is saying that women are incapable of making an adult, responsible choice. The church does not acknowledge that women are moral agents."

"Why not?"

"Habit," said Pat. "Convenience. Arrogance."

"I think," I said, "that after all this time, I am finally beginning to understand that patriarchy depends on despising women, the 'other.' Its glue is misogyny."

"Well," said Pat, in a businesslike tone, "since we are women, we had better make sure we don't despise ourselves. After all, misogyny is unchristlike. It is our responsibility to witness against it."

And so, at the end of that year, we decided we were pro-choice. We agreed to speak publicly at a rally in Washington, D.C., organized by the National Organization for Women on March 9, 1986.

Before 100,000 other men and women marching that day on behalf of women's lives, we stood on the steps of the Capitol overlooking the Ellipse. We stepped before the podium's microphones, and surprised ourselves by the strength in our voices.

"Choice is at the heart of conscience, the scriptures, and true religious freedom.

"I stand here today with you . . . proudly for that which makes us human . . . choice!"

Twenty-seven: Responsible Decision-Making

PAT

Barbara and I were glad to have at least one thing settled in our lives. Thanks to the Vatican we had spent a year studying the abortion issue. Finally, we were absolutely sure that an individual woman must have the right, unencumbered by any restrictions beyond her own conscience, to decide whether or not to carry out a pregnancy. Speaking out for choice gave us strength, very badly needed strength.

It is hard now to remember, much less to explain, how excruciatingly painful that period was for all the nuns who had signed the ad in *The New York Times*. One signer spoke for all of us when she said she felt as though "Every morning I have to get up and recreate myself as a human being."

Margie Tuite—our brilliant, beloved, vigorous Margie—understood best what was being done to us, and it was killing her. In December of 1985 she came to what would turn out to be the last group meeting of the Vatican 24 and our superiors. It was held in Convent Station, New Jersey. Margie arrived, leaning on her cane, warning us that she suspected something was going on behind the scenes. Even as we were writing a statement of solidarity, Margie was sniffing out signs that there were negotiations going on between Rome and the superiors that we were no longer being told about. But she didn't really show her old spirit. She had been betrayed by the church, and the fact was draining her, feeding the cancer neither she, nor we, knew she already had. "I feel this in my gut," she used to say, and it turned out to be literally true.

We never saw Margie again. During the winter of 1986 she came down with jaundice, something we thought she had caught during her trips to Central America. In June, she went into the hospital in New York City and on June 24 she had seven hours of surgery for what turned out to be pancreatic cancer. Word came that she was recovering well, she was cheerful and alert, but in fact the surgery had been too much for her weakened system. She died on June 28, leaving the entire community of women religious with a collective sorrow. A group of her friends carried some of her ashes to Nicaragua, where, as she wished, the women who called her *Compañera* kept vigil over the little metal container in village after village, until finally they carried their Marjorie in procession to her grave among the poor in a barrio of Managua.

For Barbara and me, the only way to deal with losing her was to keep our promises to her.

During the last few months of Margie's life, we called and sent letters and messages. I remember one particular get-well card Barbara and I picked out—before we knew how truly ill she was—with a funny picture of a huge jolly cat and a joke that said, "When you get out of there, we are going to eat all the chocolate cake in the world!" We tucked a prayer into the envelope, along with a letter, and a piece of paper on which we had written her favorite exhortations in big capital letters:

WE ARE MAKING THE CONNECTIONS AMONG FORMS OF OPPRESSION
WE ARE COLLECTING THE HARD DATA
WE ARE CHOOSING SIDES
ANALYZING, CLARIFYING, CROSSING THE STREET
AND
ACTING IN SOLIDARITY
Tell us (as you never fail to do): How can we do better?

A few days later we picked up the phone to hear Margie's old familiar laugh. "You forgot DON'T BE NAIVE. And DON'T GIVE UP," she said.

"We promise, Margie," we said. We promise.

In March of 1986, near the end of her life, Margie read in the newspapers that her case had been cleared, and that the Vatican was satisfied that she basically supported the church's teaching. She had signed nothing. She had never agreed to let the superiors of her Dominican order settle her case. We heard from a friend who was with her that when she heard the news, Margie picked up the paper and said, "They lied, they lied, they lied."

When she demanded to know why she was included in the list of nuns who had been cleared, her order refused to tell her. She went to her grave without ever seeing the letter her superiors had sent to Rome in her behalf.

The last words Margie Tuite ever spoke to us were: "Whatever you do, don't sign anything. No matter what you say, Rome will distort it to serve their own ends. Don't sign anything."

"We promise, Margie," we said.

The other day Barbara and I were looking at some of the speeches and interviews Margie gave that last winter and spring. At a Women-Church gathering in February 1986, she suddenly burst out: "They don't want us, they never wanted us, and they never will want us. I still believe that. I really do. I'm talking about the institutional church." The pain came from the fact that she was also talking about herself, recognizing herself as unwanted.

As she said in an interview, "The stress of it has been unbelievable though. I always say I am a cultural Catholic. I was born to Roman Catholicism, I went to parochial school my whole life, and I'm a Roman Catholic nun right now. It's much harder to experience repression from the temple than repression from the empire for me—because repression from the temple hits your meaning system, hits everything you care about: your ideals, your meaning, your faith structure. It's much harder to bear."

When I read those words over, I realized that Margie deeply understood the dreadful fact that was at the center of our struggle. The rest of us sensed it, like a hard pain somewhere near the heart. We even talked about it. But Margie *knew* it. Abortion was our issue, but to the Vatican it was a tool, an excuse. They really did not want us, never had wanted us. Our faith, our commitment, our years of work and dedication counted for nothing. Literally, for nothing. We could obey and be quiet and thus prove the authority of the hierarchy, or we could get out or be pushed out. I think Rome actually would have preferred that we all get out, not just out of religious life, but right out of the Catholic church. To them we were far more trouble than we were worth.

And yet, as Pope John Paul II flew around the globe, he kept repeating: "Precisely because of their equal dignity and responsibility the access of women to public functions must be ensured." Apparently equal rights, access for women, freedom of conscience, and freedom of speech were values for *outside* of the Catholic church only.

It was a miracle that any of us could even get up in the morning, still less go on recreating ourselves day after day. And it got harder as we began to hear about signers whose cases had been closed. But we weren't about to leave the church. No men in Rome have the power to make us do that. It is our church, and they are only part of the circle.

In April of 1985, Barbara's provincial team and mine had each written to Catherine Hughes in Rome, and she, in a careful observation of our own collegial process, forwarded the letters to CRIS. The letters were, of course, the result of elaborate and lengthy consultation. Pat and I were each described as sisters in good standing and as women of integrity and dedication to our mission among the poor. Both letters said that we had not meant to sign the ad as a pro-abortion statement, but as an attempt to describe the diversity of Catholic opinion on abortion and to encourage dialogue. Both letters repeated our own explanation that we had signed the ad in the context of our experiences among the poor and homeless in West Virginia and also because of "the unfair treatment of certain political candidates during the recent United States presidential election." Both letters concluded:

> We are troubled by the prejudgements implied in the [first] letter [from CRIS] and the harsh penalties prescribed.
> After consideration of the information shared with us and with the Province by Sister [Barbara and Pat] and after extensive consultation, it is our recommendation to you that there is no cause for judging Sister's action to be that of the "pertinacious upholding or spreading of doctrines condemned by the magisterium of the Church."

On May 14, Cardinal Hamer (he had become a cardinal in May 1985) wrote back rejecting our "no cause" letters. Clearly, he said, the statement we signed directly challenged the "Church's constant teaching about the immorality of abortion."

He continued: "Individual opinions may be diverse but the teaching of the Church is not subject to individual interpretation, and the statements of Vatican Council II, of recent Popes and of the Catholic hierarchy do state the only authentic or 'legitimate' Catholic position." Since the statement "was a source of confusion and even 'scandal' to many Catholics," we must retract.

But then came a subtle shift in what would be required of us.

If Sisters Patricia and Barbara were each to write to her Provincial Superior that she supports or adheres to the authentic teaching of the Church on abortion and the Provincial were to communicate her statement to the Sisters of the Province, this would *de facto* constitute a retraction and satisfy the requirement of the Holy See. In doing so it might be helpful for the Provincial or the Sister to include a statement on the extenuating circumstances of the case.

Eventually, everyone's "no cause" letters were rejected. And then, as pressure mounted, the solidarity of the Vatican 24 began to crumble. A few, *very* few, nun signers who had signed the ad out of a concern for American pluralism or a desire for discussion in the church, did genuinely agree with the church's ban on all abortions for Catholics and were willing to say so. Their cases were closed. Another signer told us that she wanted to remain a nun and to do so was willing to write whatever was needed. We had to admire their honesty.

Some cases were closed after vague and ambiguous statements were submitted. A tremendous amount of some signers' time went into crafting statements—word games, Barbara and I called them—that would not mean retraction to the signers, but would mean adherence to the Vatican's teaching to CRIS. A few signers, like Margie, never even saw what their superiors had written about them to CRIS.

In August 1985, Cardinal Hamer visited the United States and met in Washington with the presidents of the signers' communities. As usual, we the signers were not invited. Our lives were discussed without any of us being present. We heard later that one of the superiors had had a suggestion.

"Cardinal Hamer," she had said, "some of the nun signers are having difficulty with the word 'retraction.' Maybe you could use the word 'clarification.' "

"Clarification, retraction, they mean the same to me. If it helps, use clarification," said Hamer.

This "concession" was hailed in the Catholic press as a tremendous compromise, a rare and important step toward reconciliation on the part of the Vatican. But it turned out that the words literally meant the same to Hamer. At least two later statements of clarification were received by the Vatican with press releases describing them as retractions. Barbara and I, seeing that the Vatican was capable of announcing a case closed even if the particular signer objected publicly that she had not agreed, or recanted, or clarified, or whatever, were determined not to write anything or say anything or allow our superiors to write or say anything that could be misconstrued.

Cardinal Hamer flew back to Rome, leaving behind a press statement that left things exactly as they had been. He and the Vatican were not backing down, as some of the superiors tried to convince themselves and us. We were still accused of giving scandal, warned to state our adherence to the church's teaching, and threatened with dismissal. Finally, he disposed of freedom of conscience: " . . . a real value, clearly recognized as such by the Church . . . [but] conscience *cannot* be proposed as a principle to legitimize contradiction of the Church's clear and authoritative teaching on abortion.''

Diplomacy was not Hamer's strong point. Before John Paul II picked him for the job of bringing religious orders into line, Hamer had been Joseph Cardinal Ratzinger's deputy at the Congregation for the Doctrine of the Faith, the modern name for the Vatican's Office of the Inquisition. The very word ''dialogue'' seemed to them to be a signal to start piling up the wood for an *auto-da-fé*.

During Hamer's American visit, Donna Quinn tried to approach him. It was during a reception in Chicago's Holy Name Cathedral. Donna, one of the Vatican 24, and a past president of the National Coalition of American Nuns, works in a battered women's shelter. She was determined to say that she, like him, was a Dominican, that she loved her church and her community, that she had seen women suffer because of the church's policy, and to ask for a dialogue. His response terrified her. Shaking his finger, he screamed, ''You talk to me Dominican. You are not a good Dominican. You waste your time with these women.''

The struggle began to seem endless. People grew weary of one more meeting, one more question, one more of anything. The very life of some women was being sucked out of them, and they began to yearn for resolution. Barbara and I were disappointed, although we couldn't really blame them for wanting to get on with their lives. But in our heart of hearts we knew that even if we gave in, that would not be the end of it.

''This is not the right time, nor the right issue,'' our own government group argued. They tried to persuade us that the issues of dissent and interference in the life of our communities would be addressed sympathetically by CRIS ''later.'' All that mattered now was a statement of adherence to the teaching magisterium's position on abortion.

''When will it be the 'right' time?'' Barbara shouted one day as we were laboring over yet another long explanatory letter to the Sisters of Notre Dame. ''When will it be the 'right' issue? Is homosexuality going to be the issue that will get us to stand firm? Is ordination of women going to be the issue? Obviously not.''

''Why can't they make the connections?'' Barbara sighed. ''We didn't stand firm behind Agnes Mansour. We didn't protect Liz Morancy and Arlene Violet. Can't they see that the chipping and chipping, the wearing out and pushing back, is not going to stop unless we refuse to submit?''

During one of our meetings one signer told us she had heard that the file on her at the Vatican contained a videotape of her appearance on the ''Donahue'' show years before the present controversy.

''Files! I can't believe it,'' I whispered to Barbara during that discussion. ''It sounds like the C.I.A.''

Another signer, whose ministry was to gay Catholics, told us that she had received a letter from Cardinal Hamer asking her to state her adherence to the Catholic church's teaching that homosexuality is sinful.

''What next?'' Barbara said. ''Will we be asked to sign a loyalty oath to the pope?''

As it turned out, that is exactly what the Vatican had in mind.

Catholic priests had been virtually silent on our battle. In 1985, their own turn came. Charles Curran, a priest and theologian who taught at Catholic University in Washington, D.C., was declared unfit to teach theology in the church's name because of his dissident views on contraception and other sexual and medical issues. Archbishop Raymond Hunthausen of Seattle was relieved of his duties because of his tolerance of homosexuality and for creative liturgies, among other things. He was only reinstated after a long battle with the Vatican. In 1986, Jesuit Terrance Sweeny was ordered to destroy his work on a survey of American bishops that revealed that a significant minority disagreed with the Vatican's complete ban on married priests and on ordaining women as deacons.

The response to their cases made our own situation even more painful. Those of us still holding out were being pressured from all sides to settle, even by the same nuns and priests who were flocking to the defense of Curran and Hunthausen. The Leadership Conference of Women Religious (LCWR) issued a support statement for Curran and Hunthausen at their annual meeting. Yet never, ever, did they defend us publicly. "Were we not worthy also?" we wondered.

"Why Curran and not us?" many of us would ask. It was disheartening, especially when some of our own sisters would finally answer, with a disapproving cough, "Your life-style as a nun is not as appropriate."

"As appropriate as what?" I remember saying to a woman who had known me since I entered the Sisters of Notre Dame. She mumbled something about "style" and "aggressiveness."

Good grief! Next she would be telling me I wasn't being sufficiently feminine. Fighting for women's lives isn't feminine! Aha! That's what lay feminists heard all the time.

I thought Barbara would bounce right off the wall when I told her about that conversation.

"Barb," I said, trying to show a saintly patience, "you know that when people are too frightened to take a stand or don't want to agree they always dismiss the real issues by talking about style and personality."

"How does that make you feel?" she demanded.

"Demoralized," I admitted.

If it had not been for the letters women sent us, and the vocal, thoughtful, and caring support of lay Catholic feminists such as Frances Kissling of Catholics for Free Choice and theologian Mary Hunt of Women's Alliance for Theology, Ethics, and Ritual, I don't think we would have been able to hold out. Especially since we were also demoralized by the treatment of the Vatican 24 in the media, particularly the Catholic media.

As the years unfolded, we were viewed as "the abortion nuns," no matter how much we tried to explain our entire position. We went on discussing the call for dialogue, the right to dissent, freedom of conscience, and freedom of religion in a pluralistic society, and . . . the story was always about "the abortion nuns."

The sexist bias was particularly apparent in *The National Catholic Reporter*, a so-called liberal paper, and in the theoretically progressive Catholic journal *Commonweal*. Curran and Hunthausen were identified as respectable and holy men who were faithful dissenters "grounded in theology"—as they should have been. But we were "the abortion nuns," and our position was dismissed as "oversimplified" and "not responsible." As feminist journalist Brett Harvey wrote in a rare and wonderfully understanding article about the Vatican 24 in *The Village Voice*, "In other words, dissent is only legitimate if rooted in abstract theory rather than experience."

BARBARA

The Vatican spoke to our General Government Group from Rome. The G's spoke to us, and to our provincial leadership teams, from Tokyo, Johannesburg, Cincinnati, Rome. And we answered from Charleston, where we were trying to attend to the work of helping the poor, the sick, the homeless, and the frightened. It got so that we shuddered every time the phone rang or the mail slid through the slot in the front door.

May 28, 1985, from Tokyo: a letter from Catherine Hughes regarding the letter from Cardinal Hamer rejecting our "no cause" letter:

> [Hamer's] letter speaks of "this very sensitive and difficult situation" and I think this is something we would all be in agreement about. To resolve it, you are being asked to say that you adhere to the Church's teaching on abortion, and we think that in the circumstances, this is a reasonable request. We as a group could not support the opposite view, and would find it difficult to stand behind a position of non-adherence to the Church's teaching on abortion. Please understand me, Sisters, that this is not being said to put pressure on you, but simply because, as your sisters, we think we should be open with you about our position on this question. We respect your freedom but think that you also have a right to know our reaction to the letter.

June 10, from Pat and me, to Catherine, Mary, Emmanuel, Elizabeth, and Peggy (the G's), with carbons to the Boston and Connecticut teams: a lengthy and complicated letter. We ask why they had not discussed their position during any of our earlier meetings, instead of expressing it in one paragraph? We can't believe they find Hamer's request reasonable. Have they suggested to him that the process is unjust? We won't retract or put anything in writing.

"Have you ever really grappled with the abortion issue? Have you ever had doubts, problems, questions surrounding abortion and how it affects women?" we wrote them.

Are they telling us they will proceed with dismissal if we don't comply? "Do you intend to communicate your position on the abortion issue to the whole of Notre Dame? . . . Will a loyalty oath also be extracted from them in the days to come?"

June 30, from London, a letter from Peggy Loftus: She assures us they do not plan to initiate the dismissal process, and they too prefer face-to-face dialogue. They will be in touch to set up a meeting "to continue the dialogue to address with you the very real issues that have been raised."

August 6, Elizabeth Bowyer visits Charleston. Pat and I ask that all information be sent to the entire congregation, not just our provinces. We discuss the possibility of a joint letter with the G's.

August 26, from Cincinnati, a long, friendly letter from Elizabeth Bowyer reporting on the meeting the superiors of the Vatican 24 held with Cardinal Hamer on August 17—"quite a learning experience for me." She ends: "I think that we are all disappointed that no immediate end of this controversy is in sight. Probably the most important thing that we can do is to try to make each step along the way part of a process which is faithful to all that we stand for. We need to help one another in doing this."

September 10, Elizabeth Bowyer visits Charleston again. We three discuss writing a joint letter to the international SND community. We would tell our perspective, and the G's would tell theirs. On September 16, after hours of work, Pat and I send off our statement. On October 5, Elizabeth Bowyer writes from Cincinnati to warn that there may be problems on the joint letter because agreement on its contents is doubtful. "Let's try to stay in dialogue even though the situation is far from resolved and there may be some hard times ahead."

September 23, a memo from the Administrative Team to the Sisters of the Province (Boston and Connecticut) re: "The CRIS Situation." They have heard that "A Declaration of Solidarity" with the signers of the original 1984 ad is being prepared to run in *The New York Times*. "Specifically, we ask you not to publish the statement circulated by [the Committee of Concerned Catholics] for signatures."

September 30, from Boston, a letter to the G's from the new Boston leadership team reporting on a visit to us in Charleston:

> We want to tell you that we are convinced that Barbara and Pat are true daughters of Julie, that they are indeed serving the poor in a most neglected place, that they are conscientious, thoughtful, loyal and dedicated members of the Church. We do not judge that they should be dismissed from the Congregation.

October 16, from Rome, a letter from the G's rejecting the idea of a joint letter. They did not agree with our chronology, and they didn't like our analysis, as for example our accusing Cardinal Hamer of intervening in the life of the community. They wrote:

> We would be less than honest were we not to point out that we have found many of your communications non-dialogic in tone, including the material which you prepared for a joint statement. We see in your letters *a priori* determinations and judgmental statements, and we question whether these have a place in true dialogue. We admit that dialogue is a new thing in religious life and in the church as a whole and that we are all learners . . .
>
> In your reflections forwarded to us you ask: "How can one retract a factual statement or deny that there is a pluralism of opinion on abortion in our church and society?" As we understand it, a retraction is not required. What you are asked to do is to state that you adhere to the authentic teaching of the church on abortion. Such a statement would most certainly have room for your conviction that there is need for the development of the pastoral dimensions of the church's teaching; as well as the importance and value of that dialogue supported by Canon #212 [the Canon Law which regulates dissent]. Therefore the General Government Group is of the opinion that it is not unreasonable to ask you to make such a statement.
>
> We have an appointment with Cardinal Hamer at the end of this week, and we will be in touch with you again after

that. In the meantime, let us all try to bring this matter to a close in a way that respects the consciences of all concerned.

November 4, from Rome, a letter from Catherine Hughes describing the meeting with Cardinal Hamer as "cordial and, we thought, fruitful." She responded that the G's had "commented unfavorably upon the process he had initiated by his first letter." Face-to-face dialogue will be sought early on "if anything of a similar nature comes up again." The cardinal expressed concern about the pastoral problems they mentioned (i.e., the church's abysmal record of providing spiritual comfort to women facing an unwanted pregnancy). The question of dismissal did not come into the conversation. He feels that any member of the church would be asked to make the statement we are being asked to make, "either orally or in writing." Catherine concluded: "We can only end this letter as we did our last: we find the request for the statement reasonable and ask you to consider making it to your provincial teams. Our hope is that this affair will be concluded in a manner that will respect the dignity of all concerned."

November 12, from Pat and Barbara in Charleston to the G's. We thank them for speaking clearly to Cardinal Hamer.

> We respect, as we have from our first conversation, your position and views on this issue. We respect your wish to conclude "this affair in a manner that will respect the dignity and consciences of all concerned."
>
> Believing this, we share with you once again our position which has not been arrived at easily nor without anguish. During these last eleven months, we have taken time to question, dialogue and discern with many people. We have taken time to analyze and make the connections with the oppressions we see, hear, and feel each day with the homeless people with whom we work. And most importantly, we have taken time to pray and reflect on this serious issue. Sometimes we wish that our eyes had never been opened. It would make this situation so much easier and less painful.
>
> These months have led us to clearly follow our consciences and remain true to our integrity. We have never once attempted to misrepresent the truth or play word games in order to pass easily through the Vatican demands. We find it dishonest to try and manipulate words that might say one thing

to us and another thing to Rome. Our consciences and integrity have led us to stand by what we are challenged and called to in our own constitution as Sisters of Notre Dame:

> "We choose to stand with poor people as they struggle for adequate means for human life and dignity . . ."
> "We work with others to transform unjust structures and systems . . ." and
> "We dare to live this mission because we have confidence in God . . ."

It is because we believe in this process and this journey with the people of God that we cannot comply with Hamer's wishes. Our consciences and integrity will not allow us to say what we do·not believe nor simply write a statement to "get us through." To do either would abuse the very heart of what we have come to believe and trust as the word and experience of God in the lived reality of the people who have touched our lives. To comply with Hamer's wishes would violate the very depth of the challenge we have so often asked of other people, particularly the women with whom we work. We have moved with them to challenge the structures that oppress them. If a woman is willing to risk her minimum income or inadequate housing to challenge the public systems which oppress her, how can we dare speak something we do not believe in order to·save our status positions within a Church which, sadly, we think is a sinful structure and is acting in a sinful way?

November 26, from Rome, a letter from Catherine Hughes: "We regret your decision not to make this statement, while respecting your right to decide. We would certainly never want to be party to a process which in any way misrepresented the truth."

December 19-21: Pat and I attend the meeting in Convent Station, New Jersey. At least six of the signers have had their cases closed, but they attend the meeting anyway. A joint statement is released, saying "All participants expressed grave concern about continued attempts to suppress dialogue and dissent within the institutional church." A newspaper story reports: "Sister Barbara Ferraro, a Sister of Notre Dame de Namur, used blunter language. 'The only just resolution that we see is that Hamer [Cardinal Jerome Hamer, head of the Vatican Congregation for

Religious and Secular Institutes] retract and apologize,' she said in a telephone interview afterward. She said she was speaking for herself and another Notre Dame de Namur Sister, Sister Patricia Hussey.''

January 25, 1986, from Rome, a letter from the G's with copies to all the United States leadership. The statement and news story has reached them.

> You will recall that at the very beginning of this situation, we asked you not to make public statements. You have not honored this request. We feel we must express our surprise that you should consider it necessary to add anything to the agreed statement made after the meeting, and our strong disapproval of what you actually said. As women who profess to found their lives on the Gospel, we surely believe in effective dialogue and continuing effort towards reconciliation. Instead we found the form and content of your statement to be offensive, irresponsible and potentially damaging to the group to whom you have committed yourselves—your Sisters in Notre Dame.

The G's repeat that they do not support our refusal to state our adherence to the church's teaching on abortion, and add they do not support the ''way in which you make your views public.''

February 25, from Rome, a letter from Catherine Hughes and Peggy Loftus. (The tone of this letter is so much more friendly than the preceding one that we wonder if the point of the other was to produce a carbon to go to Hamer's office.) They have had yet another meeting with Cardinal Hamer ''in an effort to keep the communication lines open and to try to further the dialogue. We are convinced that we are all learners at this art of dialogue, that we even have different understandings of what we mean by it, but that we will learn to do it by actually trying.''

They report that the cardinal wondered if they had ever asked us directly if we accept the church's teaching on abortion. ''If the answer is 'yes' the whole thing is settled,'' he said. The G's had not directly asked us, but they did before we got their letter, and we said ''no.''

The G's continued:

> During the interview we pointed out again that for you it is a question of authority and unjust processes rather than a ques-

tion of abortion, to which he replied: "If they have questions on those things, let them be argued out, but not under this heading of abortion."

In fact, by that time we thought we had made it clear that for us it was a question of authority *and* unjust processes *and* abortion. Perhaps they were being diplomatic. Perhaps the dialogue was in fact just beginning. We were sure that we were beginning to be understood and that mutual respect would prevail. We even hoped our point of view would prevail. But it was certainly taking a long time.

March 3, from Wheeling, West Virginia, identical letters from the Most Reverend Francis B. Schulte, Bishop of Wheeling-Charleston, to our Boston and Connecticut provincial leaders. He wishes to inform them that we are "a source of scandal, embarrassment and confusion to many people in the Diocese of Wheeling-Charleston." (Pat observed that causing scandal and confusion is the worst thing you can do in the Catholic church. The only thing worse is having sex.)

He is particularly upset by our participation in a second advertisement in *The New York Times,* which appeared on March 2, and our local promotion of the March for Women's Lives to take place in Washington, D.C., on March 9. He enclosed a copy of a newspaper ad for the march, pointing out that it was clearly described as "a march for birth control and abortion rights."

When we read the bishop's scolding letter, we knew we were making the right decisions. Our problem would be to convince the G's of it.

The month of March 1986 was extremely busy for the Vatican 24. The Declaration of Solidarity was published on March 2. There were one thousand signatures from seventeen different countries, including at least five priests and forty women religious. The headline read: "We Affirm our Solidarity with all Catholics whose right to free speech is under attack." Pat and I signed it to support the lay signers of the original ad who were suffering continued reprisals without much public attention or support. The Maryknoll nun and we were the only members of the original group of twenty-four nun signers who signed (although many others signed a separate statement of support and thanks) despite the attempt by our leadership groups to stop us. In fact, we both rounded up our families and they signed also. Pat and I had learned that the only way to deal with threats of silencing is to speak louder.

On March 9 we spoke louder, at the march in Washington.

During the preceding week we had been getting dozens of telephone calls from the nuns who had not yet been cleared. By that time, the Vatican 24 had been reduced to the Vatican 11. They were Pat and me, six Sisters of Loretto, Judy Vaughan, Kate Bissell, and Caridad Inda.

The news was really exciting. The Vatican was coming to us! An unprecedented concession! We made enough calls back and forth for a Vatican 100.

"Do you know what is happening?" "What have you heard?" "Is it true that representatives of CRIS are coming to the United States to meet us?" "What does it mean?" "Should we go?" "How can we find out what their agenda is?" "Has your community been notified?"

Our community, the Sisters of Notre Dame, had not been notified. We discovered that we were considered "in a different category" because we had signed the second *New York Times* ad and appeared at the march in Washington. At first we were relieved, and then we resented being set apart. Our leadership contacted Mary Linscott, a staff member of CRIS and the highest-ranking woman in the Vatican, who also happens to be a Sister of Notre Dame. We received an invitation to meet. It was set for Saturday, March 22, the last day of the series.

More telephone calls. "I think we should bring our own translator." "Don't make any decisions at the meeting." "I don't think we should talk about our beliefs on abortion. Just stick to the call for dialogue and the right to dissent." "We have to demand the right to bring our own leadership people."

Pat and I decided we would not attend a meeting on the Vatican's ground, not even at the embassy. They would have to come to our turf at Trinity College in Washington which was owned by the Sisters of Notre Dame. Members of our leadership groups would be there with us. Mary Linscott would translate. She was part of the official visit, traveling with the CRIS emissary, Archbishop Vincenzo Fagiolo, the second in command. (I guess they had figured out that Cardinal Hamer was not the person to handle these delicate negotiations.)

We called Margie for advice. She warned us not to sign anything.

"You have always told us to get to the table," Pat said. We were both on the line to Margie, each on a separate phone. We said in one voice, "If the victim is not at the table as an equal, there is no real dialogue."

At last, we were getting to the table.

Twenty-eight: The Politics of Abortion

BARBARA

I don't think we would have been as hopeful as we were about the meeting with the Vatican if we had realized that it was pressure from the other side rather than our persistence that brought it about. Pro-choice groups weren't the only ones making news during March. The first week of the month a convention of the International Right-to-Life Committee took place in Rome. *The New York Times* reported that anti-choice leaders met with Vatican officials, including the pope, and asked for firm action against the nun signers whose cases remained open. They claimed that the "ambiguity" that remained damaged the political efforts of the United States' right-to-life movement.

I cannot understand why the citizens of the United States tolerate these "political efforts." Thirty years ago John Kennedy had to go to great lengths to reassure the electorate: "I believe in an America where the separation of church and state is absolute—where no Catholic prelate would tell the President (should he be Catholic) how to act . . . where no religious body seeks to impose its will directly or indirectly upon the general populace or the public acts of its officials." Nowadays the Catholic prelate doesn't hesitate to impose his agenda on the President and general populace of the United States, and no one seems to object. Is it because the President is not a Catholic? Or is it that the public hasn't even noticed—or doesn't want to notice?

Obviously, Pat and I do not believe that the church should be politically neutral. In the twentieth century, politics is the route, however inadequate, to justice. But the church's reduction of the process to a single issue—abortion: yes or no—has distorted politics, undermined justice, and debased the church's own moral authority.

The anti-abortion movement is Catholic. Conservative, right-wing *Catholic*. The Roman Catholic church began it, funded it, organized it, and sustains it. And, since no one seemed to object very strongly, or because no one noticed, the Catholic church is openly redoubling its efforts today.

Yes, there is a sprinkling of people from all the other groups. There are even "Feminists for Life." Conflict and concern about abortion is human, not denominational. But the sprinkling was deliberately turned into a smoke screen, as a calculated political tactic to obscure how far across the church-state division the movement had marched.

In 1965, the United States Supreme Court legalized birth control for the nation when it overturned a Connecticut law prohibiting the sale of contraceptive devices. The National Conference of Catholic Bishops responded by creating a Family Life Division. It was originally intended to lobby against contraception, but, as abortion laws began to be liberalized in various states and local parishes began organizing grass-roots right-to-life activities, the Family Life Division coordinated those efforts into the bishops' national campaign against legal abortion.

In 1968, Pope Paul VI rejected recommendations that the church liberalize its attitudes toward human sexuality. In turn, the faithful overwhelmingly rejected the Vatican's teaching. And the Vatican, stupidly or arrogantly, hardened its position. Thus, the social justice message of the Gospels, reaffirmed by the renewed post-Vatican II church, became trivialized and even contradicted. Banning birth control and forbidding abortions became more important to the Vatican than the great issues of peace, poverty, human rights, and economic development in the Third World.

Unfortunately for the hierarchical church, it staked its authority, and even its credibility, on only one of those issues. The wrong one.

The 1973 Supreme Court decision legalizing abortion came as a surprise to everyone. In a way, the Court's decision had preceded a national consensus. Feminists were astonished and delighted. The vast middle was a bit muddled and ambivalent, not so much about the application of the decision to themselves as about "others." And the Catholic church was appalled. The National Conference of Catholic Bishops made an unprecedented call for civil disobedience to resist laws legalizing abortion. For the first time in American history, the church began a direct, concentrated effort to influence national policy. It spawned a variety of secular organizations to work on electing "pro-life" candidates and to lobby Congress and state legislatures. The Family Life Division created an independent National Committee for a Human Life Amendment and it was critical to the founding of the National Right to Life Committee (NRLC). Enormous resources were poured into the effort, ranging from the hundreds of thousands of dollars that are on the public record to the less visible gifts such as office space, volunteers, and transportation.

In 1975, the bishops sponsored "The Pastoral Plan for Pro-Life Activities," a plan for grass-roots organizing around a single issue—passage of a constitutional amendment banning abortion. Although the grass roots were organized according to the national Catholic hierarchical structure, from the Bishops Conference to the diocese to the parishes, they claimed to be bipartisan, nonsectarian, and separate from the church. The great victory, if it can be called that, for the church was the passage, in 1976, of the Hyde Amendment to the Medicaid funding bill. Named for its sponsor, staunch Catholic Congressman Henry Hyde, the amendment cut off funding for elective abortions for poor women.

During those years of organizing, the polls showed that almost as many Catholics as the general population felt that abortion should be legal in many circumstances. But those Catholics who did not agree—many of them traditionalists eager for certainty and familiar rules—were on the march. And their activity may have been the point of the entire crusade. In her excellent book *The Right to Lifers*, Connie Paige quotes the Reverend Edward Bryce, who was then directing right-to-life activities for the National Conference of Catholic Bishops. He said to her: "Abortion is not the only issue that we could develop as a model, but this happens to be the one that has gotten the people out. With them, we are creating political cells."

Until about 1978, those cells still lacked the leadership and strategy to be a direct political force. But two conservative Catholic NRLC activists, Judie and Paul Brown, wanted to broaden the battle, to attack Planned Parenthood and sex education and the intrauterine device (the IUD prevents implantation of the zygote in the wall of the womb, which many anti-choice people insist is the same thing as having an abortion). Judie Brown's greatest contribution to the movement may have been her inspiration to tell the press that the NRLC had twelve million members. Later, she admitted that she had simply made up the preposterously inflated number, but no one had checked. The issue began to be seen as one that could make the difference in a close election.

In 1978, with the Browns' help, Father Bryce's political cells were co-opted by the emerging New Right. Paul Weyrich, Howard Phillips, John "Terry" Dolan, and Richard Viguerie, the masterminds of the New Right (all of them except Howard Phillips conservative Catholics), were completing the coalition of single-issue groups that would eventually elect Ronald Reagan. Anti-Equal Rights Amendment and pro-Star Wars defense groups were joined to anti-taxes and pro-prayer in schools groups. People opposed to school busing for racial balance were persuaded to find common cause with people offended by coed sports. Many, many of those people were white Christian fundamentalists who were already responding to an electronic, telecommunicated Christian revival, dedicated to an all-purpose solution—putting God back in government. They shared with conservative Catholics a fear of being unwanted, of being edged out of the mainstream of American culture by the gains of the civil rights and the women's movements.

Judie and Paul Brown had started a Life Amendment Political Action Committee (LAPAC). They broke with the NRLC, which refused to take a position on any issue other than abortion, and moved their offices to the cluster of small buildings in Washington which housed Paul Weyrich's various right-wing political organizations and think tanks. The most important part of the move was that they also brought LAPAC to Richard Viguerie's mailing lists.

It was Richard Viguerie, the wizard of direct mail fundraising, who had the brilliant idea of introducing the fundamentalists to the abortion issue, and the Catholic right-to-life movement to the fundamentalists. Such an alliance was no small trick. Fundamentalists, for whom the coals of the Reformation still burn bright, are traditionally anti-Catholic. But Viguerie, with the help of the Browns and Jerry Falwell, pulled it off, capping his ecumenical miracle by including the Mormons. The "Pro-Family" Coalition was complete. The pro-family agenda was purposefully anti-feminist, which was fine with the millions of people threatened by the fundamental changes inherent in recognizing the rights of women.

The primary objective of the New Right (and its beneficiary, the old right) was, as Viguerie put it, a "commitment to minimally regulated free enterprise at home"—not an aim compatible with the gospel of social justice. Christ's message was good news for the poor. The conservative message was good news for the rich. It was especially good news for rich, conservative, Vatican-centered American Catholics.

One hundred years ago Catholics were only 10 percent of the population, and the church was an embattled immigrant faith. Now we are middle class, educated and successful, politically active. Even though we are only 25 percent of the total population, we are the most powerful single minority. In Congress, 26 percent of the members are Catholics. A third of the Justices on the Supreme Court are Catholics—although only one of them, Justice William Brennan, proves that Catholicism and justice for women are not irreconcilable.

Very rich, very traditional Catholics are important contributors to the most conservative, right-wing political groups. Phyllis Schlafly is just one of those people. An astonishing number of the people in the Reagan administration were conservative Catholics, from C.I.A. director William Casey to national security advisor William Clark, to U.N. ambassador General Vernon Walters. They were establishment Catholics, not the Catholics of Pope John's "aggiornamento." Pope John Paul II, with his "restoration," his anti-Communism, and his obsession with traditional authority, was the natural ally of Ronald Reagan, with his anti-Communism, his "traditional values," and his total commitment to the authority of free enterprise.

The people who read and write for such ultraconservative Catholic publications as *The Wanderer* are the same people who supported Ronald Reagan, and who wrote frantic letters to the Vatican warning that the American church was toppling into chaos when the ad we signed appeared in *The New York Times*.

The enraged bullying that characterized the Vatican's reaction to a few nuns who signed a newspaper ad was comprehensible only if the Vatican felt that we were threatening its influence on the policies of the most powerful country on earth—which is exactly what we were doing. If mere nuns, handmaids to the hierarchy, humble peasants, would not obey, then who would?

We were uppity American women. And we were public re-
minders of the fact that despite all the Vatican's high-powered
international intrigue, the *people* of the church are shifting beneath them. The vitality of the church lies in the grass roots.

The single-issue coalitions constructed by the New Right did
not last. The New Right itself was overwhelmed by its own
victorious transformation into Reagan Republicanism. Richard
Viguerie's empire shriveled. Abortion did not turn out to be a
clearly decisive issue in the voting booth—at least not until the
1989 Supreme Court decision in the *Webster* case threw regulation back to state legislatures. The fundamentalists subsided,
or were assimilated, or retreated in confusion as many of the
electronic evangelists were disgraced. In 1982, Congress defeated the Human Life Amendment. The Catholic right-to-life
movement drew back to the church to concentrate on its own
single issue, unnerved by the increasingly obvious evidence that
the party it had relied on to force women to have babies was
also a party that was perfectly prepared to deny those women
health care and the basic necessities of life.

But where were all those newly politicized Catholics to go?
By condemning Geraldine Ferraro because of her position on
one issue, abortion, the Catholic hierarchy effectively declared
the national Democratic party off-limits to the faithful. Once
again, the church had presented Catholics with a test of its authority that it, not they, was bound to fail. Not only had American Catholics in general been moving closer and closer to the
general public's attitudes on abortion, but, as the years passed
after *Roe* v. *Wade* in 1973, the general public was moving closer
and closer to a consensus. Furthermore, the people of the United
States, including the Catholics, are profoundly committed to our
two-hundred-year-old social experiment of pluralism.

When the conservative bishops attacked Geraldine Ferraro,
it was more than an insult to a dedicated and competent Catholic
woman. It was deeply destructive and divisive, profoundly
alienating millions of Catholics and pushing Catholic women to
open revolt.

Including, of course, Patricia Hussey and me, Barbara Ferraro, faithful dissenters and dedicated thorns in the side of the
hierarchy.

" 'This is the issue that has gotten the people out,' " snorted
Pat, reading the Reverend Bryce's quote in *The Right to Lifers*.

"Yes, fighting legalized abortion got them out all right. But for what?"

"How do you mean, 'for what'?" I said. I was sorting through a box of used clothes donated to Covenant House, and for about ten minutes I had actually forgotten about our problems.

"Come on, Barb," said Pat. "For what? It's all about reinforcing the power of the Vatican. This crusade against abortion has about as much to do with saving lives as the Spanish conquest of the Aztecs had to do with saving souls."

"Whew," I objected. "Isn't that a little strong?"

"Okay, then answer this question. If *you* were a parish priest, how would you try to renew the moral consciousness of the faithful?"

I sat down on a pile of sweaters. "I know exactly what I would do. I even tried to do it in Auburndale. I would ask people to begin to meet in small circles. We would talk about the web of experience, about morals and ethics and the sacredness of *all* life. We would try to come to know the poor, and to understand the reasons for poverty. We would study Christ's message and discover how it can be fulfilled now, in our time. And, most important, they would have to learn to experience themselves as church for each other. Because, Pat, did you realize that hundreds of parishes have no priest to say Sunday mass? Catholics have to start discovering new ways to carry out the rituals because pretty soon the priests will be gone."

"And why aren't people meeting that way in American parishes?" demanded Pat. "Why is the Vatican trying to suppress it where it *is* happening, in Latin America?"

"Because the circles of the people of God have a spiritual authority greater than the Roman hierarchy," I said.

"Exactly," said Pat.

Twenty-nine: The Meeting

BARBARA

"Okay. Off we go," said Pat.

It was seven-thirty in the morning, Saturday, March 22, 1986, in Charleston, West Virginia.

"You look fine," I said. Pat was wearing her good wool pants and a tweed jacket.

"So do you," she said. I was wearing my navy slacks and a jacket.

What we wore to the meeting was important. We didn't ordinarily wear nunny suits, so we wouldn't wear them today. No special costumes for the Vatican. But we wanted to look serious and respectful. We decided to wear our best clothes. The most important thing was to be our true selves in Washington.

The plane took off at eight-fifteen. We settled into our seats, opened our backpacks, and started spreading out pencils, pens, pads of paper, our tape recorder, and stacks of notes. We went over the answers to all the questions that we had been able to imagine during the previous week of nervous anticipation.

"You know, Barbara," Pat said, as though she had just thought of it, "this is probably the one opportunity we will have in our lives to speak for the many women whose voices have never been heard by Vatican officials.'"

"Right," I said. "But what about the moment of ensoulment? Let's go over our answer to that again."

"No one knows when life begins," Pat answered. "It is a theological argument and one that is ultimately divorced from the reality of gestation, which is a long slow process depending on the physical relationship of a woman and a fetus."

"Umhmm," I said. "And what if they argue that abortion casts the fetus's unbaptized soul into limbo forever?"

"Good grief, Barbara!" said Pat. "Get hold of yourself. The church gave up on the idea of limbo years ago. If it is a soul, it is an innocent soul, and it goes straight to heaven. But is it a soul? If it is, how come the church waited until 1917 to order that miscarried or aborted fetuses be baptized—an order that is only sporadically fulfilled?"

The flight attendant offered us a snack. We were too anxious to think of eating. I managed to swallow some coffee.

"Are you nervous?" I asked Pat, nervously.

"I was doing pretty well until last night," she said.

The night before we had suddenly found ourselves all alone out on a limb. The final appointment on the Vatican's schedule was ours. As each meeting approached and concluded, all of the uncleared nun signers telephoned back and forth, planning and reporting. The first community, the Sisters of Humility, met at the Vatican Embassy on Wednesday. One of their signers, Kate Bissell, was there, and the other, Caridad Inda, was out of the country. After nearly five hours in the meeting, Kate Bissell's case was resolved. According to an article in the *National Catholic Reporter*, she had signed a statement that said she "agrees in principle that abortion is always wrong" and that she "accepts the Church's position on the issue." (By the middle of May, Caridad Inda's case had also been closed.)

That afternoon another community, the Sisters of Saint Joseph of Carondelet, met at the same place. Judith Vaughan, their only signer, took a stronger position. She said she needed time to reflect, as she usually did in her daily life, on what had happened at the meeting before she put anything in writing. (On April 1, Judy Vaughan's order announced that her case had been closed, while giving no details.)

Archbishop Fagiolo and Mary Linscott—the Vatican delegation—flew out to Denver for the next meeting on Friday with the six Sisters of Loretto. We never doubted that the Lorettos would hold firm in their position. After all, *we* had been drawing strength from *them*. When we spoke to them on the telephone Thursday night they assured us that they had spent the day strategizing and had decided to put nothing in writing and to make no decision at the meeting.

"Well, that's a relief," I said to Pat.

Imagine how I felt Friday night when, after a long day of

waiting on pins and needles, I picked up the phone and heard my friend Maureen Fiedler saying, in a joyous and elated voice, "It's over!"

My stomach flipped. "What do you mean, it's over?" I said. Pat, hearing my tone of voice, came into the living room from the kitchen and sat down on the edge of the sofa.

It sounded as though Maureen was at a party.

"We're celebrating," she said. "We won!"

"What did you do?" I asked, trying to keep the panic out of my voice.

She said they had signed a statement they had drafted themselves. Maureen eagerly read it to me, suggesting that we use the same statement and be cleared as well:

> We had no intention of making a pro-abortion statement. We regret that the Statement was misconstrued by some who read it in that way. We hold, as we have in the past, that human life is sacred and inviolable. We acknowledge this as teaching of the Church.

I wanted to shout: "How could you?" I was shocked and bewildered, and as I repeated the statement to Pat, I could see that she was really struggling to respect what the Lorettos had done. "They are playing word games," said Pat.

The Lorettos, by their own understanding of their statement, had tried not to compromise themselves. No one, they reasoned, is pro-abortion, only pro-choice. It was the Vatican that misconstrued the statement, and the Lorettos certainly regretted the fact. As for the phrase "human life is sacred and inviolable," they carefully avoided saying "*fetal* human life," but there was no way around the fact that they had used the language of the opposition. As for acknowledging the teaching of the church, well, it *is* the teaching of the church, and they did not say they *accepted* it.

"Maureen," I said, trying to keep my voice level, "I know you had no intention of stating adherence to the church's teaching on abortion. And it doesn't sound to me as though the words do that explicitly. But I am worried. We have all seen that any case that is resolved is deliberately misinterpreted as 'adherence to the official church's teaching on abortion.'"

"Oh, I don't think that will happen, Barbara," said Maureen. "We will release our statement to the press ourselves. It won't be a secret like the earlier settlements. There will be no question about what we said.''

''Well, that's good,'' I said. She sounded so relieved that I didn't have the heart to say anything more than ''Thanks for calling, Maureen.''

''Be sure and call me after your meeting tomorrow, Barbara. I'll be anxious to hear what happens to you and Pat.''

I hung up. Pat was in tears. Never, in all the time that I had known her, had I ever seen her so upset.

''They violated their own process,'' she kept saying. ''I don't understand it.''

Pat and I were the only nun signers left. We looked at each other miserably. Pat said, ''What on earth is really happening at these meetings?''

The flight to Washington was only an hour, all too short. As we fastened our seat belts for landing, Pat and I said a prayer together, the passage from Jeremiah that seemed to speak to our hope for the meeting. It comforted me, as it had for twenty years.

''God, I do not know how to speak, for I am only a youth.'' But God said to me, ''Do not say, I am only a youth; for to all to whom I send you you shall go, and whatever I command you you shall speak. Be not afraid of them, for I am with you . . .''

Our meeting was scheduled for ten-thirty. The quickest, and cheapest, way to get out to Trinity College was on the Metro. We rode along, following the flashing lights and ringing bells. The route was familiar by then. A year earlier we had followed it to our first meeting with the SND General Government Group.

Trinity College is still one of the jewels in the school system created by the Sisters of Notre Dame. Many nuns live in the convent attached to the college, and, strictly speaking, for public relations purposes, we were meeting at the convent, not at Trinity College. However it was described, the room where we met was a parlor in the original college/convent building.

We got off the Metro at the stop for Catholic University and began walking the mile to Trinity. It was a sparkling spring day. The trees were a pale green and the first flower buds were beginning to unfold.

''We are not going to sign anything,'' I said.

"Right," said Pat. "We cannot adhere to the Roman Catholic church's teaching on abortion."

"We have to talk about what our position of choice means," I said. We had repeated those lines to each other a hundred times, but since the night before when the news came from the Lorettos, we were even more determined.

"As far as we know, everyone else has talked about their right to dissent," said Pat, "but no one has talked about *why* they disagree. No one has talked about abortion."

"We can't evade it," I said. "All we can do is be honest about what we believe. If they want to clear us, or not clear us, at least we won't have skirted the issue."

We could see the Shrine of the Immaculate Conception, where Pat had stood to support women's demand for equality in the Catholic church, and where Sister Teresa Kane had so bravely spoken to Pope John Paul about women's pain. Pat stopped, and took our tape recorder out of her knapsack.

"Let's play the song by Kay Weaver," she said. "We need to muster up all our strength and courage."

And so we walked along, in the early morning sunshine, singing "One Fine Day" at the top of our lungs.

Sister take my hand,
It's with you I make my stand . . .

So many women were with us, so many women whose lives and spirits had touched us. The women in Charleston who had supported us, the women who had written to us, the women we had never met—they were all with us.

And my road is a little easier
'Cause she was here . . .

The women we knew who had had to struggle with needing to have an abortion were with us. We knew that they were good women, and they had not made their decisions lightly. They wanted their church to understand.

I see a little clearer
Through the darkness called fear,
Sister take my hand,
It's with you I make my stand . . .

For whatever reason, we were the ones who were going to speak for them.

And we'll be all we can be
One fine day.

We turned and started up the long driveway toward the entrance of Trinity College. On the threshold, we each drew a breath, smiled at each other for confidence, and then went inside.

Elizabeth Bowyer, one of our elected Government Group from Rome, came to the reception desk and greeted us warmly. Twice in the previous year she had been to visit us in Charleston. I remembered the time we had spent with her, sitting on our front porch, explaining our position. She had a tough job, trying to negotiate and communicate with us, with CRIS, and with the Sisters of Notre Dame. Now she was leading us through a maze of corridors to the parlor where the meeting would take place. I could hear Pat responding to her polite inquiries about our trip. But I was walking through time.

My shoes squeaked on the polished floors. Dark wood doors opened and closed as we moved closer to the center of the convent. I sniffed. Wax, boiled vegetables, incense . . . and secrets. I was little Barbara Ferraro again, dressed in my Sunday best, tiptoeing along with my sisters and brothers, our mother's pride and joy being taken to visit the nuns at Emmanuel College in Boston. What an honor it would be if one of us would receive God's call to a vocation!

I was a novice again, trying to walk like a nun, thumping instead of gliding silently and piously. Echoes seemed to rustle along the corridor, drowning out the pleasantries Pat and Elizabeth were exchanging. "Please, Sister Mary Kevin, may I have permission to speak?" "Barbara, *dear*, we don't ask questions here. Where is your holy obedience?"

Oh my God, I thought, how did I get in this situation? Every polished inch of corridor we passed seem to murmur in disapproval. "Barbara, dear, where is your humility? Where is your submission? Barbara, dear, who do you think you are? Barbara, Barbara, what are we going to do about you? Barbara, *dear*, it is not possible to say no to the pope."

Pat walked on ahead of me, talking to Elizabeth. They were two grown women, responsible and equal. The other voices died away. My breath came back. I was Barbara Ferraro, adult. And almost everything I was, I owed to this religious community. The Sisters of Notre Dame had given me my education. They had allowed me to discover my own mission and encouraged me to follow it. My parents taught me to trust in God, but the sisters helped me learn to keep faith with the people of God. I was among friends.

The parlor door opened, and in fact only our friends were inside. Esther MacCarthy was there from my leadership team in Boston, and Mary Rose Crowley from Pat's team in Connecticut. Esther was new to her team that year, but Mary Rose had been supportive in the struggle from the very beginning. While we were all greeting each other, Elizabeth Bowyer left to go back to the front door to meet the Vatican officials.

Pat and I began to rearrange the furniture. We were determined to sit in a circle, as equals. Margie Tuite had urged us to "get to the table," but it was going to be a low bench and little end tables placed between the sofa and the chairs. Pat noticed a coffee pot set out with some cups.

"They must expect this to go on for some time," she said.

We wanted to tape-record the meeting. Mary Rose and Esther didn't think it would be appropriate. They said something about "the international nature of the meeting" and "concern about possible misunderstanding," and we realized we were not going to win the argument. We weren't going to waste energy on it. Mary Rose promised to take careful notes. Eventually, from her notes, and from the notes Pat and I each took during the meeting and elaborated upon as soon as we got home, we put together the best record we could of what happened. But we would much rather have had an exact transcript.

Finally, there was nothing more to do. We were ready.

Mary Linscott was the first person to come through the door. She was dressed in a plain dark suit and white blouse with a matching navy blue veil. She was born in England, and by 1986 she might have been in her early seventies, but she was astonishingly unchanged, still as tall and stately as she had been when I had first met her in 1970 in Rome when she was the Superior General of the Sisters of Notre Dame. Pat had met her in 1978. She had since become the highest-ranking woman in the Vatican and worked on the staff of the Congregation for Religious and Secular Institutes (CRIS). Whether she recognized us or not she hugged us each as she said hello.

We looked behind Mary and saw a fairly tall, thin male figure in the doorway. I knew he must be Archbishop Vincenzo Fagiolo, the second-ranking man at CRIS—one of the men who can decide the very existence of women's religious communities. Behind him was another older man with gray hair whom I knew was Archbishop Pio Laghi, the Vatican's ambassador to the United States. I guess I had been expecting them to be wearing their long red robes, and to extend their hands so that Pat and I could kiss their rings. Instead, they were wearing black suits and clerical collars, and their bishop's pectoral crosses were discreetly tucked into their pockets, the chains making little gold arcs across their priestly chests. We all shook hands as we were introduced. I was relieved that no one offered me a ring to kiss. I would have had to refuse, and the meeting would have begun with a gesture of apparent disrespect. Probably they had figured that out. They were, after all, supposed to be diplomats.

It was truly remarkable that they were in the Trinity College parlor, meeting with two obscure nuns from West Virginia. The princes of the church had come to speak to the peasants. I realized suddenly how important it was to Rome that Pat and I be silenced—and how important it was for us to refuse.

As we sat down, Elizabeth pushed the heavy parlor door shut. This is it, I thought.

Archbishop Laghi opened the meeting with a prayer. Then he scooted to the edge of his seat, leaned forward, cleared his throat, and spoke.

"This meeting is meant to be a dialogue with signers who have not yet clarified their position. This is a pastoral meeting, not a juridical visit nor an inquisition. The Archbishop [Fagiolo] will say what he expects. This is a meeting of good people witnessing in the church. *But I must insist* that before this meeting is over, you put in writing that you support and adhere to the Roman Catholic church's official teaching on abortion."

So much for dialogue! In sixty seconds it was clear. Everything would be fine if we agreed with them.

A pall came over the room. Quickly Laghi said: "Why don't we go around and introduce ourselves?"

Pat was sitting to the left of Laghi, and I was to the left of Pat. The circle continued with Esther and Mary Rose to the left of me. On the couch opposite me sat Mary Linscott and Archbishop Fagiolo side by side. Elizabeth, sitting to the left of Fagiolo, completed the ring.

First, Laghi introduced Fagiolo, who did not speak English

and for whom Mary Linscott would translate. Laghi described him as a man who had been a shepherd for many years and had faced many pastoral problems, a canon lawyer who could communicate with some English and "with his heart and his eyes." Then the papal nuncio described himself as sixty-three years old, a facilitator and an advocate for a solution representing the position of the Holy Father and the church. He listed his qualifications: service in India, the Middle East, Jerusalem, Nicaragua, Angola, and Argentina, and five years in the United States in his present position. "I know the culture of the States and the mind of the States," he concluded.

Pat and I have since read in *People of God*, Penny Lernoux's final exhaustive book on the modern church, that Laghi, while posted in Argentina, had reportedly been a regular tennis partner of one of the most murderous of the leaders of the military junta.

Bright spring sunshine came into the room through tall windows. The chair I was sitting in was very uncomfortable. The murmuring had come back, echoes of my formation period as a novice: "Barbara, a nun does not think that. Barbara, a nun does not feel that. Barbara, a nun does not say that. Barbara, go to the chapel until your mind is obedient."

Suddenly, I heard Pat introduce herself.

"My name is Patricia Hussey. I have a degree in special education and a master of divinity degree from the Jesuit School of Theology in Chicago. I have worked with Barbara Ferraro at Covenant House, which is a day shelter for homeless people, for the last five years."

And then she surprised me. Firmly, she said: "And I must say, Archbishop, that I find it very interesting that you say we are here for a dialogue, and yet, to use your words, you insist that after our time together we must put in writing that we support and adhere to the Roman Catholic teaching on abortion. That does not sound like dialogue to me."

The moment Pat spoke I felt at peace. All my anxiety was gone. The line from the prayer of Jeremiah came to me: "Be not afraid of them, for I am with you." We would be able to speak!

"My name is Barbara Ferraro," I began. "I have a master's degree in pastoral studies from Loyola University in Chicago and a doctorate in ministry from McCormick Presbyterian Seminary. I have tried to find ways to revitalize parishes from a feminist perspective. In my work in parishes I have been called upon by many women who have had to struggle with the issues of birth control and abortion.''

And then I smiled.

PAT

I wasn't afraid anymore. Whatever happened was in God's hands. My job was to speak honestly. Barbara and I weren't there to deceive anyone. We weren't there to manipulate anyone. We were there to be who we were at that moment in time. We certainly had not come all the way to Washington to conclude the meeting by signing a lie. I began to feel deeply offended. Was this the best the Vatican could do? Who were these men to reject the experiences of women?

When everyone had finished introducing themselves, I took a firm grip on my pad of notes. I thought the serious work of the meeting was about to begin. Instead, Archbishop Fagiolo gestured that he wanted to interrupt for a moment. He reached inside his jacket pocket and took out a handful of little cardboard folders. He leaned past Mary Linscott and handed Mary Rose a folder, saying "A gift from his holiness, Pope John Paul the Second.''

Barbara and I rolled our eyes and tried not to giggle. It was clear that he had turned to Mary Rose first because she was the only one of us dressed in a black suit and a veil which, in his eyes, made her Mother Superior. We were all embarrassed. It had been a long time since preference had been given to someone because she wore a veil.

Esther and Elizabeth were then given folders. Barbara and I waited for ours. Instead, Fagiolo tucked the remaining folders into his pocket. I looked at Barbara and shrugged a little. Apparently the gifts were for the leadership only.

Archbishop Laghi turned the conversation to the point of the meeting.

"You speak and act in the name of the church, and you have to uphold its teachings. So it is up to you to see how you can convey to us what you meant [by signing the ad]," he said.

I answered. "The ad in *The New York Times* appeared in the context of a political election when cardinals and bishops were saying that it was wrong to vote for anyone who was not anti-abortion. It was important to state in a public forum that other Catholics and theologians hold different views on the question of abortion. Did the ad cause scandal? Perhaps for some, but for others, the scandal came from the fact of the threats of dismissal from the Vatican to the nuns.''

Barbara spoke up: "Many women saw the ad not as scandal but as a sign of hope.''

"All recognize that abortion is evil,'' Laghi said. "However, the priest does have the obligation to help women pastorally and give them absolution.''

"I have met women who have been turned away by priests. That gives scandal,'' objected Barbara. "The church has not been pastoral toward women. The church does not invite women to be part of the decisions that affect their lives.''

I said: "There needs to be discussion on this issue, just as the church has allowed discussion on nuclear war.''

"The teaching of the church after two thousand years cannot be changed,'' said Laghi.

"But there has not been a consistent teaching on abortion throughout the years,'' objected Barbara, "and the teaching is not infallible.''

"I am a theologian and a Ph.D.,'' Laghi said.

Barbara, who also has a doctorate, came right back with a learned remark on the teaching of the magisterium and the teaching of the people. "The teaching of the magisterium has not included the experience of women,'' she repeated.

The atmosphere in the room was beginning to feel tense.

"Some points can't be disagreed with,'' said Laghi. "You have rights, but also some duties.'' He was sure, he said, that if he visited us he would find our work was excellent. But, he added emphatically, "You are committed to the Holy Father.''

Somehow, I let that assertion pass. It was like a red flag, but I wasn't there to discuss the meaning of my vows, which had not included a single word about commitment to the Holy Father. I was there to discuss the church's position on abortion.

"I think we have a right to dissent,'' I said.

"You are members of an ecclesiastical group. Be noncanonical [that is, be part of a group whose constitution does not depend on Rome's approval], but don't speak as Sisters of Notre Dame.''

Barbara said: "Our community had no problem with our position until you intervened. They found no scandal and they did not threaten us with dismissal.''

A rumble of Italian came from Archbishop Fagiolo. Mary Linscott translated. "You were never threatened with dismissal from your communities. The November 1984 letter was a canonical letter to superiors to say it is a serious matter, but it was not a threat of dismissal.''

Barbara pulled copies of the letters from CRIS out from the stack of papers she had on her lap.

"The letter from November 1984 says if we refuse to make a public retraction, 'you are to proceed . . . to warn the religious with an explicit threat of dismissal from the Institute,' '' quoted Barbara. Then she read a passage from their letter of May 1985: " 'they are therefore subject to the aforementioned canon [the rule allowing dismissal proceedings] unless they retract.' ''

"Well,'' said Laghi, "if you do retract then you are never threatened with dismissal.''

What were we supposed to make of that?

There was silence in the room. After a few minutes Laghi stood up. "I only came in to get this meeting started,'' he said. "I don't think my presence here is helping, so I will leave and let the meeting continue.''

The air lightened a bit, but not for long. It was Archbishop Fagiolo's turn to lean forward in his seat. He smiled at us, and said in Italian: "I came here because of my affection for religious life and esteem for the congregation of the Sisters of Notre Dame.'' He smiled again.

We smiled back. What else could we do? And then, as he went on speaking, we regretted it.

"No member of the church, especially priests and sisters, can legitimately dissent from the official teaching on abortion because it has been a consistent teaching since the first century,'' he said, in Italian, as Mary Linscott translated. He continued talking about official doctrinal teaching, the necessity of improving pastoral responses to heal social evils so that pressure for abortions will be removed, etc.

"Make a statement in line with the doctrine of the church,'' she translated, "so that your parents won't see this as a sign of contradiction for their daughter who is a nun.''

I saw Barbara's eyebrows shoot up. She knew enough Italian to understand what Fagiolo was really saying, despite Mary Linscott's less condescending translation.

"What would your mommies and daddies think if you were no longer nuns?'' the secretary of the Congregation for Religious and Sacred Institutes had just asked us.

How dare he bring our parents into this discussion! How dare he refer to our "mommies'' and "daddies'' as though we were first-graders! But we had agreed beforehand to put our feelings on hold until we left the meeting. Quietly, we assured Fagiolo that both sets of our parents had been very supportive. "They do have questions and concerns," Barbara said honestly. "They do not agree with everything we have said on this issue of abortion, but they love us and are willing to listen and dialogue with us."

Doggedly, we turned the discussion back to the church's inconsistencies on abortion.

"I am a canon lawyer," said Fagiolo. "It is a consistent teaching in the church. We must be united on this issue." He meant: if we signed a statement, there would be an *appearance* of unity.

"Yes, we need unity," I said, "but unity does not mean conformity or an absolutist position; unity means honesty about what the reality is in our world. Certainly, reprisals against the signers of the ad are not good for unity."

"Some things in the church have no place for pluralism; for example, Trinity, Eucharist, Divinity of Christ. Abortion in the sense of the sacredness of human life does not admit of pluralism," insisted Fagiolo.

"There is no infallible teaching on abortion," Barbara repeated. And around and around we went again. Fagiolo invoked the sins of the pagans. He talked about the connection between fighting war, violence, and hunger, and defending innocent life. We argued for birth control. He mentioned that Mary had become the mother of God at the announcement of the angel. Aquinas came into the discussion somewhere. Barbara objected to Aquinas's sexist distinctions. Fagiolo talked about a friend in Japan who listened to the heartbeat of a fetus and couldn't go through with an abortion.

"But others must make another decision," said Barbara stubbornly. "Those women are adults, they are moral decision-makers."

There was another lull in the conversation. Then Archbishop Fagiolo got up out of his seat and moved into the chair left empty by Laghi next to me.

I was writing notes on a pad on my lap. Fagiolo reached over and picked up the hand I was writing with, and held on to my thumb. At the same time, he began to stroke my arm.

This isn't really happening, I thought.

I couldn't look at Barbara. If I had, we both would have laughed out loud. I wondered what would happen if I said,

"Please keep your hands to yourself!" I kept quiet. We weren't there to cause an international incident. We were there to defend a woman's right to choose.

While Fagiolo went on stroking my arm, Barbara and I took turns asking about cases of rape, incest, and an endangered life of the mother. It was almost impossible to keep the meeting focused on the fact that individual women become pregnant and not always in circumstances that permit having a child. The Vatican didn't seem particularly interested in that aspect of the discussion.

"Abortion under all circumstances is wrong, and a woman must ask for forgiveness," was the reponse each time. There was never any recognition of circumstances, a basic aspect of the theology of sin.

"But the church's position has not been consistent," Barbara said, trying one more time.

"Yes, it has," said the Archbishop. "It has always been that way since the bambino was in Mary's womb." And he moved his hand over his stomach, as though the bambino was right there in his lap.

We tried another topic. What was the church going to do to rectify the reprisals against the other signers of the ad, especially the lay signers?

"The church condemns anyone who promotes abortion, so it is inevitable and logical what happened," said Fagiolo.

Barbara said: "The church is violating a person's right to speak and is asking me and others to make a statement that we cannot. I see this as a violent act. Other signers were coerced into making such statements."

For almost the first time, Mary Linscott spoke for herself: "No one has been coerced."

"Then we must have different perceptions," said Barbara.

Fagiolo was still sitting beside me, stroking my arm, holding on to my thumb. Suddenly, for the first and only time, he spoke in English. Very dramatically, he turned to both of us and said: "I have come to the United States because I love you."

We just stared at him. He reverted to Italian. Mary Linscott dutifully translated his remarks on the evil practices of the Egyptians and Romans and Greeks at the time of Christ. He mentioned Hitler's "culture of death" and the church's respect for life. And then he turned to me and said: "Can we come to some kind of understanding in sisterly love?"

"What is your expectation of us to resolve this?" I asked.

"A statement that you accept the teaching of Vatican II and the church on abortion," he said.

"And if in conscience we can't?" asked Barbara.

"A member of the church can hardly have a conscience that would not accept it," we were told.

I argued that point for a while. "I feel very Catholic and very much part of my congregation. As part of both of these institutions, I believe I have a right to dissent from teachings that are not infallible."

Then Mary Linscott took a paper out of a folder and said it was the statement signed by the Lorettos. She suggested we consider signing a similar statement: "The Lorettos said they signed an ad but were not making a pro-abortion statement . . . it was not meant as a statement about the church's position on abortion. They regretted it was misconstrued as in contradiction to the church's teaching and in this matter they do follow the teaching of the church regarding life."

Barbara and I were amazed. The words she was reading and interpreting were neither the exact words nor the intentions of the Sisters of Loretto. The differences may seem almost invisible to outsiders, but to the Lorettos they were crucial.

"The Sisters of Loretto *did not* see this statement as 'adherence to the church's teachings,'" we objected.

They seemed surprised that we had already spoken to the Lorettos. Mary Rose said that she too did not believe the Lorettos' statement could be read as an adherence to the teaching of the church. Mary Linscott, in a barely audible voice, said in English to Fagiolo, "I knew we should have gotten a stronger statement." Later we heard her tell Mary Rose that she was surprised that the other meetings had gone so easily.

Our meeting was going nowhere. Apparently Fagiolo thought so too, because he said he was going to take a break so he could go to the chapel and pray for us.

Barbara got a cup of coffee and came over to say to me, "Who is going to believe this?"

It got worse. When Fagiolo came back from the chapel, he walked over to Barbara and pinched her on both cheeks. "You look like my grandmother," he said.

She just stood staring at him in amazement. He moved over to me, and informed me that I looked like his aunt.

"I hope she holds similar positions to ours," I said.

We sat down again. We went through all our arguments again.

What about circumstances? What about conscience? What about dissent? What about reprisals? What about dismissal threats?

It was almost one o'clock in the afternoon, time for Mary Linscott and Archbishop Fagiolo to leave for the airport. They had to be back in Rome the next day to be present for the Easter celebrations. Once more, Fagiolo asked us: "Can't you possibly make a statement of acceptance of the church's teaching on abortion?"

Over and over, all day long, we had repeated that we could not in conscience sign such a statement. And yet, later we both felt that if we had signed in that final moment, the Vatican delegation would have been delighted to close our cases. Even though we would have been obviously lying.

It made me very sad to know that the archbishops would not have cared. They had one agenda, and forcing two nuns into a moral compromise would have been a small price to pay. But sometimes I wonder if they would even have noticed. We had been allowed to speak, but no one from the Vatican seemed to have listened.

As Fagiolo said good-bye, he said he hoped we would not endanger our religious positions because "you work hard where you *teach*." After all we had said to him that day, after all our references to our work and the women we knew from our work, he had not bothered to hear us. And, it seemed to us, he really did not want to understand. He apparently was not interested in the reasons women might seek an abortion. He was interested in our obedience.

We were given until April 4 to make a written statement. "Take all the time you need," said Mary Linscott. "Be aware of the consequences," said Fagiolo. "If you can't accept the teaching, you can't continue as religious."

He then walked across the room to me, held up his hand and blessed me silently, and kissed me on both cheeks. Then he went over to Barbara and did the same thing.

Slightly dazed, we went down to the convent dining room to have some lunch with Elizabeth, Esther, and Mary Rose. They congratulated us on our dignified behavior during the meeting. We asked what was inside the little cardboard folders they had received. It turned out that they were papal coins with the head of John Paul II on each one. If we had signed a statement of adherence, we too would have gotten a coin.

That night, when I called my mom and dad to tell them about the meeting, I started laughing about the coins we didn't get.

My dad said, "It's just as well. They sound like the coins of Judas to me."

That night, as we landed in Charleston and drove home, I thought about how much more pleasant it would have been to have it all over with. We could have let our government group write a letter for us. We could have signed something that said we believed in the sacredness and inviolability of human life—after all, it wasn't as though we didn't. We especially believed in the sacredness of a woman's life. But the Vatican would use those words to "prove" that we had recanted.

We might have been able to face each other if we had found a way to be cleared. But we would never again have been able to face the people who come to Covenant House. We ask them to risk their jobs, their homes, and their fragile security by standing up for better working conditions, for freedom from violent marriages, for their basic rights as citizens. How could we do that if we failed to stand up for ourselves?

On April 4, 1986, Barbara and I traveled to Boston to meet with Esther, Mary Rose, and Elizabeth. We had reflected, as they had requested in Washington, and we had prepared a statement of our beliefs. It was, of course, a pro-choice statement. It ended:*

"We stand with those in the church who believe in all women's rights to make moral choices; who value integrity and do not compromise it; who respect conscience and do not undermine it; and who seek the truth and do not fear it."

*See appendix for statement.

Thirty: Prodigal Daughters

PAT

A strange thing happened when Barbara and I traveled to our provinces to present our statement. First Barbara was taken aside by her Boston leadership team and asked very seriously if she was acting alone or if she was being influenced by me. Barbara assured them that she was making her own decision freely.

Then the next day, April 5, we went to Connecticut to have another open discussion with my province. And this time I was asked to step aside for a private meeting.

"Pat, we want to ask if you are acting alone or are you being influenced by Barbara?" said Mary Rose.

I said I was making my own decision freely.

"What do you suppose that was all about?" Barbara said on our way back to Charleston. "Do they think they can divide us?"

I didn't want to think about it. I was tired. We had done the best we could to write a statement that explained our position, and we hoped the entire paper was on its way to Archbishop Fagiolo and to the other Sisters of Notre Dame. If he accepted it, our cases would be closed. If he didn't, at least our consciences were clear. We had been true to what we believed, and we had certainly taken the opportunity to put our beliefs *in writing.*

Elizabeth Bowyer told us it was a good statement, but, she added, "Can't you say something about the sanctity of human life?"

We sighed. She was offering us yet another chance to wriggle off the hook. Just *say* something, don't even write it, anything that will give the General Government Group a chance to tell

Fagiolo we acknowledge the church's teaching—and give him the chance to tell the world we have recanted.

The visits and the letters continued. Peggy Loftus and Catherine Hughes came to Charleston on April 15, and again we declined to write, or even say, the phrase the Vatican was after. Peggy was baffled by our refusal. "I want you to look at how far you have put yourself outside of the church and the community already," she said. "I don't know how you can continue. Why don't you just leave?"

Barbara answered, "No, Peggy, this is my church and I feel very faithful. I am very much part of the Sisters of Notre Dame. This is part of who I am and what you all have taught me to be."

On April 17, Peggy was back in Rome. She wrote to the United States' SND leadership, reporting that we had again refused, and noting:

> Should the occasion present itself, they would again take the kind of public and vocal pro-choice stance which they did at a rally in Washington, D.C., on March 9, 1986.
>
> In our opinion, this latter point shifts the focus of the issue that we have been dealing with. No longer is it simply dialogue around the *New York Times* ad. It now becomes a question of the consonance between the public witness of the Sisters of Notre Dame and activities in the public forum which support the pro-choice position in the United States. Any discussion of this position, we feel, must always be carefully situated in a moral context.

The phrase "carefully situated in a moral context" was irritating. How often had we already explained that we based our pro-choice stand on our belief that abortion is always a situation faced by a woman operating in a particular context as a morally responsible person?

The focus was indeed shifting—to us as renegade Sisters of Notre Dame, sisters who could be dismissed not because the Vatican demanded it but because we were "placing ourselves outside the community."

We wrote back, pointing out that while the SNDs certainly did need to begin discussing their stance on sexuality issues, the problem at hand remained the CRIS situation and the original ad. We included a copy of a very welcome declaration of support from five nuns in Santiago, Chile. Unfortunately, none of them were Sisters of Notre Dame. In fact, the only collective declaration of support for our right to dissent publicly that we ever got from inside our own order came from the group of twelve SNDs who formed an unofficial black caucus. It too was very welcome, but it emphasized how little most of our other sisters were able to understand the connection between the issue of abortion and the issue of the church's treatment of women. Our black sisters understood the nature of oppression.

Liz Bowyer sent a handwritten note saying that she still did not believe that our signing the first ad was cause for dismissal. But, she said, she was worried about our taking a pro-choice position without tempering our statements with references to morality and the sanctity of human life. She said we needed to talk about the implications of our position to Notre Dame's missions. She closed, "Let's keep each other in prayer. With love."

Barbara waved the note over her head. "I don't like this suggestion that we don't care about human life. Why do they have so much trouble recognizing an adult woman as human life? And how long is it since I begged them to realize that the SNDs must face this issue? Three years?"

"It doesn't matter Barbara," I said. "If it took this long, then this long is what it took. If they are finally ready for dialogue, we will just have to go through it all again."

The Connecticut team sent out a memo asking members to write to me and to the leadership team telling us how they felt. On May 23, I wrote an open letter in response to the questions they had asked:

> *Why have you let this CRIS event become your whole world?*
> I really want to get on with my work in Covenant House. However, I believe that how we respond to CRIS affects not just the Notre Dame world, but the whole church, and in a particular way, women.
> *How come you cannot express that human life is sacred and inviolable?*
> Because to do so in the context of the CRIS dispute for me would be to say I agree with the church's teaching on abortion—and I don't agree.
> *What about your vow of obedience within a papal congregation? You have been told what to do by the highest authority of the church.*
> Because I am challenging the authority of the church's teaching on this issue which has been formed without acknowl-

edging the experience and the conscience of women. I believe in the church as a discipleship of equals. Its authority resides in the people of God who are in the search for truth.

Isn't it time to move on? All of the other signers have done what they needed to do.

No, it isn't. Because then we will have to go through it again on another issue. Or the same one. We have to say "Stop! No more."

Why don't you leave Notre Dame and do your work as a laywoman?

After 19 years as a Sister of Notre Dame I won't leave voluntarily as a result of intervention by CRIS.

On June 17, 1986, Liz Bowyer telephoned us from Rome to discuss a letter and a copy of a press statement that had just been mailed to us from the G's. First the good news: the G's do not consider signing the *New York Times* ad sufficient cause for dismissal.

Then the old news: because of our public pro-choice statements, we are being asked to enter into a process of clarifying our position with them "in a spirit of search and mutual trust."

And then the bad news: The G's have already sent out a press statement about our case to the International Catholic News Service and all of the Notre Dame order. They have read the statement to Archbishop Hamer *but they have never discussed its contents with us.*

A few days later a thick envelope appeared in the Covenant House mail. It contained a copy of a three-page, single-spaced press release headlined "The *New York Times* Ad of 7 October 1984 and the Sisters of Notre Dame." First came a summary of events, which was accurate. Then came a section titled "Commentary," which stated that they believed the *New York Times* ad was signed as a call to dialogue within a particular political context and within the American tradition of open discussion. Signing the ad gave no cause for dismissal. "Nevertheless, we question the prudence of using this particular medium to initiate such a dialogue: there was a lack of clarity in the language which gave some readers the impression that it was a pro-abortion statement and that it was calling into question the legitimate teaching authority of the church."

The next section expressed appreciation of CRIS for moving "progressively from a juridical to a pastoral mode," reducing its demands to a request that the signers say they accept the church's teaching, and "culminating in a personal visit."

And then came the final section, "The Sisters." We were shocked when we read it. More than shocked. We were numb.

It began with compliments about our work at Covenant House, and then they were withdrawn. The press release that had gone out to the world without a word of warning to us read:

We regret many aspects of the way in which [Barbara and Pat] have tried to [improve women's lives] from October 1984 onwards. The sponsorship and funding of the advertisement lead to a suspicion that other strategies were operating besides those of the signers. A costly advertisement seems an inappropriate way to begin to help the dispossessed. A public stance by Sisters of Notre Dame would seem to demand prior consultation with the members of their Congregation. But beyond these considerations is the fact that from the very beginning of our discussions, the Sisters have stated that their position is "non-negotiable." We have found this attitude a block to genuine dialogue. Their frequent use of the media has been characterized by statements which are derogatory to persons in the Church and reflect a lack of respect for the Church's teaching authority. They appear to have ignored the fact that as women who have public vows and who belong to a religious congregation, they are not free to act in public as though they were private individuals. We are conscious of our covenant relationship with Sisters Barbara and Patricia. We are sisters who have made common commitment and have accepted to be in communion with one another in carrying out that commitment. We think that they have shown little awareness of their responsibility to the Congregation in their public statements and actions.

At the present time we see the Sisters' position to have changed from their original request for open dialogue on the subject of abortion. At this point they are taking a public pro-choice stance with no reference to the sanctity of life or the place of moral responsibility in decision-making and action. We believe that Sisters Barbara and Patricia's present position has serious potential for the giving of scandal and continues to reflect an attitude of intransigence rather than dialogue in regard to the teaching authority of the Church. We have grave concern in regard to the public pro-choice position which they have taken and plan to begin a process of clarification of their full position and examination of their stance in the light of the Church's teaching and of our congregational statement of mission.

So much for Liz Bowyer's "with love." Always before, in all the months of discussion and negotiation, our leadership teams and the G's had spoken to us as equals searching for truth—no matter how puzzled or frustrated they were. Now, without any warning, we had been publicly betrayed and scolded, misrepresented and accused of having hidden motives.

I sat on the brown vinyl sofa in our office and I couldn't move. I really could not believe what I was reading. After a while I realized that Barbara was so upset that she wasn't even jumping up and down and shouting. She was just sitting in the desk chair, clutching the arms and staring at the wall. Finally, she whispered to me, "How do you feel?"

"Angry. Humiliated. Betrayed," I said. "How do you feel?"

"I feel kicked in the stomach," Barbara said, and she looked so sad I wanted to cry. The deepest bond in our lives was beginning to dissolve.

The hardest part of all was that we could not call Margie Tuite for encouragement and advice. Margie was very, very ill, and we would have to rely on the strength she had already given us.

A few desolate days later we were loading a tray of strawberries into the car to take to a gathering of our Women-Church group. "Wait a minute," said Barbara, running back into the house. She came out with the envelope from Rome. "I think we need to ask them to pray with us about this," she said.

Before we could pray, we had to explain. When we finished, we were relieved to see a circle of very dismayed faces. At that point we were so discouraged that we wouldn't have been surprised to hear them say something like: "W-e-l-l, they do have a point."

"That press release might have been written by the Vatican," said Karen.

"Actually, it sounds like it was written *for* the Vatican," said Mary Kay.

"Do you mean it was written for the Vatican to read?" asked Connie.

"No, I mean something worse," said Mary Kay. "I mean

the G's are doing the Vatican's work for them. The Vatican has succeeded in turning women against women.''

Somehow that explanation gave us the energy to begin dealing with the second part of the package that had come in the mail. That part was titled ''Proposed Guidelines for Process of Clarification.'' In view of our public pro-choice statements, we were being asked to respond in writing to certain questions—with the counsel of a moral theologian if we wished. Our responses would be submitted by the G's to ''a few'' moral theologians for comment.

After we answered their questions, and after theological consultation, the G's would like to meet with the two of us to discuss the answer to the question: ''Is [our] position tenable in our Congregation where we live our mission according to the norms of Church teaching?''

We had no problem with their questions.

Are you saying that a woman should not be hampered by law from having an abortion? *Or,* Do you recognize any objective moral norms which would guide her decision? What are they? Are you saying that the Church has no teaching role in regard to morality? Are you saying that Catholics have no obligation to take the Church's teaching seriously in the formation of conscience? Are you saying that a Catholic woman has no obligation to be attentive to the teaching of the Church in regard to abortion?

Good questions, ones we had spent twenty years studying. But the G's wanted our answers by August 1, which suggested to us that someone's deadline was more important than the slow process of understanding.

Our problem with their request was that, in light of the G's public statements about us, we had begun to wonder if they were looking for a reason to dismiss us. If our signatures on the ad were insufficient cause for dismissal, perhaps they were going to satisfy the Vatican by acting on our abortion position.

We wrote back saying that we were glad they had courageously decided not to start dismissal proceedings. But we also said: ''We believe that if true dialogue is to occur, it must happen with all or many Sisters of Notre Dame and not simply focus on personalities. The issues are broader than the two of us.'' Before beginning such a sensitive discussion we wanted to know if CRIS was going to issue a statement that we have been cleared so that we could proceed in an atmosphere free of fear and coercion. And, we deeply regretted that the first communication the whole international congregation of SND's received was the press statement. It was unfair to them, and it was certainly unfair to us.

We were being shut out of the information network of the Sisters of Notre Dame. Our letters were not distributed, or published in the order's international newspaper. And then Liz Bowyer wrote to tell us "Since we are beginning a new phase of talking together, we have decided not to make our correspondence to you public. We would like to move away from giving the impression that we are having a public controversy through letters to just being able to write to one another as sisters." Presumably as a sister she also said, "We realize our comments [in the press release] must have been hard for you to read, and we regret that. However, we felt it necessary to be as honest as possible in presenting the ambiguous position in which we found ourselves."

On July 10 we wrote back, beginning with an expression of sorrow over Margie's recent death. At the end of May we had traveled to Washington to discuss our situation as the last two uncleared nun signers with Frances Kissling, Mary Hunt, and Maureen Fiedler. As we arrived at Maureen's house she got a telephone call telling us that Margie was dead. It was a dreadful moment but it was some comfort to share it with the three women who would offer us the greatest support in the months to come.

"Truly," we said to our SND sisters, "it is in her spirit and because of her life that we write to you regarding a furtherance of our conversation together."

That said (and, in the fact of our continuing to write, acted upon), we asked again if we were to be cleared before beginning the extensive dialogue suggested. Shouldn't the process involve the entire congregation since the issues are critical to all? Isn't a question-and-answer format too limited? What about *our* questions? For example, "Do you believe that any one of us as Sisters of Notre Dame can publicly dissent on any other controversial issues that are presently part of the official church's teaching, e.g., birth control, ordination of women, human sexuality issues?" "Could you help us to understand why our answers would be given to moral theologians? Who are they? Will we see their responses, or get to sit down and talk to them?"

Finally, we urgently wanted to know "Is there any way this pastoral process could turn into a juridical one?" (On the telephone, Liz Bowyer told us she hoped not, but the G's had no control over CRIS's actions.)

Just for good measure, we repeated all our questions again. Since we seemed to be required to repeat every previous letter, we figured we might as well get a head start on this one.

On July 21, the Vatican tried to give us a shove by issuing a press release. "The Holy See is closely following the efforts of the general government group of the Notre Dame Sisters with the hope that the cases will be resolved without having to begin formal disciplinary procedures in accord with Church Law." Cardinal Hamer was quoted as saying, "The Vatican accepted public declarations of adherence to Catholic Doctrine from the twenty-five other Catholic nuns, priests and brothers who signed the ad and considers their cases closed."

Eleven nun signers, including the Lorettos, promptly tried to come to our support by issuing a furious statement categorically denying that they had ever made public declarations of adherence to the church's teaching on abortion. But the fact remained that Barbara and I were the only signers whose cases had not been closed, and the Vatican was still determined to patch up an appearance of unity. Barbara and I realized again that it was essential that we not put anything in writing, not even the answers to the G's questions. We were afraid that our answers might be used against us.

Letters and phone calls, letters and phone calls. It was a dreadful way to spend the summer. On July 26, Liz Bowyer sent us a chatty letter saying that she really hoped for clarification because "Although the statements are clear to you, they are not clear to some of us and to people who have talked or written to us. The statements come across to some as pro-abortion . . . It is important that we talk about this. If an SND were making public statements defending nuclear warfare or apartheid, I would feel that we would have a serious responsibility to ask for clarification and to question how these statements fit into our shared mission as SNDs."

Barbara looked bewildered when she read that letter. "How can anyone equate defending women as moral agents and responsible decision-makers with defending apartheid and nuclear war? I don't know, Pat, I'm beginning to think the Notre Dames are so out of touch with the issue of the status of women that they are incapable of understanding us."

"It doesn't matter," I said. "We have to go on talking."

* * *

The G's had apparently decided that we were refusing to talk. On August 16, from England, Elizabeth (not signed "Liz" this time) wrote to say, "We regret the fact that you have refused to participate in the first step of the clarification process." (We had in fact merely refused to answer in writing.) They also felt sad and embarrassed to read remarks quoted by us in "angry and abusive language," and they find the quality of theological thought in our press statements inadequate for a Sister of Notre Dame. However, they are still willing to dialogue, and suggest our meeting with them in Washington in September.

By then I was beginning to feel like a prisoner who has been kept awake for seventy-two hours. All night thoughts ran around my head: sign a statement, quit the community, run away, burn the mail, get it over with. Luckily, Barbara and I rarely felt discouraged at the same time. She was busily writing the speech she was planning to give at the Boston province's annual assembly at the end of August. I hoped they would all stand on their chairs and cheer when she finished, but I was too tired to do anything but mumble "good luck."

BARBARA

Once more I was attending an annual assembly of the Boston Province of the Sisters of Notre Dame. The talk I had been laboring to write was not going to be heard by an anonymous audience. These were my *sisters*, two hundred and fifty women I had known for most of my life. It was very disconcerting to realize that I had to start my explanation from the most basic level of consciousness-raising—from my own experiences in knowing good women who had had to struggle with the issue of abortion and had been turned away by their church. Where had my sisters been for the last decade? I wondered. They certainly were up-to-date on the struggle in Nicaragua. How had they failed to develop an understanding of their own struggle?

As I began speaking, a thought flashed through my head— We have grown apart from this community—but I repressed it. My mission at that moment was to bring us together.

I asked them to think about the implications of a secular public policy that would criminalize abortion for all American women. I reminded them that the church has never spoken infallibly on abortion. Pro-choice is not pro-abortion—what woman would ever consider getting pregnant just so that she could experience having an abortion? Nor is pro-choice limited to abortion. Being pro-choice requires working for alternatives, for prenatal care, family support, day care, job training, health care, decent jobs at living wages. The right to abortion does not replace the need for better sex education and family planning programs. My work in Covenant House is essentially trying to provide choices for people with too few. As a religious order, we work for choices through civil and equal rights, by joining in the battle for self-determination of Nicaraguan and South African peoples.

Last of all, I discussed the broader implications of the process we had all been undergoing since the first letter threatening dismissal came from CRIS. I listed power and powerlessness, domination and submission, dissent or quiet acquiescence, shared versus imposed authority, conscience or coercion of conscience, the autonomy of our community.

I quoted from an article published in the magazine *Women and Power*, in 1985 by Mary Daniel Turner, a former superior general of Notre Dame: "We must continually ascertain whether we are participants in generating life-giving systems or collaborators in preserving death-dealing ones. We must particularly examine our understanding and practice of virtues commonly associated with women; e.g., obedience, loyalty and docility."

Make the connections, I pleaded. As an example of questions we must ask, I wondered why the church can discuss war—a man's issue that affects women and children—but not abortion? I wondered also at our docility the previous March when Archbishop Pio Laghi moved to suppress the Women's Ordination Conference on the grounds that it was questioning church doctrine. Do we as women abdicate certain rights when we become members of religious communities? Are we to uphold teachings of the church for the sake of the church's teaching when they are unenlightened and lacking in truth, such as the issue of ordination?

In 1979, another distinguished Sister of Notre Dame, Marie Augusta Neal, had written an article titled "Sociology and Sexuality . . . A Feminist Perspective" for the magazine *Christianity and Crisis*. I quoted from it:

So concentrated is the question of sexuality on the issues of birth control, abortion and divorce, as well as on the issues of premarital sex and the possibility of married clergy, that men are not yet aware of the general problem of a male-dominated theological language, liturgy and the religious education that is denying to women a place to celebrate life in the church . . . My discipline of sociology in theory and research confirms that the major sexual problem for consideration by the church is the human rights of women in the consciousness of men . . .

Finally, I asked them to consider the more complex meaning of the question Pat and I had been asked by the G's: were our positions tenable in our Congregation where we live our mission according to the norms of church teaching? I hoped they would begin to wonder if part of our mission was, of necessity, questioning the norms of church teaching.

Never before or since had I shaken out my soul so thoroughly in public as I did that day before my province. I had given them all I had, and after I finished I waited for responses. There was no chance of their standing on their chairs and applauding, as Pat wished for me, but they did clap warmly and supported my ability to share on such a personal level. The meeting then went on to the next topic. A while later a woman stood up to say, "We have got to start doing something about what the church is doing to people like Charles Curran." Talk about failing to make the connections!

Something even worse happened after the meeting. A nun came up to me and said she strongly disapproved of my "using" Mary Daniel Turner and Marie Augusta Neal "in that highly manipulative way." Apparently in her eyes I was so thoroughly discredited that I was not entitled to any corroborating wisdom—especially not SND wisdom!

In September we met again with the G's at Trinity College. Again we explained "pro-choice." This time, the G's said they were satisfied with our explanation; however, they asked us to refrain from making further public statements. We told them their request for silence was impossible.

By September 25, the G's were writing to us from Rome. They used their old one-two approach. First the good news: "We heard in your clarifications that your basic stance is not a pro-abortion position, but rather that you reject efforts to make abortion illegal and that you cannot accept the teaching of the Church which states that abortion is immoral in every circumstance. We believe that your basic orientation of respect for human life is consistent with our shared mission as Sisters of

Notre Dame." Pat and I saw progress there, although we still had to write back and point out the distinction between "pro-choice" and "pro-abortion."

But then the bad news. Because they find our public statements at times "abusive and disrespectful of persons," they request that we refrain from making further public statements that do not fully convey our position, that we refrain from using abusive and disrespectful language, and that we discern with our provinces before making further statements until our provinces have developed a policy regarding public dissent. From this time on, those three points became the basis for the G's demands, repeated over and over again.

In October we wrote back at some length, saying we believed it was particularly important to continue to speak out while the church was attacking our right to dissent. We also planned to continue to reflect and discern personally and communally in the same manner as we had for the previous five years with the group of SNDs and other nuns living in West Virginia. Apparently our letter was too long. Back came another letter asking for a "yes or no" answer. We sent back our previous letter, marked with yellow highlighter.

Three months went by without a letter from Rome. It was wonderful. Then, on April 3, 1987, we each got a copy of the same letter from the G's. Two individual copies signaled a serious new step. It was a long letter listing the various things we had refused to do (submit written answers to questions) or not do (stop speaking publicly): "The majority of sisters who have corresponded with us about you have been opposed to your methods of public dissent because your public statements contain language which is abusive and disrespectful of persons, and your statements are read as being pro-abortion." The main point was near the end: "You owe obedience to the lawful authority of the Congregation by virtue of the vow of obedience you have made. In now invoking that vow, we are exercising our authority for the common good of the Congregation." We were being ordered to be silent.

A statement repeating the letter was sent to the entire international order. We wondered what a Japanese nun or an African nun would think when she read that we had used language abusive and disrespectful of persons, especially when the G's helpfully included a list of some of our public activities. What kind of picture would those distant nuns have of us, running amok while making a keynote address in Connecticut, abusing the interviewer on the CBS news magazine program "West 57th," raving disrespectfully in a *Village Voice* article?

When the "West 57th" show appeared a little later, I had a wonderful fantasy of being able to send videotapes to every SND convent. Pat and I were in excellent form, which I thought would translate to our sisters as strong instead of abusive—although I must in honesty admit that I recall wanting to make a remark about the cardinals in their red hats and their red dresses. In fact it was the other side that was abusive. Speaking for the hierarchy was one Monsignor William Smith, a moral theologian from New York and a close pal of Cardinal O'Connor. He explained to correspondent Meredith Vieira, "What you got there are, you got two girls who are pimping for Planned Parenthood basically" who "should have their heads unscrambled." When she suggested that we believed the male hierarchy of the church does not care about women, Smith snapped: "That's a cheap shot by cheap sisters."

It was Pat's turn to draft a reply to the G's. The typewriter was smoking by the time she got to the end of the first paragraph. "We all know that we are at this point in our common histories because of an ad calling for dialogue on abortion. The Vatican has caused all this and we are frankly shocked at your participation in this process. Your judgments are complete and our names have been damaged. There is nothing we can do. It seems that you are involved in a process of justification for what is going on."

Pat wrote that the Congregation had only seen the G's side of the correspondence (no wonder they didn't like our methods of dissent. If, in fact, they didn't). We had repeatedly said we were willing to dialogue, contrary to the G's version. To us, obedience is understood as honoring the belief in a discipleship of equals, and we were disturbed by an authoritarian vocabulary, telling them, "We will not obey commands as if we were part of a military regime." We regretted the horizontal violence being done to us and considered it a result of the sense of powerlessness that comes from our canonical status. To abdicate our responsibility to dissent is unacceptable, and "to invoke a vow of obedience based on the style of dissent rather than the substance of dissent is ludicrous." The mission statements of Notre Dame call on us to transform unjust structures: "Does that mean *only* those structures outside of the church?"

On May 21 letters were sent issuing us a first canonical warning of dismissal procedures. We never received them. They were reissued and on June 19 the dismissal process officially began. Meanwhile, we gathered up our strength and sent off a letter asking for specific examples of our abusive and disrespectful language. We also said we considered the demand that we discern with our provinces to be artificial, since we live a thousand miles away. It would also have been almost impossible. The Connecticut province, struggling to invent a workable solution, wrote suggesting that we at least discern with the leadership team before we made a public statement. If they could not support us, we could invite two sisters and they would invite two sisters and also a facilitator to help resolve our differences. They admitted a conference call might be necessary. All in all, quite a childish and elaborate arrangement to obscure the fact that we were being silenced.

In July, Catherine Hughes wrote with an example of abusive and disrespectful language. Apparently the G's had a newspaper clipping in which we said, "Margie was a nun signer, along with us. She went to her grave never knowing what her Superior said to the Vatican that cleared her. They basically lied to the Vatican and misrepresented her position to clear her."

Pat said: "Since when is naming the reality abusive?"

We were left hanging. We wondered why the dismissal process had been halted. Was the real reason a desire to avoid bad publicity during the Pope's visit to the United States that fall?

On September 25, Pat and I informed our provinces that until our situation was resolved we had decided to withhold the monthly payments of $500 we had each been making to our provinces. After nearly three years we had begun to worry about our futures. Nuns, like housewives, had always believed their commitment would reward them with being taken care of in their old age. Like housewives, we were beginning to suspect that reality was going to turn out otherwise.

Meanwhile, the Connecticut and Boston provinces had belatedly asked that the G's, the leadership teams, and Pat and I sit down and dialogue. Possibly they were at last ready for true dialogue. But we felt that the idea of dialogue had become confused with the request for discernment and that both words were masking the true choices we were being offered: either return to our provinces for a kind of reeducation in silence and submission, or refuse and appear to be placing ourselves outside the circle of the community.

By September 1987 we had written our statement to the Vatican explaining our position. We had met with the Vatican and met countless times with members of our order. We had written a small folio of explanatory letters. And still they asked us to dialogue. We *had* dialogued, yet no one seemed to be listening. How many times could we repeat the same thing? We began to believe that to the Sisters of Notre Dame the only satisfactory dialogue would be one in which we were willing to say what they wanted to hear.

By October 22, 1987, none of us were feeling particularly charitable. We were furious that the G's had characterized us as "intransigent," "offensive," "abusive," "disrespectful," and "destructive." We wrote to the G's saying that we wanted a public apology before we even considered entering into dialogue again. There had been enough meetings—a plague of meetings. Far from refusing to dialogue, we had been doing most of the talking. We wanted some responses to the issue of justice for women from the Congregation.

We also wanted a decision about our membership. "It seems so simple. 'Can we continue to disagree publicly with official church teachings as members in good standing or can't we?' You must answer that question for us and for others in Notre Dame who will dissent in the future."

In January 1988, we got two new letters officially warning us of dismissal. The process had started again. In the letters, Catherine Hughes suggested we ask for an indult of secularization: "You would then no longer be bound by a vow of obedience to religious superiors and you would have that capacity 'to live and act freely' which you desire."

We wrote back that since we had done nothing wrong we would not leave the order. Also, we were dismayed to see our ideals of collegiality and dialogue replaced by demands for obedience to the "lawful orders" of religious "superiors." Looking back, I remember that we were not only dismayed, we were surprised. Vatican II seemed to be slipping further away from the Sisters of Notre Dame with every letter. There were times when I felt foolishly old-fashioned, harping on about conscience and justice.

We received our second warning in February and responded with a long letter restating our call, in conscience, to bear public witness to a woman's right as a moral agent to make decisions about her own fertility, including the act of abortion. We repeated that we had not refused either to dialogue or discern with our Sisters. However, because we were still under a threat of dismissal unless we complied with demands to state our adherence to the Vatican's teaching, we were continuing to refuse to participate in a coercive process.

March and April of 1988 passed in the now familiar way. We worried, we answered letters and took phone calls, and we tried to focus what energy we had on the people that came to Covenant House. Then, on June 1, we each received a letter from Catherine Hughes saying that the G's had decided not to proceed with the dismissal process. We were so relieved that we tried to ignore the indictment against us that was part of the statement the General Government Group sent out to the Congregation and to the press:

> We regret that you have disregarded your responsibility to be accountable to the religious community which you have freely chosen to join. You have assumed an intransigent position which has consistently blocked attempts at dialogue initiated by the general government, the leadership of your province, and other Sisters of Notre Dame. This implies that you no longer value your membership in the Congregation nor wish to fulfill its basic requirements. You have, in practice, placed yourself outside the life and mission of the Congregation.

It didn't seem to matter what our governing group thought of us. We were proud of them. They had honored our desire not to be secretly cleared and they had refused the Vatican's demand that we be dismissed. They had shown both courage and responsiveness to our side of the dialogue. On June 9 we held our own press conference in Washington and declared the decision "an enormous victory for all women, particularly women in Religious Congregations."

Happily, we announced, "You can be publicly pro-choice and still remain a nun."

As it turned out, by refusing to dismiss us, the Sisters of Notre Dame had freed us to leave.

For the first time in nearly four years we had time to think about something other than resisting the Vatican. And we discovered that both of us were thinking the same thing: "What now?"

The struggle had changed us. We needed to understand what

had happened and who we had become. We needed to listen to the Spirit within us to learn where we were being led.

The early summer of 1988 was hot in Charleston—suffocating, crushing, baking hot. We started jogging in the relative comfort of the early morning, running up and down the Kanawha River, looping around the state capitol building, feeling "home" in our feet. A few weeks after our victorious press conference in Washington we began to face the fact that we were still nuns in name—had in fact fought like tigers to remain nuns—but we were no longer Sisters of Notre Dame in spirit.

We looked at the fine print in the letter from the G's telling us we would not be dismissed, and we found the words "*at this point*." Would it ever end? Would we, every time we spoke out on any issue at all annoying to any member of the male hierarchy, be asked to discern and consult and obey? Probably so. The Vatican was chipping away the freedom of religious women, and we would be permanent problems of intransigence. We would drain energy and focus away from our sisters, and, frankly, we did not want to spend our lives in a constant debilitating internal argument with other women. They were not our enemy. The patriarchal system was. Covenant House was our mission, a life-giving one. Nundom, on the other hand, seemed to be dying.

The Vatican was squeezing the vitality and hope out of religious communities. It wasn't just their demands for a return to religious dress and convent living. Truly ominously, the new Constitution of the Sisters of Notre Dame would not be approved without inclusion of a new "Oath of Fidelity" for the membership—a loyalty oath to the pope already required of the hierarchy, but now newly extended to nuns. We could not possibly agree to such an authoritarian arrangement. It would contradict twenty years of our lives, and abrogate the four years of struggle we had just lived through. Nuns—neither priests nor lay, neither fish nor fowl—were beginning to seem a vestigial remnant of the Middle Ages, something like an appendix to the faith.

We could no longer be a part of the hierarchical system, even though it was the system that defined us as a part. The Catholic church has no respect for women. Daily, some member of the American hierarchy reinforces that impression. Cardinal O'Connor, for example, has grown fond of saying that one of the most dangerous environments in the world today is the mother's womb. Surely not. Surely the truth is that God gave women the ability to have children because she knew we would exercise the privilege with common sense and responsibility.

Sadly, the final straw that separated us from our community was a series of attacks on us by two of the other nun signers. They were women we had admired as strong feminists, tireless activists, and determined intellectuals. And yet, beginning in September 1987, they felt moved to circulate letters criticizing our decision to carry our protest to its end. The letters turned into an "analysis" published in a religious women's newsletter, and finally into a lengthy article in a liberal Christian magazine published six months after our order refused to dismiss us. The authors' cases had been closed, by what means we still do not know. And yet they accused us of operating out of a male model of dissent, of refusing to dialogue with our order (although they had never heard our side of the dialogue), of failing to consider the good of the whole community. We were sick at heart when we read what they had to say. To us, the "whole community" was the women of the world, not just nuns.

Nuns, not even of our own community, were suggesting that we had let ourselves be used by Catholics for Free Choice, when in fact CFFC had been our greatest support. In the name of sisterhood we were being told that our conscience stand was nothing more than recalcitrance. *Nuns* were accusing us of having a "death wish" and being "profligate siblings." They were publishing lengthy papers designed to show that they, not we, had practiced *responsible* dissent. Apparently, we had been traitors to our class. And all of these insults were couched in nunny language of "anguishing deeply" and "healing" and "reconciliation." We were urged to forgive our oppressors. One particularly saccharine and intrusive letter to us referred to the writer's meditation on the parable of the Prodigal Son (or daughter): "My prayer is that you may, like the prodigal parent, forget the past and give each other rings for the fingers and shoes for the feet." Or perhaps, we wondered, we would be given papal coins?

Who had supported us since we signed that fateful ad? Laywomen. Who were the women who were actually *doing* what they preached? Laywomen. Who were the least privileged, most powerless, most despised people in the Catholic church? Laywomen.

From now on, we wanted to stand with them, free of the false privileges of nuns, free of the ungodly restraints of religious life.

On July 13, 1988, we wrote to our sisters in Boston and Connecticut and resigned from the community of the Sisters of Notre Dame. We said there were two reasons for our decision. To truly stand with people who are struggling, one must be in a relationship of equality with them. Thus, for us to stand with women, we need to renounce the differences, limitations, and even privileges that are part of membership in a religious community in a patriarchal church.

And, sadly, we had realized that the violence of the process used with us by the leadership, the lack of respect and understanding of our motivation for the good of the whole church by many in the community, are for us insurmountable barriers to the reconstruction of a positive covenant relationship.

We thanked those of our sisters who had given us their support and prayed that in the future fear would not paralyze any of us.

It was very hot in Charleston. The women in the sewing cooperative in the back room of Covenant House moved slowly around their tables. People came in looking for a cold shower and a little shade. The Ferraros and the Husseys called to tell us that we were loved. It was just another day.

The first day of our entire adult lives as laywomen.

Thirty-one: Circles

PAT AND BARBARA

We live inside the circles now.

The pain of cutting ourselves off from an institution that was dying has begun to disappear. We never hear from the Sisters of Notre Dame. It was hard at first to accept that our years of community and service to the order could be reduced to a final sharp exchange of letters concerning payments we were owed for our Social Security account. Now we know what a divorce feels like.

But gratitude has replaced sorrow, and we have been rewarded with a life fuller than we ever imagined. The Spirit has brought us to the joyous process of creating something new, of trying to realize a small part of the world without patriarchy.

Charleston, West Virginia, is still our home. We have been confirmed in our mission. These people—at Covenant House, in the valley, in this state—are the people we continue to fight for and with. Covenant House has expanded its programs to the homeless in rural areas surrounding the city. It has opened the first residence in West Virginia for people with AIDS. Already we are looking for the means to purchase a second home. We continue to support choice on all issues. With others, we have begun two new state organizations supporting reproductive rights: West Virginia Catholics for Choice and West Virginia Clergy and Laity for Religious Freedom and Reproductive Rights.

We are Catholics. The Vatican's version of Catholicism is a culture of oppression, a church that is only about itself. We stand with the church of the people, of the scriptures, the Catholic church of service, solidarity, justice, and charity. We stand as members of the circle.

We pray with our Women-Church group. Some of us are Catholics. The important connection is that we are women, and we are trying to heal and empower ourselves by naming the sacred in our own lives.

The meaning of life lies within us. The beginning of the search for truth lies in each person's story. To truly hear one another is to respect one another. If we help each other to listen to the Spirit within and to see the power of God in ourselves and in others we can work together to transform the world into a holy and just place for all people.

Recognizing our shared experiences, defining them, learning to trust them as real and valuable—in that lies the beginning of clarity and change. In that process we move toward justice.

This book is our story until now. When it is read it will become part of a greater story, and come back to us as something richer. The circles will hold.

Appendix

A DIVERSITY OF OPINIONS REGARDING ABORTION EXISTS AMONG COMMITTED CATHOLICS.

A CATHOLIC STATEMENT ON PLURALISM AND ABORTION.

Continued confusion and polarization within the Catholic community on the subject of abortion prompt us to issue this statement.

Statements of recent Popes and of the Catholic hierarchy have condemned the direct termination of pre-natal life as morally wrong in all instances. There is the mistaken belief in American society that this is the only legitimate Catholic position. In fact, a diversity of opinions regarding abortion exists among committed Catholics:

- A large number of Catholic theologians hold that even direct abortion, though tragic, can sometimes be a moral choice.
- According to data compiled by the National Opinion Research Center, only 11% of Catholics surveyed disapprove of abortion in all circumstances.

These opinions have been formed by:

- Familiarity with the actual experiences that lead women to make a decision for abortion;
- A recognition that there is no common and constant teaching on ensoulment in Church doctrine, nor has abortion always been treated as murder in canonical history;
- An adherence to principles of moral theology, such as probabilism, religious liberty, and the centrality of informed conscience; and
- An awareness of the acceptance of abortion as a moral choice by official statements and respected theologians of other faith groups.

Therefore, it is necessary that the Catholic community encourage candid and respectful discussion on this diversity of opinion within the Church, and that Catholic youth and families be educated on the complexity of the issues of responsible sexuality and human reproduction.

Further, Catholics — especially priests, religious, theologians, and legislators — who publicly dissent from hierarchical statements and explore areas of moral and legal freedom on the abortion question should not be penalized by their religious superiors, church employers, or bishops.

Finally, while recognizing and supporting the legitimate role of the hierarchy in providing Catholics with moral guidance on political and social issues and in seeking legislative remedies to social injustices, we believe that Catholics should not seek the kind of legislation that curtails the legitimate exercise of the freedom of religion and conscience or discriminates against poor women.

In the belief that responsible moral decisions can only be made in an atmosphere of freedom from fear or coercion, we, the undersigned,* call upon all Catholics to affirm this statement.

The ad from *The New York Times*.

STATEMENT BY
BARBARA FERRARO AND
PATRICIA HUSSEY

In September, 1984, we signed the Catholic Statement on Pluralism and Abortion which was published in *The New York Times* on October 7, 1984. Since that time, we have been engaged in discussions and negotiations with our General Government Group in an attempt to respond to the demand of the Vatican Congregation of Religious and Secular Institutes that we retract our signatures from the statement on Pluralism and Abortion or face dismissal from the Sisters of Notre Dame.

On March 22, 1986, for the first time, we met representatives of CRIS in the persons of Archbishop Vincenzo Fagiolo and Sister Mary Linscott. The meeting was described to us as a "pastoral," not a juridical or canonical, visit. During that meeting Fagiolo clearly told us that no one could be or remain in religious life if they dissented from the hierarchical magisterium's teaching on abortion. In addition, we were told that the resolution of our case required that we declare our adherence to that teaching.

One formulation suggested to us was that attested to by the Sisters of Loretto on the preceding day. Because this demand in content and in process is, in our opinion, inappropriate within the Catholic community and does not reflect the truth as we know it, we are compelled to make the following statements.

We believe that the Vatican in characterizing the *New York Times* ad as a pro-abortion statement has deliberately chosen to misconstrue it.

   (1) The ad spoke of a diversity of opinions on abortion among committed Catholics and called for dialogue.

We regret that the official Church has taken part in repressing open discussion within the church and demanding obedience to authoritative rule without allowing legitimate dissent.

We believe that dialogue is essential for the very life of the church. If we are serious about the search for truth, this can only happen when true dialogue occurs. Dialogue needs to happen in an atmosphere free of fear and coercion.

   (2) The statement alluded to legitimate Catholic positions on abortion other than that held by the hierarchy.

We regret that the male, celibate Church is ignoring and trivializing the experiences of women. We regret that the official Church cannot deal with women as full persons and moral agents in our own right. We regret that the official Church is neutralizing and negating the serious reflections of Catholic theologians and theologians in other faith traditions on the issue of reproductive rights.

We regret that the official Church is continually repressing dissenting voices and seems to be acknowledging only the view of the religious right within Catholicism.

We believe that women are to be affirmed in their reproductive decisions on the basis of individual conscience and personal religious freedom.

We believe that by the official Church's inability to deal with birth control in practice it promotes the high abortion rate it claims to abhor.

We believe that Catholic theological reflections and ecumenical exchange on the most conflictual subjects including reproductive rights are essential for the life of the church.

We continue to believe that there are other legitimate positions on abortion that are theologically and ethically defensible within the framework of Catholic tradition. Theological inquiry and ecumenical exchange even on the most difficult issues are essential for the life of the church.

We believe that dissent on all controversial issues, including reproductive rights, is essential for the life of the church. We believe that dissent falls within the rights and responsibilities of all Roman Catholics. The official Church has a responsibility to foster a climate in which faithful dissent is incorporated into the ongoing life of the community.

(3) The statement said that those who publicly dissent from hierarchical statements and explore areas of legal and moral freedom on the abortion question should not be penalized by their religious superiors, Church employers or bishops.

We regret that the official Church is prepared to and has used force, threats and violence to obtain submission. We regret that the official church which speaks of religious liberty, freedom to dissent, equality of persons before the law in society fails to apply these same human rights to the Church itself.

We believe that the integrity of legitimate church authority has been threatened. We believe that the hierarchy has given scandal by: their disruption of and intervention in women's religious communities; extracting what amounts to loyalty oaths; attempting to compromise the integrity of many religious signers; and deliberately misinterpreting and miscommunicating nun signers' statements to the public.

We are also concerned by the punitive actions taken against many lay signers affecting their economic livelihood and academic freedom.

The cornerstone of the Catholic tradition is the search for truth. Unfortunately the actions of the official Church thwart that goal and are totally contrary to our ''vision of church as a discipleship of equals.''

Our statements come as a result of both reflection and challenges from: the experiences of women we have known and worked with; the scriptures and our studies of theology and the history of the Roman Catholic Church. They are also the result of 19 years of Pat's experiences and 24 years of Barbara's experiences as members of the Sisters of Notre Dame.

We stand with those in the church who believe in all women's rights to make moral choices; who value integrity and do not compromise it; who respect conscience and do not undermine it; and who seek the truth and do not fear it.

Patricia Hussey, SND
April 4, 1986

Barbara Ferraro, SND

About the Authors

Barbara Ferraro and Patricia Hussey run a daytime shelter for the homeless in Charleston, West Virginia, as they have for the past eleven years.

Jane O'Reilly is the author of *The Girl I Left Behind* and a frequent contributor to numerous periodicals. She lives in New York City.